The Greatest Templar Tale Never Told

The Greatest Templar Tale Never Told

The Sinclair / Wemyss Journals

By Scott F. Wolter

North Star Press
www.northstarpress.com
Since 1969

ISBN: 978-1-68201-162-1

First Edition
Second Printing

Printed in the United States.

Type set in Carta Marina, IM Fell English, and IM Fell English SC.

North Star Press of St. Cloud Inc.
www.NorthStarPress.com

Visit Scott's website at:
www.ScottFWolter.com

Back cover Author photo credit: Hayley Ramsey

Interior and exterior book design by Liz Dwyer of North Star Press.

The Greatest Templar Tale Never Told
Resource Center

Scan this QR code for exclusive access to the resource center. Here you will find supplementary materials, documentation, high-resolution images, and additional research referenced in the book.

This resource center will be continuously updated with new materials, documents, and discoveries, so check back often.

Previous titles by Scott F. Wolter :

Oak Island, Knights Templar, and the Holy Grail: Secrets of the Underground Project Revealed | 2024.

Cryptic Code of the Templars in America: Origins of the Hooked X | 2019.

Akhenaten to the Founding Fathers: Mysteries of the Hooked X | 2013.

The Hooked X: Key to the Secret History of North America, |2009.

The Kensington Rune Stone: Compelling New Evidence | 2005.

Dedication:

To my two precious children, Grant and Amanda,
along with my amazing grandchildren,
Jack, Kinzlee, and Poppy.

Contents

Foreword I

By Don Shelby

There is nothing so delicious as a mystery. Humans are built with manic curiosity. The mind grows strong and nimble when we feed our curiosity. That is how crimes are solved, but it is also how life-saving medical breakthroughs are discovered, and how engineers dream and construct ever taller buildings. It is why we figured out a way to fly to the moon, and maybe, one day, go to Mars. Curiosity propels us forward.

But there is one area where curiosity fails most Americans—our history. For most of us, there is no room for curiosity when it comes to the one certain truth we have been taught. When you are schooled by teachers and parents and society that there is one revealed truth about America, and that teaching becomes part of our DNA, there is no need to look further. We don't wish to find facts that differ from the legends and myths on which we depend and with which we have grown comfortable.

But what happens when we encounter facts that don't fit neatly into our doctrine? What happens when we are forced to consider those facts? I have learned that one cannot un-know a fact. It eats at you, disturbs your peace and tranquility, it challenges everything you think you know and believe. Often, the reaction is resistance to the new fact—anger toward to revealer of the fact, or even fear. Our brains try to combat the new fact as our immune system responds to a pathogen.

In reading this book, you will have a bodily response. You will try to make the facts you are about to digest untrue. You will question the veracity of the words, the source material, and the very premise of what you are about to learn. And, well, you should. Bring to this work your most critical eye. That is what the author has done, but not done for you.

Scott Wolter, a noted scientist and historian, brings to us in *The Greatest Templar Tale Never Told* a compendium of fresh facts. It is your job as the reader, to make sense of it for yourselves. Do not be afraid of new facts, even if this material challenges everything you have been taught to believe about the founding of America.

You will read names you have never heard before in our textbooks and founding documents. It may be scary.

I spent nearly fifty years as an investigative reporter, and I have been scared a lot. But curiosity propelled me past my fears. I read *The Greatest Templar Tale Never Told* with the same growing apprehension. Fear that I was about to have my confidence shaken in what I though was true.

I cannot, personally attest that every word of *The Greatest Templar Tale Never Told* is true. That is because I didn't conduct the investigation myself. But I trust the scientific methods used by Scott Wolter and his vast understanding of the mysterious and cloaked world this story seeks to reveal. When reading the first draft of Scott's book and seeing the documents upon which it is based, I said to him, "If this is true, it changes everything."

Enjoy this journey. Have your fill of this remarkable examination. If you are like me, you will find this real-life mystery delicious.

-Don Shelby
September, 2025
Emmy and Peabody award-winning journalist

Foreword II

By Janet Wolter

We all think we know the story of how our beautiful country came to be. In school we learned there was a revolution by the British subjects living in the thirteen colonies in an attempt to gain their freedom and independence from the British crown, worn by King George III. War broke out and the King tried in vain to subdue his subjects by force, but the desire to govern themselves, have individual rights, and worship what deity they chose was stronger than the fear of punishment or death for most. It was the dream of people who were subjects, not only of British royalty but many other crowns throughout Europe, to break the back of the feudalistic system and be beholden to none but their deity. And so they did. The Americans won, followed by the French, and the whole system eventually fell apart and Democracy became the way across Europe. But here is what we were not taught, because our teachers did not know: in reality, that was the end of a very long untold secret story, one which really began over 600 years earlier, fought by a group of people we coined the "Venus" families. Why Venus?

Venus, as viewed from Earth, is the third brightest object in the sky, after the sun and the moon, and the traditional representative of the sacred feminine, known as the eternal consort of the Sun. She follows or leads him as an evening or a morning star depending on where she is in her eight-year cycle. A cycle in which she traces a pentacle, or five-pointed star, in the sky. Ancient cultures around the world observed this celestial relationship for countless centuries and many emulated the dualistic nature of these deities of the heavens in their own cosmology and lives. The Venus families as related to the story you will read in these journals begins with the Scottish/ Norwegian Saint Clair (Sinclair) family in the fourteenth century. Earl Henry Sinclair, the writer of the first three journals began writing down his story at the important age of eight, a special age where training can begin for children deemed worthy of a special destiny, and a sacred number in many traditions, and also related to Venus.

Henry Sinclair and his family, you will read, often celebrated many special days that relate to the Goddess while at the same time observing the required doctrine and holidays as taught by the Roman Catholic Church in their day. But they kept the old ways and teachings alive, like those of the Ancient Mystery schools in Eleusis and Egypt, as passed down by their ancestors, usually quietly and in secret. They were also a part of the Templar and Freemasonry Orders of their day, Knights and lay brothers and sisters who secretly kept the ancient dualistic traditions and teachings alive, right under the nose of the Church officials, often through artifacts, temples, and symbols hidden in plain sight, such as the number thirteen seen throughout the journals—a number of the Goddess and lunar cycles, demonized by the Church.

You see, at some point in history, going back to the time of Jesus and his wife Mary Magdalene, their descendants and followers made a pact with the Great Goddess called a Covenant, or a promise to Her that if She helped them find and found their New Jerusalem where they could practice their worship of Her freely, they would keep Her always present, but carefully veiled, and Her wise teachings alive and well. Jesus and Mary Magdalene were the physical embodiments of this dualistic philosophy in their time, the beginning of the Great Age of Pisces, when Jesus became known as the Fisher King. You get it, right? His mentor and cousin before him was John the Baptist, who is always shown in a wool shawl, with a staff and a lamb, because he reigned at the end of the Great Age of Aries, the ram. Make sense? If not quite yet, don't worry, Scott will be teaching you more about this in this book. It is the key to the history of religion and always has been since humans began to track the heavenly bodies.

The Medieval Knights Templar, and the Venus families, including the Sinclairs and others such as the Wemyss, Haliburton, and Stewart clans among many others, and their ideological descendants—the Freemasons—tell their story of their quest to found what they called their "Free Templar State." Their vision was a place where the rights of an individual reigned supreme, where the Goddess and God of one's choosing could both freely be worshiped, and democracy *by the People, for the People* would be the system of government. They had tremendous patience, and over countless generations passed on their sacred Covenant with the Goddess, a tradition in their case that involved moving and hiding large portions of the Templar treasure to this side of the Atlantic. This was the real beginning of the North American part of this "Templar Tale Never Told" and the founding of the United States and you will be stunned to learn what the treasure was, where it was placed, and who carefully guarded it. And in the end, we learn who the real heroes were: those who moved, brought, guarded, recovered, and hid the wealth of the Templars without which the heroes we are all familiar with, like George Washington, Paul Revere, Ben Franklin, Thomas Jefferson, George Mason, and many others, could not have had the funds to enlist the help of the French, such as General Lafayette, and others who helped turn the tide in our favor. War is expensive. The Templar treasure served its intended purpose.

The sacrifices of long separations and deaths of loved ones made by these families was a tremendous price to pay without which we would not be enjoying the freedom and rights we are privileged to have today. If every American read these journals, it would be my great hope that all would feel a renewed sense of why these selfless men and women found the principles they lived and died for to be so worthwhile. We have come to take our rights they fought so hard to preserve for granted in this time. They lived under oppression and tyranny, something I pray we never have to experience because we have the right to vote, a tremendous opportunity and privilege to be heard, and to choose our leaders. Read these beautiful journals of the past and appreciate what you have. For it can be gone, discarded, or taken away from you in an instant. The Venus families knew this all too well, and worked to make life better for their descendants... and all of us.

And thank you to Diana Muir for bringing these journals to our attention. While we know full well they are surrounded by controversy, as is

Diana herself–the journals must stand alone. I feel there are simply too many things that a modern, uninitiated individual would not know about Templarism and Freemasonry which we have long been a part of. We have researched the places and people within the journals for years. Finding the school room where Ben Franklin led a secret Freemasonic meeting, unknown to history, was unbelievably moving. We even met with the modern day Masonic Templar Grand Archivist in Halifax who allowed us access to old meeting notes and rolls, due to our affiliations and friendships, and we found several names of brethren from the journals, thus confirming their existence. He said nobody else has asked him to see those records in the thirty years he has guarded them. That was pretty convincing and that is why these journals must stand alone, regardless of controversy surrounding them. But you can decide for yourself and do your own study of them, as we continue ours. Let us know what you discover. Enjoy the story and Scott's annotations and analysis of other related sites and artifacts, especially the Kensington Rune Stone, all of which support this story of the Templars in America.

-Janet Wolter
August, 2025
Co-Author of *America Nation of the Goddess: The Venus Families and the Founding of the United States*

Introduction

The biggest and most obvious question I have wrestled with over the past nine years of vetting these journals is their veracity. Is this real and legitimate historical information written by one of the most important historical figures in history and his descendants, or is this an incredible work of fiction? The implications of the answer to this question are profound indeed. On one hand, we have arguably the most important historical information of the previously unknown details, spanning over four centuries, of what happened to the Templar Knights who disappeared into history on October 13, 1307. We also know what happened to the treasures they took with them that served as the tangible and symbolic cornerstone to the mission of establishing a sanctuary they called, "The Covenant."

Before we get ahead of ourselves, the reader needs to understand exactly what the Sinclair/Wemyss journals are. The trove of documents is comprised of twenty small books ranging in size from 4" x 6" to 6" x 8" in the later four books made of linen paper. The first thirteen books are written in Latin, the next two were written in Old English and the last five books are in modern English. The journals chronicle the secret activities of two Scottish clans over a period of 417 years that span five generations of the Sinclair clan and ten generations of the Wemyss/Weems clan. Their mission was to use the Templar treasures that disappeared from France at the port of La Rochelle on the evening of October 13, 1307, to establish a new sanctuary in a land "...far to the west." That land would eventually be called the United States of America, and this is the previously unknown story of how the nation was founded. The stories told in these journals are nothing short of incredible, although whispers of Knights Templar treasure making its way to North America have been heard within Masonic circles for over two hundred years. This story brings the popular movie, *National*

Treasure to life in an eerie similar way, suggesting the modern descendants of the people you will meet in this book knew more than they let on.

How the journals first came to my attention is an interesting story and important to understand in the context of their authenticity. The following is a summary of how the journals made their way to me, and Diana Muir's story about what she did leading up to it.

Chance meeting with Jeffrey Irving

In the fall of 2015, after completing her translations of the journals, Diana contacted the Lagina brothers, the stars of the History Channel show, *The Curse of Oak Island*. A year later in June of 2016, the brothers invited her to visit them on the island in Nova Scotia to show them the journals and the lambskin map in her possession. Unfortunately, when she reached the Canadian border, she was denied entry due to her felony conviction in 1987 for lying on her student loan application. At this point Diana contacted Jeffrey Irving who lived in the border town of Saint Andrews, NB. Jeffrey was a Templar/Oak Island researcher who she had been in contact with who also appeared on the show in Season 3. Jeffrey then offered to cross the border from Canada into the United States to meet with Diana and look at the documents she brought with her.

Jeffrey met with Diana on June 4, 2016, and examined the lambskin map (see page 32) and a few of the crew lists she had with her. During their meeting, Jeffrey expressed skepticism about the crew lists but had a favorable opinion of the map. He then took photographs of the items he later shared with me that were extremely helpful during the vetting process over these last several years. I asked Jeffrey if I could interview him to get his thoughts on the journals and his meeting with Diana and he shared the following comments:

> *"There were two things that struck me as I examined the crew lists and the lambskin map Diana showed me that day. The first was the names seemed to fit perfectly, almost too well. Like a genealogist had looked them up, and well, Diana is also a genealogist. Second, I was struck by how the ships drawn on the map looked childishly drawn. They didn't strike me as believable."*

Jeffrey and I talked about the visit with Diana and his comments in a phone conversation on July 28, 2025. He readily admitted his initial thoughts were hardly solid proof against the veracity of what Diana had shown him. Jeffrey also admitted he was concerned about Diana's shady past, but while concerning, it wasn't evidence of wrongdoing on her part.

After her meeting with Jeffrey, Diana traveled back through Massachusetts and said she stopped in Westford, Massachusetts, to see the Westford Knight and the Westford Boat Stone. Both are artifacts I have studied in the past and have concluded the man-made carvings are centuries-old and are connected to the activities of the Templars in America. Since I had concerns about Diana's credibility, whenever I had a chance to check on the veracity of statements she made, I resolved to do so. Her claim of visiting Westford provided such an opportunity. Sure enough, when I looked at the visitor list of the Westford Museum Diana's name was there where she signed the list a few months earlier.

This might be a good time to talk about the Westford Boat Stone, which is an extremely compelling artifact that, in my view, is connected to the Knights Templar and their activities in this area. It should also be noted the Boat Stone was found at the intersection of ancient indigenous trails mere blocks away from the Westford Knight carving. I will delve deeper into the connection between the Westford Knight—it's actually a carving of a sword only—and the local legend of its connection to a fallen

Visitor Log

Date	Name	Address/email	Purpose
5/22/16	Sue Moser	LionLily@onemain.com	Visitor
"	WA Hist Soc	[illegible]	
5/23/16	David K. Weight	6 Red Brook Ln, Ledyard, CT	Visitor
5/25/16	Jeff Wetherbee	Pepperell, MA	"
6/5/16	Becky Hanson	Quincy, MA	visitor
6/5/16	Diana Muir	E. Moline, IL	visitor

On October 31, 2016, I traveled to Westford, Massachusetts while on a trip to the East Coast. Inside the Westford Museum I photographed the visitor log to see if Diana's name was there. I was checking the veracity of the story she told of seeing the Westford Knight and the Boat Stone a few months earlier in June. Her name was indeed there. (Wolter, 2016) fourteenth-century Templar Knight named James Gunn. James Gunn's name appears on the crew list of the *Perequin* during the expedition to the Western Lands in 1395.

The Westford Boat Stone is one of the least well-known, but most compelling artifacts, in my opinion, ever found in the Northeast that are connected to pre-Columbian activities of the Knights Templar in this area. I learned about the artifact in 2005 and first saw it in September of 2006. In 2007, I offered to conduct a forensic investigation into the relative age of the weathering of the carvings, in a similar manner to what I had successfully done on the Kensington Rune Stone a few years earlier. The stone was shipped to my laboratory in June of 2007 and, after drilling a core sample out of the back of the stone and conducting my examination and testing, I issued my final report to the Westford Historical Society on October 12, 2007. My investigation incorporated the following background information provided by then Westford Knight Committee member David Brody:

> *"Regarding Boat Stone and its age, David Goudsward in his book ("Ancient Stone Sites of New England," p 125) notes that in the 1960s, Frank Glynn interviewed both William Wyman, who found the stone in 1932, and Edwin Gould, a longtime Westford, Massachusetts, resident. Both recalled seeing the stone along the side of the road when they were teenagers, some 60 or 70 years earlier. That dates to stone back to at least circa 1900."*

I have published my 2007 report on my website[1], but my bottom-line conclusion is the weathering of the man-made images and characters are quite advanced and certainly not of modern origin (after the early 1900s).[2] The man-made pecked lines exhibit weathering that predates the early 1900s by at least several decades and could well be several centuries old. Further, the advanced weathering could also be consistent with a circa 1400 CE origin. In layman's terms the artifact is authentic and historically important.

It is my opinion the artifact was created as a directional indicator meant to be understood by colleagues with the same knowledge and understanding

1. www.scottfwolter.com

2. https://scottfwolter.com/wp-content/uploads/2024/08/06557-Bat-Creek-Stone-web.pdf

The Westford Boat Stone sits on a metal stand inside the Westford Library in Westford, Massachusetts. The carvings include a medieval ship, an arrow, and three symbols interpreted to be: a "1", a vertically aligned fish or a Hindu Arabic number "4", and the Arabic number "4" or possibly the astrological symbol for the planet Jupiter. (Wolter, 2006)

of certain signs and symbols. One of the symbols that will be discussed in greater length in Chapter 9 is the esoteric knowledge of sacred numbers. Arguably the most important sacred number to the medieval Templars is the number 8, which is featured in the number of cannon ports on the side of the carved ship and lines on the fletched end of the arrow. This is clearly not coincidental and along with what are likely the astrological symbols of Pisces and Jupiter at the bottom, the stone could be signaling a rendezvous at a ship, at a particular point in time calculated in the heavens.

It should also be noted that the proximity of the Boat Stone to the Westford Knight (Sword) is likely not a coincidence. In fact, if the story of the broken sword carving is related to the legend of a fallen knight in Westford being Sir James Gunn is true, then it serves as powerful evidence to support the story relayed in the forthcoming journals. That means the two stones are likely connected and the Boat Stone was carved by a member of the exploration parties sent inland by Earl Henry Sinclair looking for colleagues who had traveled to the Western Lands from Norway in 1358. This story will be fleshed out in book one of Earl Henry Sinclair's journals in Chapter 4.

To say that I have been one hundred percent objective and completely detached from the story would be a lie. I want this story to be true, probably more than anyone. It would add conclusive supporting evidence to the work I've dedicated my life to for the past twenty-five years. This includes providing context, and answers the questions about *who*, from *where*, and *why* the artifacts like the Kensington Rune Stone and the Newport Tower—which already stand tall from a mountain of factual evidence that confirms their authenticity and fourteenth century origin—exist. Together with the vast trove of Cremona Document material we now know the complete, six-hundred-year-long true story of the founding of the Free Templar State, The New Jerusalem, or what Francis Bacon called, "The New Atlantis"—the land now known as the United States of America.

The mission to establish what would be called the United States of America was called the "Covenant", was born from the suppression and dissolution of the Knights Templar order by the King France who was aligned with the Roman Catholic Church in 1307. The surviving order went underground and longed to establish a new home "far to the west" where they and their ideological descendants could live free from the tyranny of the monarchs of Europe and persecution from the Church. This is why America fought a revolution against a monarchy and why there is a separation of Church and State in the Constitution. People have forgotten our own history and if we don't remember and learn from the past, it will be at our own peril.

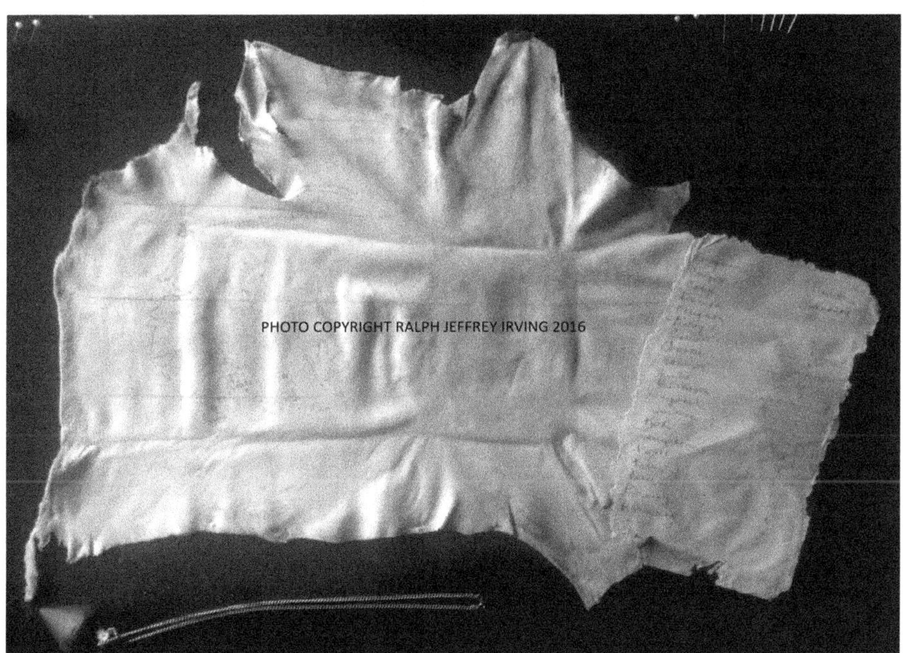

Jeffrey Irving took this photograph of the lambskin map when he met with Diana Muir on June 4, 2016. Jeffrey's and my photographs of the lambskin map and are the only known photographs that survive. The crew list in the photograph is from the *Perequin.*

Diana Muir and Jeffrey Irving pose for a selfie on the day they met, June 4, 2016. Photo courtesy of Jeffrey Irving.

1

Diana Muir

To fully understand the Sinclair/Wemyss journals one must start at the modern day beginning of the story and how they first came to my attention. It all began with a series of emails I received from a woman I did not know named Diana Muir.

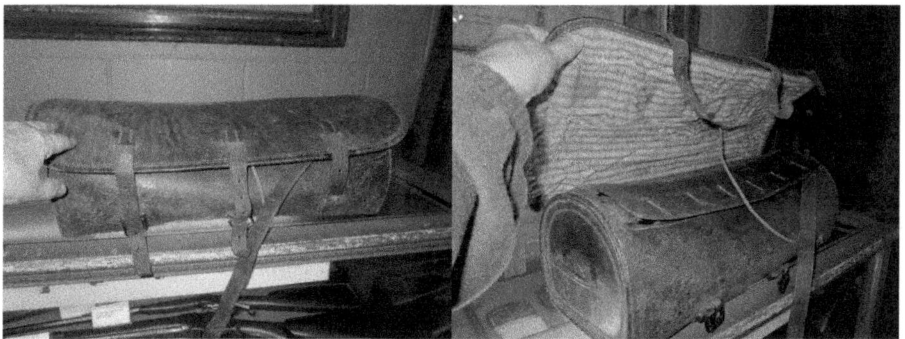

When Diana told me the story of how she found the journals she said they were inside an old leather saddlebag inside an old trunk. She later forwarded these photos, the second of which has the letters "US" stamped on the side, along the bottom edge. This suggests it likely belonged to a courier with the government sometime after the final entry was written in July of 1770, since the United States had not yet become a country. (Courtesy of Diana Muir).

Nauvoo

What started off as what I believed would be the first of many opportunities to see, feel, and touch the journals and lambskin map, turned out to be the one and only time I would have time to examine them. That day was September 21, 2016, only two months after Diana and I made contact. My friend and fellow Masonic brother, Matt Cranston, joined me for the roughly six-hour drive from Chanhassen, Minnesota, down to the Mormon Temple in Nauvoo, Illinois.

Diana had reserved a room at the library building that gave us a private opportunity to examine the lambskin map and John Weems Jr's third journal of four he wrote, which was book nineteen of twenty total. Before getting started, I set up a tripod with a video camera to record the entire meeting and examination of the articles Diana had brought with her. I started by unrolling the lambskin map that looked like a burrito, according to Diana. The skin was smaller than I imagined and had tiny hairs protruding from the edges and a few areas on the open surfaces. Once unfolded, I leaned in to get a close look at the markings that appeared to be made with either a lead or charcoal pencil. It quickly became apparent the side I looked at first represented a fairly accurate depiction of the southern shoreline of Nova Scotia. There were drawings of eight ships with a series of dots between the boats likely representing the routes taken during the expedition in 1395. I knew this was the date as it was drawn in Roman numerals on the end of the right foreleg of the lambskin.

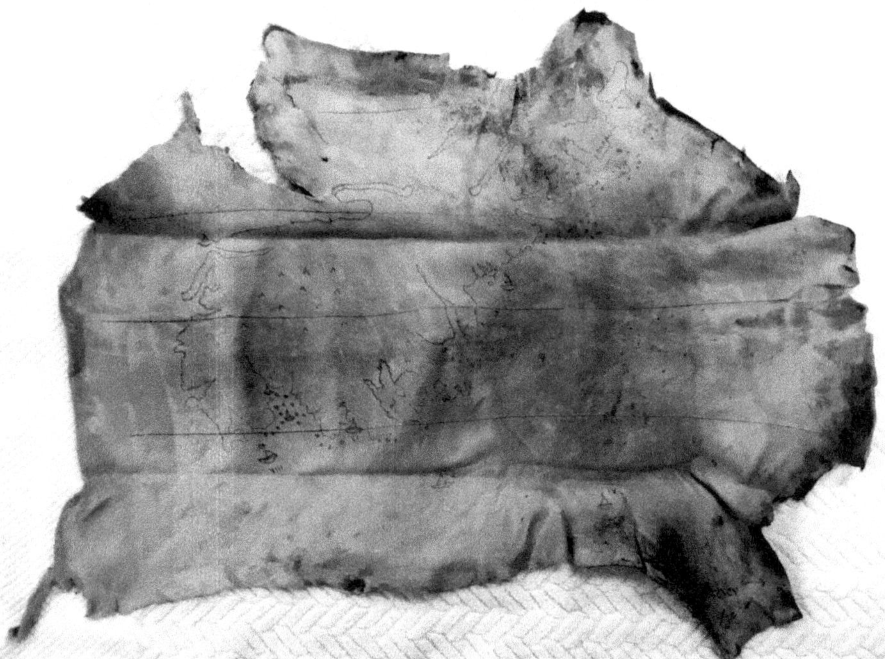

Above and opposite: The front and back show a reasonably accurate depiction of primarily the southern shoreline of Nova Scotia and other islands, respectively. Small ships and lines of dots appear to indicate routes sailed by Earl Henry's fleet of eight ships which were mapped by navigator and cartographer Antonio Zeno. We'll take a closer look at the five islands drawn on the back side in Chapter 9. (Wolter/2016)

At this point, it seems fair to hear from Diana herself and let that be the final word in this chapter. In May of 2022, I asked Diana if she would write an honest history of how she obtained the journals and her actions involving them since that time. I found her narrative to be factual as far as I could determine, and she seemed honest in her comments even when it wasn't personally flattering. In the end, the veracity of the journals will be determined by internal evidence and facts that can be documented on the ground. Read her narrative and decide for yourself. The pictures in this section were added by me to give additional context.

Henry and I

> *"It would be easy to say that I made everything up in my head since Day 1. No journals, no map, no translations, no anything. But that would be the biggest lie of all and too easy. It would make my life a lot simpler, but it just wasn't so. They really did exist. A lot of people had seen different parts of them, and I didn't know enough about Henry, Freemasonry, the Goddess or anything else when I first received them. I couldn't have written them, even if I'd wanted to.*

There are lots of questions about the journey I've taken over the past 15 years. Yes, it's been at least that long since I visited Greeneville, Tennessee, on Mother's Day weekend in 2005. I've been a genealogist ever since I joined the LDS Church in 1972 and had taken genealogy classes while a student at BYU. I knew my 3rd great-grandfather, John Weems, came from Baileyton, Greene Co., Tennessee, but no one knew anything about where he came from. On Mother's Day that year, I was living in Atlanta, GA, working for Intelligent Education and my home in Iowa was too far to go in just a 3-day weekend. So, I chose to visit the graves of my 3rd and 2nd great-grandmothers instead in Baileyton, Tennessee. And now to answer your questions:

How I discovered them in Tennessee.

After visiting the cemeteries in Baileyton – there are 2, the old and the newer one by the Methodist Episcopal Church, I decided to go to Greeneville to the T. Elmer Cox Historical and Genealogical Center to see if they had anything new in their collection. I arrived about 11AM only to find out that they closed at Noon on Saturdays.

The T. Elmer Cox Historical and Genealogical Library in Greenville County, Tennessee, where Diana Muir obtained the Sinclair/Wemyss Journals on Mother's Day in 2005. (Wolter, 2017)

I quickly surveyed the family files in the cabinet, perused the books on the shelves, and could see that there was nothing new since my last visit a year or two before. There was only one attendant that day, a young man in his 20s who was sitting behind the desk doing something to keep busy. No one else was there.

So, I asked, "Is there anything else that you know of that relates to the Weems family from Baileyton?"

He looked up and said slowly, "Well there's an old trunk in the basement that says, "property of John Weems", but it's never been catalogued." He hesitated for a moment, "I'm not supposed to let anyone down there, but I have a moment." He looked at his watch and quickly motioned for me to follow him. We descended a steep basement stair, and he pointed to the far southeast corner.

He said, "It's been in a fire and really stinks. That's probably the reason no one has messed with it." (I learned later that it had been rescued from the basement when the old German Methodist Episcopal church had burned down in about 1880.) Looking at the tag that marked the trunk he released the lock and lifted the top of the chest. The smell of fire and tar wafted out, making my eyes burn for a second or two. Looking in, we could see a small leather bag with a flap enclosing the contents. Lifting the flap, we could see several small books, or journals. There looked to be at least a dozen and being small (about 4" x 5"), they fit easily within the bag. I reached for the top one which looked very old and lifted it out, opened the cover only to find that it was written in Latin, and I couldn't read a word. All I could make out was Henricus Santo Claro. The rest was gibberish to me.

"May I take them upstairs?" I asked.

"Sure." He responded. "I'll put them away later."

Taking the small bag out of the trunk, we headed back upstairs where I laid the bag on the floor next to my chair and took a couple of the small books out and put them on the table to look them over. Looking at my watch, I could tell that it was 5 minutes till noon and saw that the attendant was leaving to go lock the doors.

Not wanting to miss the chance to review them, I put the books back in the bag, lifted the bag into my arms and headed towards the door with my purse over my shoulder. I hoped that by the time he returned, I'd be gone. Holding the small bag to my chest, I went out the door, opened the trunk to my car and slid the bag in, covering it was a small blanket that I kept in the trunk for cold weather.

I know I shouldn't have taken them, but I really wanted to look at them. I justified it by saying they didn't even know they had them, and since they'd never been catalogued, they didn't know what they were missing. I hadn't told him my name and so I hoped I'd get away with it. I told myself I'd return them to the library after I'd looked at all of them, but I never did.

I told others that he had offered to let me take them, but it wasn't true. He had no idea. I asked years later about the young man that used to work there, but they said he was no longer working there and had moved away a long time ago. I also checked with the local police department to see if anyone had ever reported a theft from the historical society, but they hadn't. I suppose he just let it go. At least I hoped he had.

Translating them.

When I first began to transcribe them, I started reading those written in English, the journals of John Weems Jr. I didn't get very far before I realized I needed to start at the beginning with the earliest ones. So, I looked at the dates and lined them up as best as I could. I then started with the one in Latin written by Henricus Sancto Claro starting in the 1350s.

I used Google translate to translate them, and because the grammar is totally different for Latin and English, I had to restructure the sentences to make sense. I also used the internet to translate the Middle English. I know the translation wasn't entirely accurate and there were a few words here and there that didn't translate at all. I tried not to change the meaning of the sentences and luckily the last four or five were in modern English and easier to read. At the time, I wasn't trying to be historically accurate. I just wanted to know what they said and how they related to the Weems family of Greene Co., Tennessee.

Who did I contact?

Once I knew it was talking about Prince Henry Sinclair, I joined the Sinclair family Facebook group. I asked questions about him and his genealogy, because at the time genealogy was still my main focus, trying to connect him to my own family from Greene Co., Tennessee. After a while I started to post some of the things I'd found in the journals, including ship's crew lists. Some people told me the journals were fake, and others told me that the crew lists were full of family names from the Orkney islands who were loyal to Prince Henry. One of those people was Robert (Rob) Sinclair who thought they were real and with whom I'm still in contact today.

I soon started my own private group called "Fellowship of the Map" and published a couple of pages from the first journal. Terry Deveau told me it sounded like someone trying to write a book and I quickly shut it down. I wasn't up to more criticism at the time. I'd also published a couple of crew lists on the Prince Henry Sinclair group but don't remember publishing anything else. I've since reopened the Fellowship page but have made it private with just a few individuals who I'm working with to vet the journals.

I began transcribing the journal because I'd been watching The Curse of Oak Island *on the History Channel and heard them mention Henricus Santo Claro. That's when I tried to translate them and figure out what they were. I contacted* The Curse of Oak Island *team, but it took them over a year to respond to me. By then I'd been introduced to Scott Wolter and although I talked with Rick Lagina for over an hour on the phone, nothing came of it.*

I had planned to visit Oak Island in June of 2016 and had made arrangements with Rick for a private tour of the island. He wanted me to join the tour, and I was looking forward to it. I had the transcription with me and the map, which I had pinned into a shadow box so it wouldn't get damaged. I put it in the trunk of my rental car and headed towards Canada.

First, I stopped in Boston, Massachusetts, to see my daughter Becky. I showed Becky the map in the back of the car and told her about my planned trip to Oak Island. That weekend she took me to see the Westford Knight Stone in Westford, Massachusetts. It was only about 14 miles away from where she lived. We stopped at the town square and then drove around a bit as it was a Sunday, and the Museum wasn't open until noon. It was also graduation weekend as we could see a party going on across the street.

Once it opened, we went inside, and I signed in and began looking around. Because we were the only ones there, the docent began talking and I told him I had the Prince Henry Sinclair journals and was looking for information on artifacts that had been found, including the Boat Stone. He suggested I talk to David Brody, as he was an expert on the Westford Knight Stone and a writer. He tried to sell me some of his books that were by the front door, but I resisted. He gave me his contact information, but I never contacted him. After stopping at the Westford Museum, Becky took me on the Concord trail to Boston that had been used during the Revolution.

After the weekend, I continued my journey. However, when I got to the border, I was stopped by the border patrol. I had forgotten to sign my passport and was taken into the border office for further vetting. It was then they learned of my felony conviction from nearly 40 years ago for lying on a student loan application and so I was turned away.

Instead, I decided to stay the night in a local motel there and called Jeffrey Irving, a good friend of mine that I'd been corresponding with for over a year, who lived just across the border. He came to see me the next morning, and we met in the dining area of the motel (which was closed for construction) and I showed him the map and a couple of the crew lists which I also had with me.

I told Jeff about my difficulty getting over the border and he called Jack Begley, a member of the Oak Island crew, that he knew personally. He explained the problem and told Jack that as far as he could see, the map was real. He asked Jack to let Rick know that I wouldn't be coming up that weekend, which was a huge disappointment to me.

After a few hours, I said goodbye to Jeffrey. He headed back over the border, and I took the northern route back home to Illinois. I remember that for almost June, it was freezing cold in Vermont, and I stopped to buy a fleece jacket at a small gas station.

When and why, I contacted, you, Scott Wolter.

Right before I reached out to the Oak Island team the first time, I also sent an email to Scott Wolter after watching one of his shows; America Unearthed *on the History Channel. At the end it says something like "If you have something you think I should see, please contact me..." He never responded until my neighbor Shaundra sent him a couple of pictures of the map (which she'd seen in my apartment) and he finally became interested.*

Our initial meetings

Our initial meeting was at the Wolter home in Chanhassen, Minnesota. I drove up to meet him and brought the transcription that I had completed. He seemed disappointed that I hadn't brought the originals, but I didn't know him and wasn't certain I could trust him. I had heard a lot of different things on the internet about both the Oak Island team and Scott Wolter. I didn't bring any originals because I didn't want to lose them. During that weekend in Chanhassen, I accompanied Scott and his wife Janet to a meeting of Freemasons at the Scottish Rite Temple in Minneapolis. I explained what I believed I had and asked for their opinions as to whether it was worth pursuing. They all seemed to think so and gave me instructions on how to handle the documents (like a museum Archivist would with gloves and such) and insight into what Henry Sinclair meant to the Freemasons. I made arrangements later to meet up with Scott and one of the men he'd introduced me to at the visitor's center in Nauvoo, Illinois, to review some of the actual documents. When I left that weekend, I left a copy of the transcription with Scott so that he could read it more thoroughly.

Diana Muir tells her story about finding and translating the Sinclair/Wemyss journals to a group of Freemasons and researchers at the Scottish Rite Temple in Minneapolis, Minnesota, on August 13, 2016. (Wolter, 2016)

The next time we met was in late September at the Nauvoo, Illinois, Visitors Center. I arrived first and made arrangements with some of the attendants there to use the conference room on the 2nd floor for our meeting. I had brought part of John Weems Jr's journals, written in English, that described what he remembered being buried in the Vault outside of Washington DC, on Theodore Roosevelt Island, and the lambskin map which Scott had only seen pictures of.

His friend, Matt (Cranston) from Minneapolis, took a video and showed me a green stone slab that mimicked an artifact talked about in the journals (The Emerald Tablet). After Scott examined the pages from John Jr's journals and the lambskin map, he said he was very impressed and wanted to set up another meeting to see more. Unfortunately, that follow-up meeting never happened.

Diana Muir, Scott Wolter, and Matt Cranston, pose next to the lambskin map and book number 19 of the 20 Sinclair/Wemyss Journals Diana showed to them in a private space at the Mormon Visitor's Center in Nauvoo, Illinois on September 21, 2016.

About a week later, I panicked after Scott had declared them 'most likely real' because of the content and decided to end my association with him. It scared me to think of getting involved in something that could change history, that might very well turn out to be a hoax. I didn't want to be the person accused of perpetrating a hoax, and I didn't want to deal with it any longer. It had basically taken over my life; constantly researching, talking with skeptical people, and being told I was a liar by people on the internet. My skin wasn't thick enough and I had my own doubts about the authenticity of the journals. Things had happened in my past that were similar in nature, and I didn't want them to become known. I knew that I would be blamed for 'creating' the journals and map and I wanted it over.

After visiting the Temple, I visited the nearby park and almost put the journals, and everything associated with them into a trash can but changed my mind. I was afraid someone would find them before the trash was emptied. I would wait till later when I could put them in a dumpster that someone wasn't going to go through. I drove back to East Moline, tossing my phone out the window when I went over a small stream and bridge and tried to think of what I was going to say when I got back.

What I did with the journals in October of 2016.

When I got close to East Moline, I went to a low-income apartment building where I knew a few people lived, and which was next door to my church. I tossed the bag containing everything (including the map) associated with the journals into the dumpster. The dumpster was empty, and I remember hearing the thud in the bottom. I quickly left because I didn't want to make the decision to retrieve them.

The three pages I found and gave to Scott shortly thereafter.

Scott didn't believe that I had really thrown the journals away. At one point he was scheduled to go to Washington DC and present his story to a television network and needed something concrete to show the panel. He insisted that I check everything and everywhere to see if I had anything left that I hadn't thrown away. (Even though he believed I still had them.) By then we had vetted a good share of the journals, and I began to realize that even though many people told me they were fake, the events, people and circumstances in the journal really did happen. Scott had found many similarities to Freemasonic teachings and there were things in the journals that I could not have invented. We had spent a lot of time and effort creating affidavits for him to take to the presentation and I wanted to help him get the television show.

So, I went back and searched through everything I had. At one point I had taken the pages of some of the journals apart and put them in transparent page holders. Although I threw the binder of pages away, I had put three of them into a blue folder that I used to carry with me when I was doing research. They each had signatures on them, and I wanted to see if any copies of their different signatures still existed so I could compare them. They were still in the binder, so I took them to Minnesota to give them to Scott.

Field research from the last couple of years tracking down various Weems descendants.

For the past couple of years, besides vetting the events and people in the journals, I've been trying to track down other descendants of John Weems Jr. who might be able to corroborate information in the journals or have other stories or pictures to add. I knew that the main family had come from Greene Co., Tennessee, and had already spent a lot of time talking with Greene County relatives including my cousin Betty Edwards who told me about her uncle who'd been to Wemyss Castle where he'd been told that they were smugglers at one time. Most other Weems in Greene County have no idea they're even related, much less that John was a Freemason. They do recognize that many of the Bailey men (who married the oldest daughter Lizzie) were Freemasons.

I was able to make friends with many of them and still keep in touch with many of them. The history of Greeneville is amazing and lends credibility to the idea that the journals were copied to save them from falling into Confederate hands during the Civil War and being lost. Greeneville had been a hotbed of activity and had actually changed hands from Union to Confederate five times. A local college had been burned, the Masonic Hall had been used as a Confederate billet, and bridges, churches and buildings had been burned throughout the county by Confederate and Union sympathizers alike.

Another group of Weems, descended from one of John's younger sons (Thomas Louis Weems), went to Southern Illinois, which is where David Weems is from. I have tried to track down as many of them as possible but still have a long way to go. I've been there twice now and have visited many cemeteries and family members. I've been to the local library there, but the family records there only go back to about 1850 when the family arrived. One of my cousins from this group is Barbara Weems Hawkins who used to live in the Ozarks but now lives in upper Michigan. Although she's had a stroke, she helps me as much as possible and believes the journals are real. She told me of a vision her mother had that told her that someday the Weems family would impact the world. She introduced me to many more cousins from Southern Illinois including the one who gave me the daybook of Sister Agnes from the Catholic library. Still, they know nothing of the journals, only that some of the men were Freemasons.

The third group of Weems is from grandsons of John Jr. (George Wright Weems and Jones Weems) who went to Stella, Missouri, with some of the families of their wives from Greene County. This group is the most interesting because this is where I learned that the journals had been copied to preserve them and sent in three directions with each group. This meant that what I had found was most likely a copy. And that there were 2 more copies out there. When I arrived in Missouri and checked into the Super 8, I mentioned to the girl at the desk that I was in town to do genealogy on the Weems family. (I always talk too much and offer too much information). She mentioned she knew someone named Weems, Sean Weems and that I should call him. I did and we talked for about half an hour, and he told me some of the stories his grandfather had told him. (He was descended from George Wright Weems the 3rd b. 1817 in Greeneville and died in Wanda, Missouri, in 1881. George Wright Weems III was both a Freemason and a member of the KGC). Sean was the one who told me that there were 3 copies and there was one buried in the Weems Lot in the old cemetery. His great-grandfather was notorious for his KGC affiliation, so he remembered a lot of the old stories. The other copy was probably in southern Illinois, which meant I needed to go back to Illinois at some point.

I spent the next day at the local library where I learned about David Burnell Weems, who was on his death bed. I decided in my head that he was Sean's grandson (even though he only had a daughter) and the information had come from him. Instead, I lied to Scott and Janet and said that I had spoken with him, instead of Sean.

While researching the Missouri Weems, I found that many of the Weems were Freemasons and one in particular had been raised to be a 32nd degree by Albert Pike, the Grand Master of the Southern Region and a member of the KGC during the period leading up to the Civil War. Several of the Weems cousins had been part Native American and had served under General Pike. Given that Andrew Johnson had come from Greene Co., TN and had been in the lodge the same time as the Weems and Bailey, and that he was a confidant of Albert Pike, it held to reason that there might be a connection, or shared knowledge between Albert Pike and the Weems of Missouri. I'm still working on that.

The next summer I returned to southern Illinois to do more research and to track down more of the Weems descendants. It was while having lunch with a cousin that she gave me Sister Agnes daybook. It talked about the journals and how Sister Agnes was translating and transcribing the journals that James Alston Weems, a 'shouting' preacher from Stella, MO (that's a preacher who stands on the corner and shouts his message to passers-by) in exchange for wood and hay for the Catholic priest. She was originally from Scotland (so knew Gaelic, was a Catholic nun so she knew Latin) and seemed to become good friends with him, even though they came from different churches. She also seemed to know some about the legend of Prince Henry Sinclair and Templar treasure from Scotland. She had gone to Canada as a novice and then was sent to Illinois when the church was beginning to grow. The daybook also gave insight into the life of the Weems from that time period and why they came to Illinois. I still need to check out other entries such as marriages and births to see if they are accurate.

The Darren Weems journal story appears to still be unfolding

" In southern Illinois, there was a Weems (JCE Weems who went by Edward) who was a 47-year-long member of the Masonic Lodge whom I thought may have known something about the diaries. I thought maybe they had passed to him as he was a Freemason and next in line. I tracked down his

grandsons through his obituary and was able to set up a dinner meeting with Darren Weems, a captain in the Air Force stationed at Scott AFB in East St. Louis while I was there that week. I met him and his wife, a girl from Thailand, who were about to be transferred to England the next week. He told me of his grandfather and that he (Darren) had a copy of the journals. However, he had taken it from his father's house (his father was apparently a drunk and a thief) and believed it to be a fake. He believed his father and his girlfriend were copying the book that his grandfather had in order to sell it to the highest bidder. He found it at his dad's house after his grandfather died and took it. It was among the things that he had packed to go to England, but he had a picture of it that he had taken, along with pictures of all his other belongings that were being shipped. He shared that picture with me, and I sent it to Scott.

When Darren arrived in England, he was coming home for the holidays and asked me to meet him at Andrews AFB near DC so he could give me the journal personally. I agreed to drive to DC and meet him at the air terminal on base, because he was flying 'space available' on military flights. Being a veteran, I have a Veterans' ID and was able to get through the gate fairly easily after explaining that I was meeting a relative at the air terminal. Although we had asked him not to open the package, he'd been required to open it when going through customs but had stapled it back together in its white padded package. He handed me the package; we spoke for a few minutes and then he was back on his plane to go to Scott AFB. Since then, he's been transferred to Poland as part of the NATO forces. He is a pilot and flies transport planes. Because of the Ukraine-Russian conflict, I haven't heard from him for a while but hope to hear from him as soon as he's able to communicate. Since then, it's become obvious the book he had was a modern copy, but the content is virtually the same as the transcript that I created from the first copy. Although words and grammar are different, the story is basically the same."

In summary, I felt Diana had been transparent in her write-up, but because of her inconsistent answers to certain questions over the years I asked to do an interview with her in early 2024. I did this for two reasons. The first was to try and glean additional information she may have inadvertently left out in her narrative. The second was to ask some of the same questions to see if she gave the same answers. In the end, as you will see in the interview, her answers were consistent, and it seems she was being truthful.

While I cannot condone Diana's behavior in stealing the journals from the historical society in Greenville, Tennessee, it is a separate issue from determining the veracity of the journals.

Interview with Diana

1. How did you acquire the journals?

"I found them in an old trunk in the basement of a distant relative in Greeneville, TN where John Weems Jr had lived, while I was on a research trip to TN and NC on Mother's Day Weekend in 2005."

2. Where did they come from?

"Answered above. They were written by generations of John Weems' ancestors, and himself. They've traveled from Scotland, to Jamaica, to Canada, to Colonial America, and finally to Abbeville, North Carolina, and Greeneville, Tennessee."

3. How were they stored?

"The journals were in an old saddle bag, probably from the Civil War era, inside the trunk, and were in the basement of an old house. There were no special storage precautions."

4. When did you realize the importance of what you had?

"I acquired them in 2005 but it wasn't until about 2015 that I realized what they were. It wasn't until after I spoke with Scott Wolter that I realized how important they might be."

5. What did that realization feel like?

"It made me feel ignorant as I didn't know anything about the events or context that they were talking about. I barely knew who Prince Henry Sinclair was and only heard of the Knights Templar but knew nothing about them."

6. How did you translate the Latin and Old English journals?

"I used Google and Bing translation programs on the internet. Then I put the sentences into modern grammar so that they would make sense. I had no thoughts of ever publishing them when I did the translation. It was for myself, so I knew what they were saying. I didn't do it as a professional translator would have done, and I'm sure a lot of mistakes were made."

7. What challenges did you have as you did the translations?

"The Old English translated a different way every time I did it. There aren't any good translation programs and so I went with the translation that seemed to make the most sense."

8. What have you done to investigate the veracity of the journals?

"I had started with transcribing the journals that were written in modern English (John Sr. and John Jr.) and then realized I needed to go to the beginning in order to make sense of what they were saying. As I read, I started to do research on the people and events that they talked about. Still, before I took the transcription to Scott Wolter, I hadn't done a lot of research. I had verified the names of the author of each volume, and their relationship to the next but had done little on the events of the time or the Templars that they talked about.

I asked several people on the Sinclair Family Facebook group and got a lot of reactions.

A) That I couldn't have known the names of the Orkney families who were loyal to Prince Henry. Therefore, the ship lists of sailors had to be real because I didn't have any way or resources to learn who they were.

B) Most people said I was full of crap and wrote them myself.

C) Some said they were a hoax from the 18-19th century when Templars were being scorned by academics.

D) Niven Sinclair, the head of the Sinclair family at the time, believed in them. Many others who had done a lot of research believe in them, but were still skeptical, waiting for more research to be done."

9. Why did you contact me?

"I contacted the Lagina brothers first, because I had been watching the show and heard them talk about Prince Henry. I thought they might be interested, but at first, they never called back. It wasn't until after I contacted Scott that Rick Lagina called me on the phone. Rick wanted access to them, but in the NDA, it was exclusive to them, and I would have lost all rights. In the meantime, I had talked with Scott and agreed to work with you on validating the journals."

10. Why did you only bring one of the journal books and the lambskin map when you met with me at the Mormon Temple in Nauvoo, Illinois?

"I still wasn't certain of how much I wanted to share with Scott and so I only brought what I thought was most important; the journals that talked about the vault on Mason Island and what was contained in the vault. I brought the map because it was unique and showed places where they said the treasure had been buried throughout the bay."

11. In September of 2017, you said that you threw the journals away. Why did you do that?

"I did them because someone in the Sinclair group convinced me they were fraudulent. I didn't want to be accused of presenting a hoax. Plus, I was overwhelmed by how important everyone thought they were and unprofessionally I had treated them and doing such a bad job of translation. I had also been introduced to a world of esoteric knowledge and practice that I knew nothing about and was uncomfortable with because of my Church affiliation (LDS). Trained as an academic in History,

archaeology and sociology, everything convinced me that they were fraud, so I threw them away (although I kept the transcription a couple of pages with signatures that I had wanted to verify)."

12. Do you think the Journals could still be recovered?

"The waste management group seems to know exactly what hill of trash they would be in at the city dump, but garbage is treated with chemicals to make it dissolve, so I doubt they'd be salvageable even if we found the bag they were put in."

13. In 2019, when I asked if you had any of the original pages, you were able to produce three pages of originals. Where did they come from?

"The three pages that I had kept were in a blue binder that I hadn't had with me when I threw the rest in the trash. I fact I forgot about them until he asked if there was anything left. Then I went back through all the binders and found them."

14. By producing three original pages, doesn't that cast doubt on your claim that you threw them away?

"Certainly, but I DID throw them away and have nothing more to present."

15. Tell us about your discovery at Banning State Park?

"In September of 2019 I went to pick up my little brother, Brian Shover, in Monticello, WI to bring him to live with me. He was an alcoholic, jobless, and homeless, but he was family. On the way back he and I stopped at Banning State Park to camp out for the night and then took the trail to the ice cave, along the river. I told him a little bit about the story and how I had figured that if the Templars in 1665 came to the end of the Lake Superior, somewhere along the river in Duluth, that the first major river they would come to in their trip west would be the one going through Banning State Park. It also squared up with the coordinates left in the journals. The cave was written about on the internet, so I thought it was a good chance, that was where they'd left part of the treasure. Later, I

learned that if you drew a straight line from the end of the bay in Duluth, directly to where the Kensington Rune Stone was found, Banning State Park is on that direct line. They appear to have been headed to where the Kensington Rune Stone was.

While walking down the trail to the Ice Cave, Brian used a metal detector, mostly for fun to see if he could find anything. He did, mostly beer tabs, and a couple of pennies and a nickel. As we got to where the trail is blocked by a pile of rocks, there is a smaller cave to the left. I was trying to inspect that when I saw him digging next to the entrance to the left side of the cave. He was determined to get whatever it was out so we used a garden trowel I had in the car to dig deeper. About 6-8 inches down we found a silver coin, with Templar markings on it. I found another one among the tree roots near the entrance to the small cave. Brian wanted to search further but I convinced him that without witnesses, it wouldn't mean anything, and we should wait and tell Scott what we'd found. We didn't go any further to the ice cave. It's locked and we didn't have any tools with us, plus it's full of bats and I didn't want to crawl over the pile of rocks blocking the rest of the trail.

Instead, I took compass readings where we'd found the coins and send a pic[ture] *to Scott. Then as we looked up, we could see the sketch of an Indian head on the cliff above. It took a few minutes, but then could I see the outline of an 8-pointed star 'behind' the sketch of the Indian head, like the head had been drawn over it. It's very faint, and irregular but it's there. I took several pictures of it and then we started hiking back.*

We called Scott who asked us to meet him somewhere and showed him the coins. He showed us a few of the coins he had and verified that they had [T]emplar markings on them. I still have them in my jewelry box."

16. What personal connection do you have with the journals?

"The last writer of the journals, John Weems Jr. born about 1745, died 1812, was my 3rd great grandfather, who died in Baileyton, TN. He was a direct descendant of Prince Henry Sinclair. I descend through his oldest daughter/child, Elizabeth who married Thomas Bailey. I've been

to Greeneville, TN and Abbeville, SC and Hillsboro, NC to research the family many times."

17. What does this all mean to you?

"I've learned through further research that my family was crucial in the recovery of some of the Templar Treasure which was used to fight the Revolutionary War. Also, history isn't what they teach us in school, there is always more to the story. Since then, I've learned the history behind the journals and the men who wrote them, the natives they interacted with, and the men who came with them to the Americas. I've also learned that they were most likely a copy (although the map was original). The place they lived in, Greeneville, TN, changed hands from Union to Confederate 5 times during the Civil War. They were most likely copied to keep the knowledge safe. I've since learned that several copies were made. I believe there were 3 copies; one went to Southern Illinois with a younger son, and another went to Stella, Missouri with two grandsons. The question remains, where are the originals or were they lost during the Civil War? It is well known that the Confederates burned the Masonic Lodge, local college, and bridges during the Civil War. I'm still doing research on all of this.

The men who wrote them knew other Important men like Albert Pike, who interacted with the Weems family in Arkansas and southern Missouri, and Andrew Jackson who was a member of the same lodge as the Weems and Bailey (family by marriage) in Greeneville. What took place between them all, we'll probably never know."

18. Being a Mormon, how does the "Covenant" fit in with your beliefs?

"The rituals of the Freemasons mirror those of the Templars and many native American tribes. It's not something that is ever discussed in the Mormon faith. Mormons become Freemasons but I don't know if they understand the esoteric meaning of some of the things Scott has taught me. The covenant of protecting the knowledge and treasure to create a free Templar state fits right in with the Mormons trying to set up their own free state in the state of Utah. I've never really shared what I learned

from the journals with a highly placed Elder in the LDS Church, so I don't know what they would think of them."

19. Where did the Sister Harkin notebook come from?

"It came from a distant cousin in Olney, IL who worked at the Catholic Church in the library. She said it had been left there for years as part of the history of the local Catholic Church."

20. Do you think the Harkin notebook is authentic–representing events that actually happened?

"Yes, I've researched several of the mundane passages, such as marriages, deaths, and births and they are all accurate within a day or two. I also know that James A Weems was an itinerant preacher for the Methodist Episcopal Church of that time and verified with their church archivist. It turns out that John Weems Jr was a Methodist Episcopal preacher and several of his son were as well. They spread out to southern Illinois and Missouri, many still setting up their own churches."

21. Why did you present a modern leather journal as old when it was obviously modern?

"At the time I presented it, I didn't know that. I hadn't done any research on the leather journal itself."

22. What is this journal and who did the writing in it?

"It appears to be a copy of the original journals. I believe the girlfriend of the man who had it, did the writing."

23. Assuming the journals are legitimate, what role do they play regarding American history?

"They explain how intricately involved the Freemasons were with the founding of America, and where some of the funding came from."

24. Given your difficult past, has it made bringing the journals public more difficult?

> *"Absolutely! I didn't want to be accused of writing them and presenting a hoax. It's never been about the '15 minutes of fame', being on TV with the Laginas, or even the money. Just about the truth. I never intended to publish it in the first place. I just wanted to learn more about my family."*

25. What do you say to people that might accuse you of creating these documents?

> *"In order to have written them, I'd have to be a lot smarter, knowledgeable of Templar rituals, the belief in the Goddess and other things that I simply didn't know about as a traditional academic. All those things were – to me – fringe science. Some things, like the comet in the sky above Nova Scotia, you would have had to be there, and I wasn't. To write the journals, I'd have to be a genius and divinely inspired. I'm neither."*

While I appreciate Diana's candid and seemingly honest responses there are still plenty of reasons to question her honesty about a number of things. That said, I do not believe Diana had anything to do with the creation of the journals as the internal evidence is too compelling and accurate for ANYBODY to have created them. The veracity of the journals is confirmed by their content which will be discussed in detail in chapter 9.

2

The Sister Harkin Journal

Diana Muir believes the original journals, last in the possession of John Weems Jr., who died in 1812, were copied by three members of the Weems family just prior to the Civil War. This means there must be at least two additional copies out there somewhere. If Diana had one copy, and possibly the original lambskin map, the Sister Harkin copy would be the fourth copy—this one fully translated into English.

Diana claims the Sister Harkin journal was given to her by a distant cousin who lived in Mount Vernon, Illinois and who worked in the library at the Catholic church. She said it had been left there for years as part of the history of the church. The diary contains several entries chronicling her four-month-long efforts to translate the Latin and Middle English into modern English for Reverend James Alston Weems (1828-1908). Weems was a street preacher who didn't have a church but was recognized and ordained by the church, and who must have inherited the journals from a family member. Reverend Weems was a great grandson of John Weems Jr.

According to Sister Harkin's diary, she agreed to do the translations of the journal entries in return for firewood and hay on January 31, 1885. She started with the Latin books and had them completed by the end of February. In her entry on February 26, she noted she asked Reverend Weems if "*...he knew anything about the Templars, he said no.*" Clearly, she understood what she was translating and must have been blown away by the story being told. One can only speculate how she felt about the alternate history conveyed in the journals—especially being a nun in the Catholic Church. Later entries into her diary give some indication into her psyche as she did this work.

In her May 13, 1885 entry it's clear Sister Harkin understood the importance of the story and appears to have felt compelled to report the information to Church authorities. However, she writes that she honored her agreement, most likely with Reverend Weems, to keep the information about his ancestors secret. Apparently, Sister Harkin was so caught up with the story she decided to transcribe the remaining five books written in modern English by John Weems Sr. (Book sixteen) and John Weems Jr. (Books seventeen through twenty). Despite her notes, the modern copy Diana received from Darren Weems does not have translations of the Middle English or modern English entries Sister Harkin says she included. That means Darren's father's girlfriend must have chosen not to copy the rest of the journals, or she copied a different version that didn't have the last seven books transcribed.

Upon completion of her work, Sister Harkin was clearly moved by the story to the point of skepticism. One can appreciate this position because the same thing happened to John Weems Jr. as he wrote in his own journal upon his return from Nova Scotia in 1769. He too found the story told in the Sinclair/Wemyss journals involving nine generations of his own family to be incredible to the point of being unbelievable. It wasn't until he was taken to the Newport Tower in Newport, Rhode Island that he was convinced the story was true.

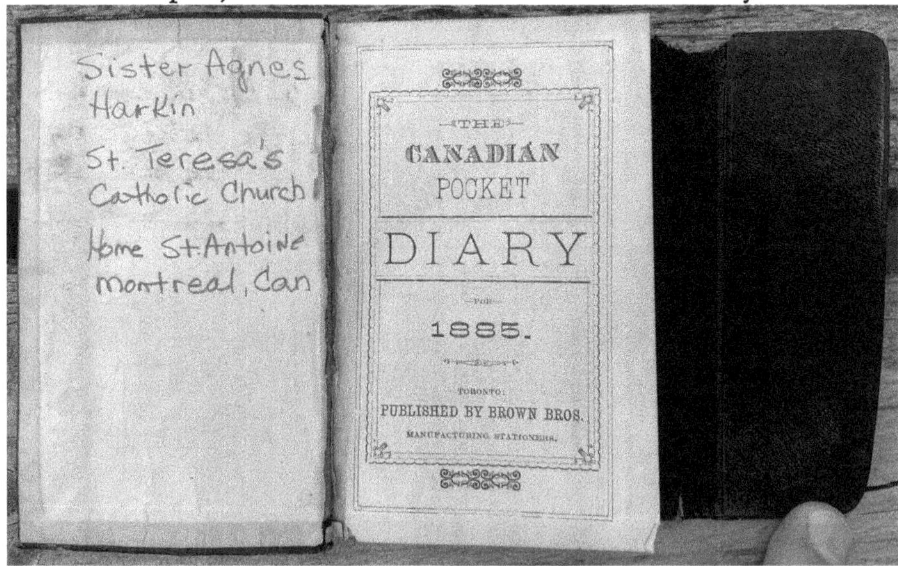

The original Sister Harkin pocket diary from January 31 to May 30 1885 which contains numerous entries and commentary on her translations of the journals for Reverend James A. Weems. Diana Muir produced this journal for the author on July 22, 2021. (Wolter/2021)

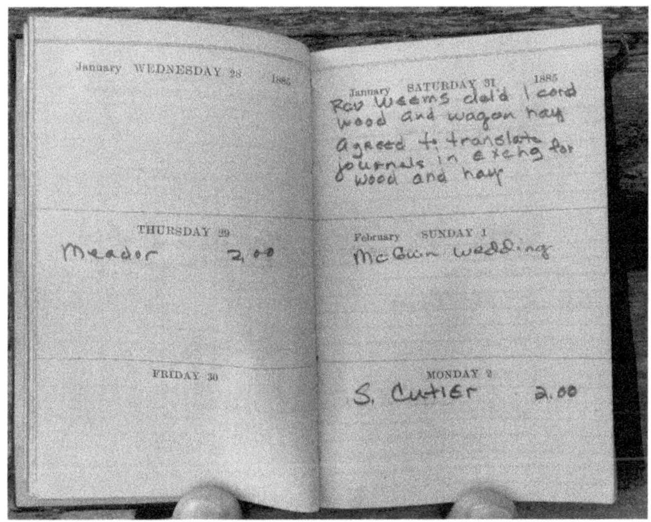

On January 31, 1885, Sister Harkin wrote in her diary that she had reached an agreement with Reverend James A. Weems, to translate the Latin and Middle English entries in his copy of the Sinclair/Wemyss journals into modern English in exchange for firewood and hay. (Wolter/2021)

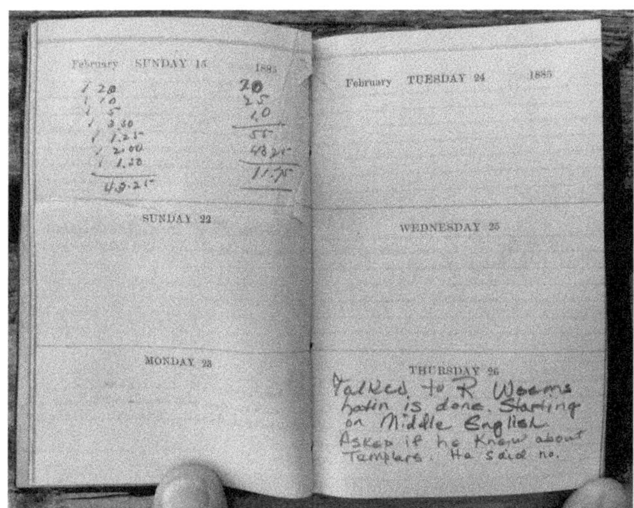

On February 26, 1885, Sister Harkin wrote that she had completed the Latin entries in the first thirteen journals. She obviously understood the essence of the story and asked Reverend Weems if he knew who the Templars were, to which he replied "No." (Wolter/2021)

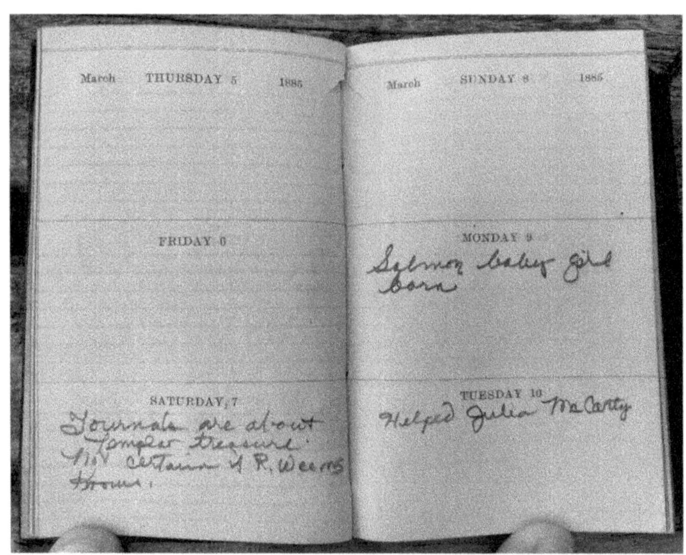

Sister Harkin's March 7, 1885 entry makes crystal clear she understood the mission of transferring Templar treasure to North America and appears hesitant to discuss with her client Reverend Weems. (Wolter/2021)

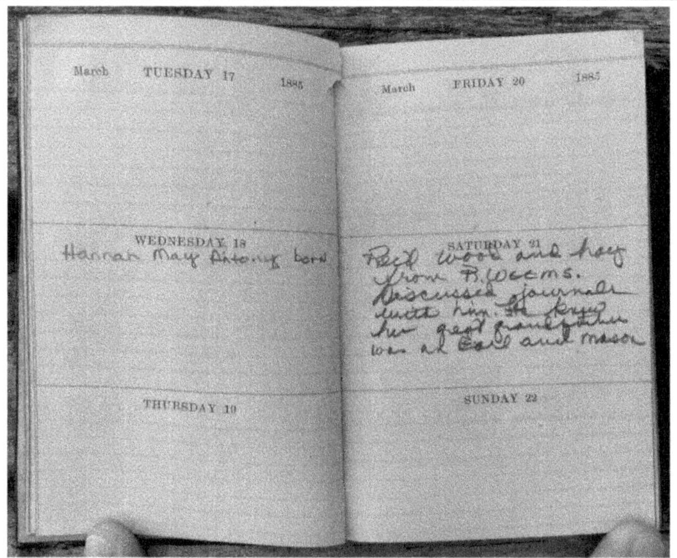

Two weeks after writing she understood the mission of the "Covenant" it appears she talked to Reverend Weems about the contents of the journals she was translating. How much she conveyed to him is unknown. (Wolter/2021)

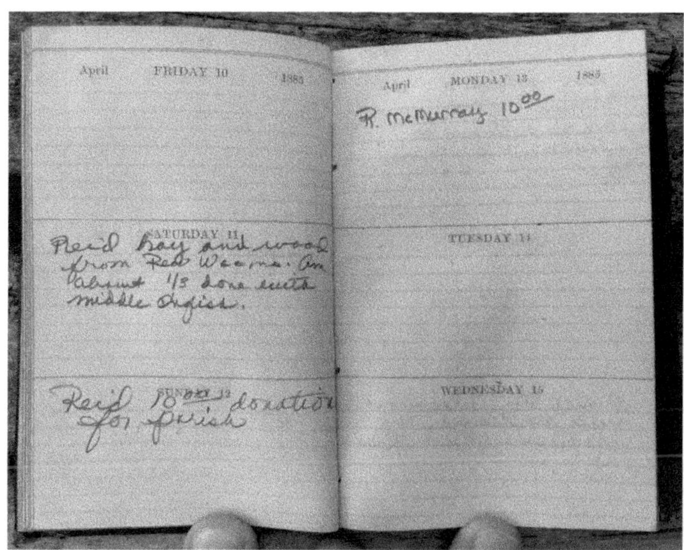

In this April 11, 1885 entry Sister Harkin writes she received more hay and wood from Reverend Weems and was one-third of the way through translating the Middle English. (Wolter/2021)

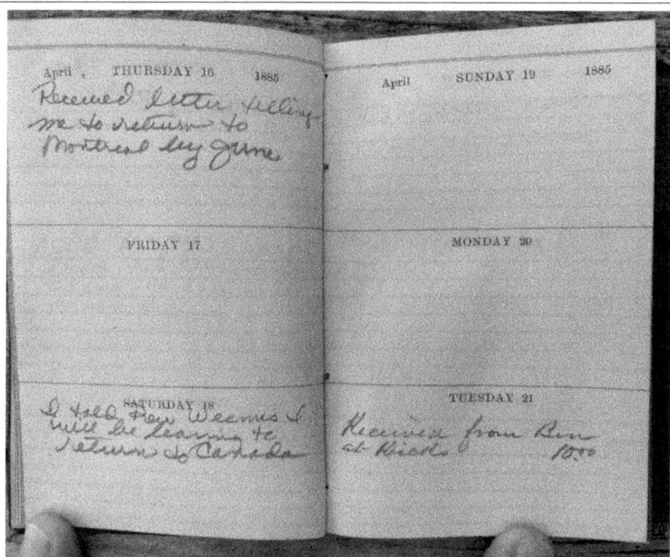

Two entries made on April 16 and 18, 1885 reveal Sister Harkin had been summoned by the Church to return to Montreal by June of that year. She conveyed this news to Reverend Weems who likely asked her to complete her translation work before leaving. (Wolter/2021)

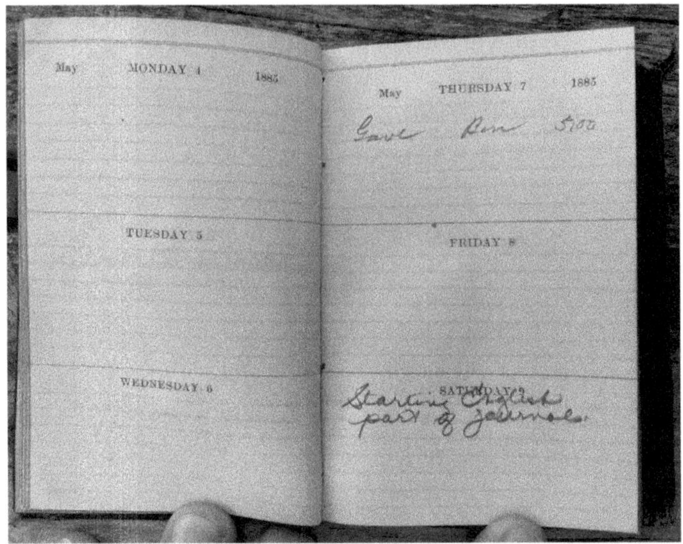

On May 9, 1885 Sister Harkin had completed her translations and decided to transcribe the final five books written in modern English by John Weems Sr. and his son. I suspect she was enamored with the story and wanted to finish it for the reverend, or it was part of their agreement. (Wolter/2021)

The entry Sister Harkin made on May 13, 1885, is extremely interesting as she apparently felt obligated to report the story of the Covenant to Church authorities. It appears her conversations with Reverend Weems resulted in an agreement to keep the story involving his family a secret. (Wolter/2021)

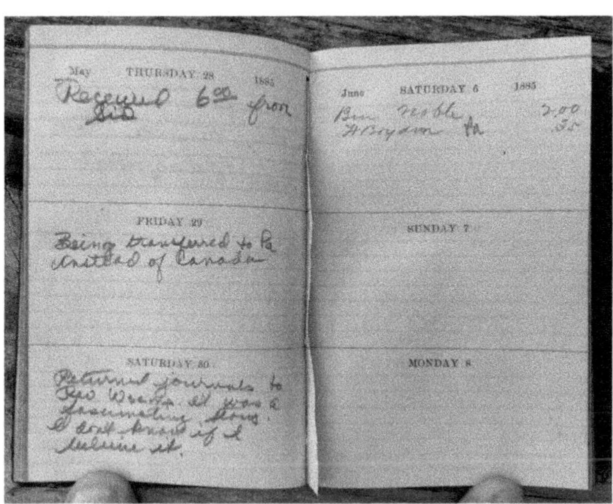

In her final entry on May 30, 1885 Sister Harkin returned the journals to Reverend Weems and was clearly moved by what she had read. One can appreciate her skepticism as the story truly is incredible. (Wolter/2021)

Dearest James,
I am being sent to Philadelphia and must say goodbye to you, my friend. You have brought me back memories of home and I will miss your lively conversation. I wish I had time to tell you of the stories of Templar treasure beneath the altar at St Antonies. Your story is amazing and God has told me it is true. I only translated that which was not in English. You should be able to read the more recent ones.

I have left your original in the Church Library for you. May God bless you and your family.
Agnes

In the journal Diana presented on January 18, 2022 there was a handwritten note (likely a copy of the original done in 1885) that adds additional context to her work, *"Dearest James, I am being sent to Philadelphia and must say goodbye to you, my friend. You have brought me back memories of home and I will miss your lively conversation. I wish I had time to tell you of the stories of Templar treasure beneath the altar at St. Anthonies. Your story is amazing, and God has told me it is true. I only translated that which was not in English. You should be able to read the more recent ones. I have left your original in the church library for you. May God bless you and your family. Agnes."* (Wolter/2022)

3

The Reverend James Alston Weems Copy

In July of 2021 Diana received a copy, likely a copy of a copy, of the Sinclair/Weems journals that was originally made by Sister Agnes Harkin for Reverend James A. Weems between January 31 and May 30, 1885. The whereabouts of the original copy produced by Sister Harkin is unknown, but this most recent modern copy was given to Diana from Darren Weems, the 4th Great grandson of Reverend James A. Weems. Darren explained to Diana the origin of this modern copy was that it was made by the girlfriend of his father sometime within the last ten years. The following genealogical list is presented to help clarify the relationships of Darren to his ancestor, Reverend Weems, and his relationship to John Weems Jr., the last generation to write the journals. This genealogical information was provided by Diana Muir.

John Abraham Weems Jr. (Born: April 1, 1741, Died: October 27, 1812)[3]
Thomas Lewis (Lacy) Weems (Born: Feb. 2, 1777, Died: September 7, 1829)[4]
John Wesley Weems (Born: August 23, 1797, Died: April 13, 1884)[5]
James Alston Weems (Born: February 16, 1828, Died: August 9, 1908)[6]
William Jesse "Bill" Weems (Born: July 31, 1864, Died: August 20, 1920)[7]
John Franklin Weems (Born: November 26, 1887, Died: August 24, 1960)[8]

3. https://www.findagrave.com/memorial/100099720/john_abraham-weems

4. https://www.wikitree.com/wiki/Weems-827

5. https://www.geni.com/people/John-Weems/6000000102345032845

6. https://www.findagrave.com/memorial/30073018/james_alston-weems

7. https://www.findagrave.com/memorial/56621520/william_jesse-weems

8. https://www.findagrave.com/memorial/132408543/john-franklin-weems

Howard Edward Weems (Born: October 12, 1908, Died: June 23, 1946)
JCE Weems (Born: May 12, 1933, Died: August 20, 2019)[9]
Charles Duane Weems (Born: March 20, 1957, Died: 2018)
Darren Weems (Born: 1982 to Present)

Diana was told John Weems Jr's copy was then copied by three different individuals shortly before the Civil War. These individuals were reportedly Thomas Bailey (1760-1832), a 32nd degree Freemason who lived in Baileyton, Tennessee, and married one of John Jr's daughters. The second person was Reverand Grandser Weems (1803-1876) who was the pastor of the Methodist Episcopal Church in Baileyton. Diana believes Grandser

Reverand James Alston Weems poses with his fourth wife, Louisa J. "Eliza" Jessap, whom he married in April of 1894. His previous wives were Nancy Trout (married 1849), Nancy Ellen Freeman (married 1851) whom he had seven children with and died in 1888, Mary E. Baker Owens (married 1889) who died in 1894.

9. https://www.legacy.com/obituaries/name/jc-weems-obituary?pid=193701983

Weems was likely the person who rescued the trunk containing the leather saddlebag with John Jr's journals from the church that burned to the ground around 1880. The third individual is unknown but was believed to have also been a Freemason who worked at Tusculum College in nearby Greenville, Tennessee.

One copy went with Thomas Lewis Weems (1777-1829), one of the sons of John Jr., who moved to Iuka, Illinois circa 1820 and died in 1829. The second copy went with Jonas Weems (1792-1880) and his brother George Weems (1796-1839) to the tiny town of Stella, Missouri. The whereabouts of the third copy is unknown. Upon his death, the Thomas Lewis Weems copy went to his oldest son, John Wesley Weems (1797-1884). Due to rampant death in the Civil War, the John Wesley Weems copy should have gone to his oldest son, but he was killed 1862. His second son died in 1858, so his copy of the journals went to his third son, Reverand James Alston Weems in 1884 after his father's death.

In March of 2017, I traveled to Baileyton, Tennessee to find the graves of John Weems Jr., who died in 1812, and his wife Kitty. Locals told the story of a greedy land developer who hired a bulldozer to remove the gravestones of the deceased on the land seen behind this sign that overlooked Lick Creek. The author found the nubs of the gravestones of John and Kitty Weems on land that was never developed. (Wolter, 2017)

The Reverand James Alston Weems copy most likely went to his son, John Lewis Weems (1866-1951) who then gave his copy to JCE Weems (1933-2019) who was Darren's grandfather and a Freemason for over sixty years. Diana suspects JCE Weems' copy was likely inherited by Charles Duane Weems (1957-2021). This means the leather journal Diana shared with me on July 22, 2021 was not the original version Sister Harkin copied in 1885, as this journal was clearly modern. Diana claims the copy she shared with me was given to her by Darren Weems and was copied by his father's girlfriend. Diana suspects they were trying to sell a copy of the journals that were passed down to them from JCE Weems, who also lived in Illinois. Darren Weems (1982-present) inherited the copy his father's girlfriend made. Where the JCE Weems copy is she used to make her copy is unknown.

On January 18, 2022 I met up with Diana Muir in Waterloo, Iowa, to see the copy of the Sinclair/Wemyss journals purportedly written by Sister Agnes Harkin in 1885. I had already seen Sister Harkin's diary on July 22, 2021 and was very excited to see the work she had done 137 years ago. One exercise that occurred to me when vetting Sister Harkin's work was to compare her translations with Diana's. If the entries were identical, it would be a huge red flag, suggesting this recently discovered modern journal was copied, word for word, from Diana's work. In fact, since Diana used modern computer programs like Google Translate, and Sister Harkin was formally trained in Latin, most likely by the mid-nineteenth century Catholic Church, the translations are sure to be different. Indeed, starting with the very first entry made by an eight-year-old Henry Sinclair, the translated messages, while similar, were not at all the same.

Throughout the journals you are about to read I have presented the transcribed entries together, ***Diana's italicized***, **Sister Harkins' not italicized**, to show the differences in their translations.

I provide commentary where I felt it was appropriate, in shaded boxes like this one, especially when I had personal involvement with a location, a specific point, or idea I could shed light on. I invite you to dial in and enjoy reading the personal diaries of these important historical figures—a few known but most unknown to historians—who were involved in one of the most exciting, important, and improbable ventures of the past millennia.

4

Journal of Earl Henry Sinclair

Book 1

November 5, 1353

Diana's Translation (Italics): *My father gave me this journal for the celebration of my 8th birthday. He tells me to write about things I want to remember when I am a man. This year Father Dominic will teach me Latin, French, Gaelic and Norwegian. Father has promised to take me fishing with him in the spring. I can't wait to see the western banks and want to catch lots of fish.*

Sister Harkin's Translation (Plain): My name is Henricus Santo Claro, my father gave me this journal to celebrate my 8th Birthday. He says to write about things I want to know when I am older. Father Dominic will teach me Latin, French, Gaelic and Norwegian this year. Father has promised I can go fishing with him in the Spring. I am impatient to see the western lands and want to catch many fish.

The Author's Commentary (Shaded Box): In this very first entry we have a subtle but very telling clue that speaks loudly in support of the veracity of the journals. Young Henry receives the book from his father on his eighth birthday, which is a very sacred age for those initiated in the Templar tradition, and which Henry's father obviously was. I will explain this in greater detail in the Sacred Numbers section in Chapter 9, but right from the start we see a very important clue that resonates throughout the journals.

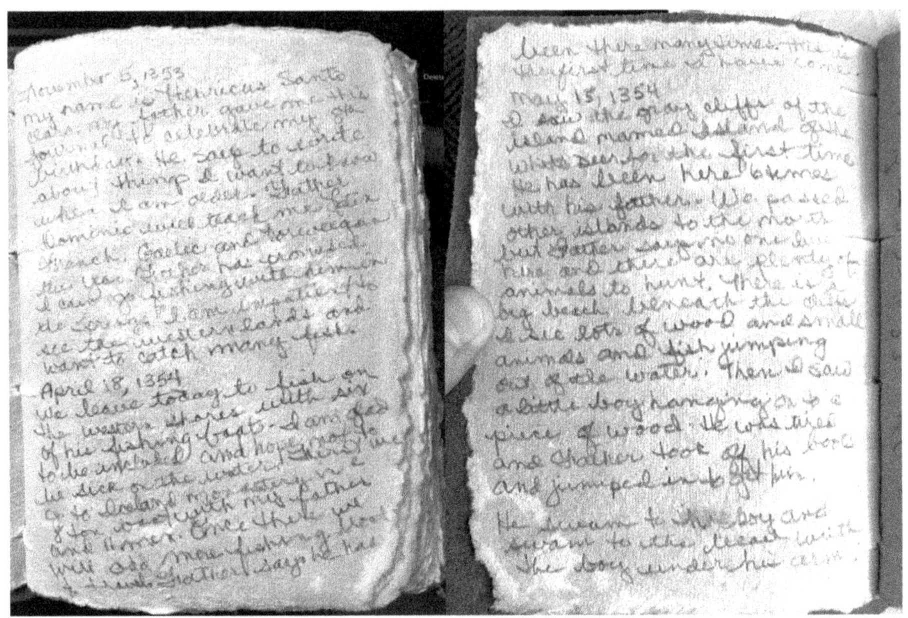

The first two handwritten pages of the recopied Sister Harkin journal translations contain the first three entries made by eight-year-old Henry Sinclair. He apparently wrote "Henricus Santo Claro" which is not in Diana Muir's translation. (Wolter/2022)

April 18, 1354

This day we leave to fish on the western banks with my father and six of his fishing vessels. I am excited to be included and will try not to be sick of the rough water. We are to travel first to the monastery in a barque of 8 tons with my father and eleven men. Once in [Iceland] *we will travel with additional fishing boats to the western banks. Father has been there many times, but this is the first time I have been allowed to accompany him.*

We leave today to fish on the western shores with six of his fishing boats. I am glad to be included and hope not to be sick on the water. First, we go to Iceland monastery in an 8-ton boat with my father and 11 men. Once there we will add more fishing boats to travel. Father says he has been there many times. This is the first time I have come.

The important takeaway in this entry is the mention of Henry's father, William Sinclair II of Rosslyn, having traveled to the Western Lands

"...many times."[10] This confirms the information in the Cremona Document that the Templars had been traveling to North America repeatedly since at least the middle of the twelfth century. By this time, in the mid-fourteenth century, it was commonplace for Templars to be in North America. This is also supported by the numerous controversial artifacts that are consistent with this, such as the Kensington Rune Stone, Spirit Pond Rune Stones, Narragansett Rune Stone, In Hoc Signo Vinces Stone, Westford Boat Stone, Westford Sword (Knight) and the Newport Tower.

May 15, 1354

As evening came upon us, I saw for the first time the gray cliffs of the island my father calls "Isle of the White Stag". He has been there six times with his father. We had already passed other lands further to the north, but Father said this island was uninhabited and offered small animals as they search for food on the shore. As we approach the beach good game. There is a wide beach at the bottom of the cliffs and further to the north I can see much wood and I see many birds and see the fish jumping in the water. It was then that I saw a small child clinging to a piece of driftwood. He looked exhausted and Father kicked off his boots and jumped overboard to help him. He swam to the boy and then swam with the boy under his arm to the beach as the barque pushed onto the shore a small black haired naked man came running down the beach with his arms outstretched. He knelt in front of Father with his arms outstretched and his head down, hoping this strange man would return his son. Father placed the boy in his arms and the small man placed his right hand on my father's chest in gratitude before carrying his son up the beach and onto the cliff face.

I saw the gray cliffs of the island named Island of the White Deer for the first time. He has been here 6 times with his father. We passed other islands to the north, but father says no one lives here and there are plenty of animals to hunt. There is a big beach beneath the cliffs. I see lots of wood and small animals and fish jumping out of the water. Then I saw a little boy hanging on to a piece of wood. He was tired and Father took off his boots and jumped in to get him. He swam to the boy and swam to the beach with the boy under his arm. The boat came ashore and a small naked man with black hair ran

10. Sinclair and Me, Pages 278-285, 2018.

down the beach with his arms wide open. He stopped in front of Father with open arms and a bowed head probably hoping the odd man would return his son. Father put the boy in his arms. The little man put his right hand on Father's chest to show thanks before he took his son and ran up the cliff.

Here we learn Henry's father had already been to North America six times with his father Sir Henry Sinclair I of Rosslyn (1299-1336), who likely also visited the Western Lands with his father and so on. We also learn about the Island of the White Stag—which I have concluded is Janvrin Island—which is in the southwestern section of Cape Breton, Nova Scotia. In August of 2019, I visited Janvrin Island with my friend and Masonic brother Tom Colvin. We spent three days searching the shores for the boulder the Templars reportedly carved the dates on during their many visits to North America. After talking with locals who said the shores in this area erode at a rate of one foot per year, and seeing the clay-rich sand, gravel, and boulder glacial deposits that make up the island and mainland in this area, it seems likely the boulder now sits on the bottom of the ocean 600 years after it was carved

The rescue of the native boy named Askoosh was the beginning of a lifelong friendship, which subsequent entries by Earl Henry will bear out.

Janvrin Island and the mainland in the southwestern part of Cape Breton are glacial sediments comprised of clay, sand, gravel, and boulders that rapidly erode from wave action at a rate of roughly one foot per year according to locals. (Wolter, 2019)

Tom Colvin and I spent three days searching the shores of Janvrin Island for the boulder Earl Henry Sinclair and other visitors carved the dates of their visits to the Western Lands on. Tom and I swam out to the island—seen behind us—and back on a blow-up raft, but concluded the boulder has since been taken by the sea after eroding out of the soft glacial sediments that make up the island. (Wolter, 2019)

May 16th, 1354

We have set up camp and I was asked to collect driftwood for the fires. I saw many different types of birds and they seem unafraid. Father promises to teach me how to determine latitude this eve.

We have set up camp and I was told to collect firewood. I saw many different birds, but they weren't afraid. Father said he will teach me how to find latitude after supper. The natives laugh at sailors making beds on the sand. The tide washes them away and sailors scramble up the cliffs.

May 17, 1354

The small black-haired man returned today with his son much recovered and another man. They brought with them a large deer as an offering to our dinner. They also showed us how to find roots and bake them in the coals of the fire. It tasted much better than the dried fish we have [been] *eating during our voyage. Father only knows a few of their words but they communicate mostly with their hands and drawing in the sand. He showed them how to make nets out of the vines to catch the fish and offered the man some animal skins to wear against the cool weather. The boy is about my age. His name is Askoosh, and he showed me how to dig for clams.*

The little man with black hair came back today with his son who was well and another man. They brought a big deer for our supper. They showed us how to dig roots and cook them in the fire. It tasted much better than old fish we had been eating. Father only knows a little of their language and they talk with their hands and draw in the sand. Father taught them how to make nets from vines to catch fish and gave them some animal skins to wear in the cold weather. The boy is my age, and his name is Askoosh. He showed me how to dig clams.

May 21, 1354

Today we celebrated the Bright Mother Goddess Day with our new friends. They too celebrate the Great Goddess who brings life to them throughout the year. We have many similarities.

We celebrate Bright Mother Goddess Day today. They celebrate the Great Goddess also who brings rebirth to them during the year. We are a lot alike.

This entry is the first of many that mentions the Great Goddess as a deity both the indigenous people and the Templars venerate. This served as the basis for a deep spiritual bond between the two that allowed the Templars essentially free reign to roam that continent, traveling with their brothers. This also led to strong trust the indigenous people would guard the treasures, which they would do for over four centuries.

July 6, 1354

Our visit to the Western banks has ended and our boats are filled with the codfish we found in the deep waters off the Isle of the White Stag. I have learned much from my friend Askoosh and have given him a knife made from whalebone to remember me. He has taught me many of his words as I have taught him some Gaelic. We sail home the same way we came and by months end should return to Orkney if the weather cooperates.

Our trip to the western lands is done and we have filled the boat with Whitefish we found in deep seas off the Island of the White Deer. Askoosh has taught me much and I have given him a whale bone knife to remember me. I learned many words from him, and I have taught him some Gaelic. We will go home the same way we came and if the weather is good will reach home by the end of the month.

August 28, 1354

We have returned home to Orkney. Half of the ships have returned to Caithness while the rest anchor in Kirkwall Bay. We stopped once again in Groenland and [Iceland] *for provisions and were delayed by storms. Now that we are home Father must return to Midlothian as King David is still imprisoned. I have been instructed to assist the dock Master in preparing the fish for winter.*

We are home in Orkney. Some boats went to Caithness and others anchor in Kirkwall harbor. We made stops in Groenland and Iceland to reprovision and to wait out storms. Father will return to Midlothian because King David is still in prison. I have been told to help prepare fish for winter.

September 16, 1354

Today we celebrate the Greek festival of Demeter. I wish I were old enough to participate in the rituals but am happy my father includes me in the festival.

We celebrate Festival of Demeter a Greek festival. I want to be older so I can take part but am pleased Father allows me to go to festival.

The festival of Demeter mentioned here is an ancient Greek religious festival that honors Demeter which occurred in the late fall and was called Thesmophoria.[11]

11. https://en.wikipedia.org/wiki/Thesmophoria

March 9, 1357

Today my mother participated in the festival to honor all Mother Goddesses along with my sister Margaret. Father Dominic is teaching me about the old religion and is also teaching me Greek. It is difficult and I much prefer Latin.

My mother went to festival to honor all female Goddesses with my sister Margaretha. Father Dominic is teaching me Greek and about the old religions. It is hard and I prefer Latin.

August 1, 1357

Today is the festival of the grain harvest in Orkney where we celebrate Demeter and Ceres. There are so many festivals and so much food. I will soon be fat as a pig.

The festival of grain harvest celebration of Demeter and Ceres is today. There are lots of Festivals and food. I will get as fat as a pig.

September 29, 1357

We celebrated Michaelmas today.[12] *My younger sister Annabelle celebrated her birthday. I gave her a wooden box I carved myself. She is ten years old today.*

Today we celebrate Michaelmas. My youngest sister Annabelle celebrated her 10th birthday. I carved a wooden box for her.

November 22, 1357

I spent the day at the forge with my father learning about the feast of Weyland the Norse God of the Smiths. I am clumsy at the forge but respect those who are very clever. The smiths are creating nails and rivets for a boat to travel to the west banks in the spring. Father Dominic says that Father Richardus will accompany them with the seven new Acolytes.

12. https://en.wikipedia.org/wiki/Michaelmas

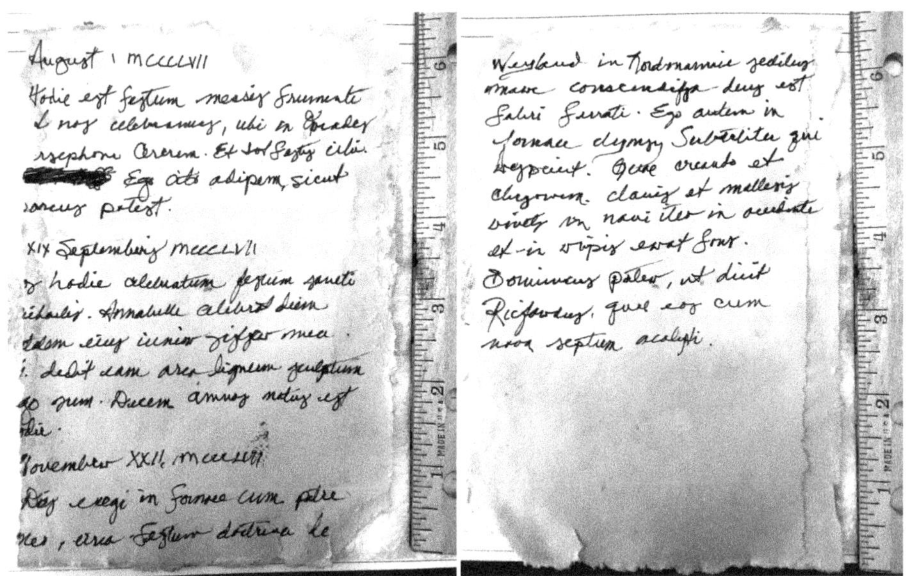

In March of 2018, Diana Muir found three pages of the journals she had that included one page from Earl Henry Sinclair's entries written in Latin from August 1, September 19 and November 22, 1357. The November entry could be an inadvertent mention of the monk who may have been the author of the Kensington Rune Stone inscription in 1362, Father Richardus (Richards). (Wolter/2018)

I spent the day at the forge with Father who taught me about the Feast of Wayland who is Norse God of the Smiths. I am bad at the forge, but I respect those who are good. The smiths are making nails and hinges for a boat that will journey to the west shores next. Father Dominic says that Father Richard will go along with 7 new priests.

It wasn't until the second reading of the journals that I caught the significance of this entry. Henry wouldn't learn till later in his life about what we call the Kensington party, having left Norway for the Western Lands in 1358. Armed with this knowledge, reading the entries the second time through led to a starling realization. The only boat mentioned that needed nails and rivets for traveling to the Western Lands in the spring of 1358 was the one used by the Kensington party that left from Norway. This discovery is interesting enough, but the real bombshell was in the last sentence.

The reader might recall the first line of the Kensington inscription reads, "8 Goths (Gotlanders) and 22 Northmen (Norwegians)..." If the journals are a reliable indicator, the eight Goths might be the "*...men of the Craft including monks with herbal knowledge...*" mentioned in Henry's July 26, 1368, entry. According to my own research into the esoteric and symbolic aspects of the Kensington inscription, it appears the "seven new acolytes" and Father Richardus are being acknowledged and intentionally singled out using what many runic scholars have called "strange runes."

November 30, 1357

Today I received word that Alexander de Ard has been proclaimed by manifest as the legitimate heir of my grandfather Earl Malise. He is my cousin, but Mother and Father are angry because they think it should have been my right to inherit. They say I must grow up fast in order to protect my heritage.

Today we learned that Alexander de Ard has been proclaimed heir to my grandfather Earl Malise by Manifest. My parents are angry because they say it is my right to inherit. He is my cousin. They tell me to get older in order to protect my legacy.

April 25, 1358

Father has left for London where he will sail for Europe. He promises to be home by the end of the year. Today is the Roman festival for Ceres and Demeter. Father Dominic celebrates the old religion and teaches me there must be a balance between the old and the new.

Father will go to London and then sail to Europe. He says he will be home by the end of the year. The Roman festival of Ceres and Demeter is today. Father Dominic celebrates the old religions but teaches me there must be a balance between both.

September17, 1358

Father was killed in battle this day. Mother has sent myself and sister Annabelle to live with our sister Margaret for a short time. Sir Thomas Stewart, her husband, is to teach me my duties when I become Earl.

The Kensington Rune Stone has seven "g" runes with a single punch in the upper half, and one "u" rune with one short horizontal line on the lower part of the vertical stave and two punch marks in the upper half. Both are unusual Scandinavian runes. Could these eight runes allegorically represent the "seven acolytes" and Father Richards by symbolizing the new initiates and their Master? (Wolter, 2002)

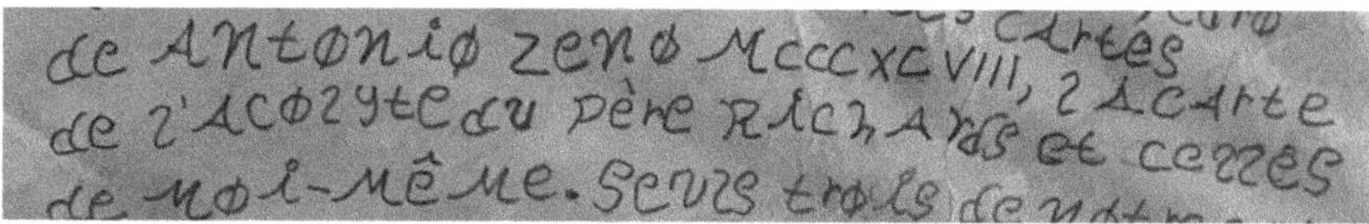

This section of the narrative written in French by Clyphus Lucinus Yzarbo XVI (16th) was found on the back of Map 8—which was copied onto paper by Dan Spartan and his son from the rotting animal skin original circa 2015—and includes the following translated into English, "*...of Antonio Zeno MCCCXCVIII (1398), the map of the acolyte of Father Richards, and my own.*" The mention of Father Richardus supports the veracity of Henry Sinclair November 22, 1357, entry where he mentions Richardus. (Wolter, 2021)

Today we learned that Father was killed in battle. Mother has sent me and Anna belle to stay with my sister Margaritha for a small time. Her husband is Sir Thomas Stewart and will teach me the duties of an Earl.

This entry is important in putting to bed the controversy as to when Sir William II died. The authors of *Sinclair and Me* argue William II and his colleagues likely died in battle in Lithuania in 1367. They present highly speculative evidence William II was alive and witnessed a charter in Edinburgh in 1362, after which he disappeared from the records.[13] Based on this entry, the legend of Sir William II dying in battle in 1358 is actually true.

September 21, 1358

Mother's counselors have proclaimed me Earl of Rosslin and say that I must now take my father's place as Lord. Sir Thomas promises to guide me in my duties when I return home to Rosslin. In my absence, mother will rely on Lords Halyburton and Wemyss for counsel.

Mother and her council have named me Earl of Rosslyn and tell me to take my Fathers role as Lord. Sir Thomas says he will guide me when I return to Rosslyn in my duties. Until then mother will listen to Lords Haliburton and Wemyss for counsel.

September 29, 1358

My sister Margaret has welcomed us to her home, and we once again feel as a family. Today we celebrate Michaelmas in the chapel. Sir Thomas is a stern master, but his lands are well managed, and he is well respected. He is much older than Margaret, but he treats her well. I hope to learn a lot from him so I may return to my mother's side as soon as I am able.

My sister Margaret has invited us into her household, and we are a family again. Sir Thomas is a hard Master, but his lands are well managed, and he is revered. He is many years older than Margaret but is good to her. I hope to learn a lot so I can go home to my mother soon.

13. Sinclair and Me, Page 283, 2018.

November 11, 1358

Today we celebrate St Martins Day.[14] *My sister's kitchen is well prepared, and Sir Thomas continues to give advice on how to manage an estate as well as my future home.*

We celebrate St. Martin's Day today. Margaretha's kitchen is well stocked, and Sir Thomas still gives advice on managing the estate and my future home.

December 5, 1358

I return home to Rosslin today in the company of my mother's counselors and Sir Thomas Stewart. It is important that I be in Rosslin for the celebration of St. Andrews Day, the patron saint of Scotland.[15] *It is a big celebration where I will be recognized by my people that I am their Lord.*

I go home to Rosslyn with Mother's advisors and Sir Thomas Stewart. It is important I be there for St. Andrews day. He is the patron saint of Scotland. It is a big celebration my people must recognize me as Lord.

February 1, 1360

Today I must appear at the manorial court with the freeman to discuss the matters of the estate. I have reviewed the map of the estates and am prepared to discuss the upcoming planting season.

Today I go to manorial court with the free tenants to talk about estate matters. I have gone over the map of my estate and will talk about planting this season.

March 13, 1360

My brother-in-law Sir Thomas Stewart has been accused of killing [the] *King's favorite mistress and has been imprisoned in Dunbarton Castle. They say he is to lose his head.*

---

14. https://en.wikipedia.org/wiki/St._Martin%27s_Day

15. https://en.wikipedia.org/wiki/Saint_Andrew%27s_Day

Sir Thomas Stewart, who is my brother-in-law, has been accused of killing the Kings favorite concubine and has been put in Dunbarton Castle. They say he will be beheaded.

April 15, 1361

We received word today that Sir Thomas Earl of Angus has died at Dunbarton Castle of plague. My sister Margaret grieves.

Today we received word that Sir Thomas Earl of Angus has died of plague at Dunbarton Castle. My sister Margaretha grieves.

May 3, 1362

Today is Holy Rood Day and we celebrate in the chapel with Father Dominic and Father Christoph.[16] *My mother spends a lot of time in the chapel, and I fear is becoming melancholy. It is my hope that she remarries soon as she is still a young woman.*

Today is Holy Rood Day and we celebrate with Father Dominic and Father Christopher in the chapel. My mother spends a lot of time in the chapel, and I think she has become depressed. I hope she remarries soon as she is still a young woman.

May 13, 1362

We leave this day to travel to Denmark to attend the marriage of Princess Margaretta. I have only met her once and she is still a young child. My councilors tell me that I too must marry soon to produce an heir. I hope it will not happen soon as I do not feel ready.

We go today to Denmark to attend Princess Margaretta wedding. I have only met her once and she is still a young child. My advisors tell me I must marry soon to have an heir. I do not feel ready and hope it will not happen soon.

May 19, 1362

We have arrived in Denmark where the local people are celebrating a local

16. https://en.wikipedia.org/wiki/Feast_of_the_Cross

holiday. They offer us food and drink in preparation for our meeting with King Magnus. I am nervous as I have not seen him since I was a young lad.

We have landed in Denmark where locals are celebrating a local festival. They give us food and drink to prepare for our meeting with King Magnus. I have not seen him since I was a small boy and am scared.

June 1, 1362

At the insistence of my Lord King Magnus, I have been married this day to Princess Florentina who is just an infant. When she is of childbearing age, she will join me in Orkney. King Magnus is highly pleased.

Lord King Magnus insisted I be married to his infant daughter Princess Florentina today. When she is of childbearing age she will come to Orkney. King Magnus is very pleased.

Feb 8, 1363

I have received word that Princess Florentina the daughter of King Magnus has died.

I have been told that the daughter of King Magnus, Princess Florentina has died.

July 1, 1364

I am to be married this day to Elizabeth of Strathearn my cousin who is 14 years old. She will live at Rosslin until she delivers our first child. Then we will move to Kirkwall in Orkney. She adheres to the Christian religion and talks constantly of God and Christ. I have been instructed by Sir Hugh Halyburton as to my duties on my wedding night. I hope I do not disappoint.[17]

I am supposed to be married to my cousin Elizabeth of Strathearn who is 14 years old. She will live at Rosslyn until she has our first child. There we will move to Kirkwall in Orkney. She practices the Christian religion and

17. The internet has confusing information that is incomplete, versus what Henry has recorded in his journals. Here is one example, https://www.wikitree.com/wiki/Sinclair-201

Left: The three virtues in Freemasonry that have long been represented by three pillars—as seen on this tracing board—are Wisdom, Strength, and Beauty.
Right: The virtue of Wisdom is also symbolized by the Master of a Masonic Lodge, who imparts knowledge and wisdom to members of his lodge, as we see in the Master's Chair at Garnet Lodge in Forrest Lake, Minnesota. (Internet, Wolter, 2024)

talks of God and Christ all the time. I have been told of my wedding night duties by Hugh Haliburton. I hope I do well.

September 29, 1364

Today we celebrated Michaelmas which my expectant bride has enjoyed very much. She is happy and well and looks forward to becoming a mother. Tomorrow I must ride to the nearby villages where they celebrate the Feast Day of Saint Sophia.[18] *She is the mother of Faith, Hope and Charity and is known as the Goddess of Wisdom. I pray that she grants me wisdom in becoming a father and a good Lord to my people.*

We celebrated Michaelmas today with my pregnant bride. She is well and happy and looks forward to being a mother. Tomorrow, I have to ride to the nearby towns where they celebrate Saint Sophia the mother of Faith,

18. https://en.wikipedia.org/wiki/Sophia_of_Rome

Hope, and Charity. She is called the Goddess of Wisdom. I pray she grants me wisdom to become a father and a good leader for my people.

As a Freemason, the mention of Faith, Hope and Charity resonates loudly as they represent the three virtues so important within Freemasonry. Although Henry had not yet been initiated into what is obviously a tradition that embraces Masonic teachings, these positive virtues appear to be important in the Scottish clan culture he was raised in. The initiations he will soon describe appear to be an early tradition of Freemasonry long before its official founding in 1717. Most knowledgeable Freemasons already know Masonic tradition existed before 1717, but to read about Earl Henry's experiences in the middle of the fourteenth century is truly remarkable.

May 1, 1365

My bride Elizabeth has died of a fever but the girl child she has delivered thrives. I am saddened at the loss of my bride. The child, Margaret, will be well cared for by her nurses. She has red hair and blue eyes like her mother. Tomorrow is Holy Wells Day, a Norse holiday celebrated by my mother's family. We will bury Elizabeth on the following day in the Churchyard here at Rosslin.

My bride Elizabeth has died of a fever, but the baby girl thrives. I am saddened by the death of my bride. The baby Margaret will be well cared for by her nurses. She has blue eyes and red hair like her mother. Holy Wells Day is tomorrow and is a Norse holiday celebrated by my mother's family.[19] We will bury Elizabeth the next day in the Rosslyn churchyard.

May 31, 1365

Today I was made a knight by Sir William Halyburton and instructed in my duties to those who are in need. I pray that I am worthy and am thankful for this opportunity. Now I may take my rightful place at the Scottish Parliament as Mother has wanted.

19. https://shirleytwofeathers.com/The_Blog/pagancalendar/holy-wells-day/

I was made a knight today by Sir William Haliburton and taught my duties to those in need. I pray I am worthy and am glad of the chance. I can take my rightful place as mother wanted in the Scottish Parliament.

June 1, 1365

Today was spent in the chapel receiving the instruction from the Seven Brethren the Secret Masters and investiture of obligation to the Holy Mother and to the preservation of the ideals and principles upon which we live and believe. I must remember to use the Key of Intelligence within the Circle of Reason to prepare myself for the Lord's will. Father Dominic's instruction in the old religion has prepared me well to appreciate the symbolism and rituals of the Craft.

This day was spent in the chapel receiving instruction from the 7 brethren and Secret Masters and installation of vows to Mother Mary and to the continuation of the ideas and principles that we practice in life and believe. I must strive to use the Key of intellect in the Circle of Reasoning to be ready to do the will of the Lord. Father Dominic's teaching in the ancient religion allows me to know the symbolism and rituals of the Order.

It is crystal clear that Earl Henry has been knighted and begins his initiation into what he calls the "Craft." This is the word we Masons still use today to describe Freemasonry. This definitively proves Freemasonry existed long before it's "official" founding date of 1717.

August 3, 1365

Today we celebrate the festival of Artemis the Goddess of the Hunt and of the Moon.

We celebrate the rites of Artimus the Goddess of the hunt and the moon today.

August 15, 1365

We celebrate the Assumption of Our Lady Mary in the chapel.

We celebrate the Assumption of Our Lady Mary in the chapel today.

October 18, 1365

This day I am raised to the next degree by the Craft and have learned the meaning of the architecture of the chapel. I have also been instructed on the manner of the Honorable Hiram Abiff's burial beneath the temple.

Today I am elevated to the next level in the order and have been instructed in the meaning of the architecture of the chapel. I have also been taught about the death and burial of Hiram Abiff's beneath the Temple of Solomon.

Both versions indicate Henry received what in Freemasonry today would be the second (Fellowcraft) degree, and possibly the third (Master Mason) degree as well. The architecture of the chapel in this context could either be learning about the five types of capital styles at the top of a building column which are Tuscan, Doric, Ionic, Corinthian, and Composite. The architecture of the chapel could also be referring to the ancient, sacred feminine architecture that was secretly incorporated into religious structures, and which honors the feminine aspect of the Godhead so prevalent in Gothic cathedrals constructed in the medieval times–much to the chagrin of the Roman Catholic Church. To the best of my knowledge, this is the first historical mention of Hiram Abiff in a Masonic initiation context ever.

March 1, 1366

Today we celebrate the birthday of my daughter Margaret who is now 1 year-old and the death of her mother Elizabeth. She is a happy child with red curls. I am reminded that I must marry again soon.

Today we celebrate the death of my wife Elizabeth and the birthday of my daughter Margaret who is now 1 year old. She is a jovial child with red curls. They remind me that I must marry again soon.

June 1, 1366

Freeman's court was held today. I make preparations to travel to Scone for the Scottish Parliament at the request of the King.

A freed man's court happened today. I prepare to travel to Scone at the request of the King for the Scottish Parliament.

October 4, 1366

The Craft met this day and advanced me to the next level.

The Order met today and elevated me to the next level.

It is unclear what level (degree) Earl Henry is referring to. It could be the Master Mason (3rd) degree, but it likely is a different, higher degree possibly related to what we now call the York Rite Degrees. However, without more details it is impossible to know.

February 2, 1367

Today we celebrate Candlemas in the chapel.[20] *My daughter Margaret was present and is an unruly child. I suspect I was much the same when I was a child. I enjoyed watching her and gave her a sweet to keep her quiet.*

We celebrate Candlemass today in the chapel. My daughter Margaret was there and is a naughty child. I think I was like her when I was small. I had fun watching her and gave her a sweet to quiet her.

March 2, 1367

My daughter Margaret is 2 years old today. I must think of marrying again soon. My councilors stress that I must have a male heir.

My daughter Margaret is 2 years old today. I think I must marry again soon. My advisors say I must have a male heir.

June 24, 1367

Today is St John's Day and I have spent the day traveling throughout the villages to hear the complaints of the people. They seem well satisfied with their lives and it delights me that they seem well pleased. The crops are doing well, and we have been blessed with rain this past month. It should be a goodly harvest.

Saint John's Day is today, and I have gone today through all the villages to hear the complaints of the people. They appear happy in their lives, and it delights me they are pleased. We have been blessed with much rain this past month and the crops are doing well. The harvest will be good.

20 https://www.britannica.com/topic/Candlemas

In Templarism and Rosicrucianism, which evolved into modern Freemasonry, John the Baptist is *the guy*. All Masonic lodges around the world today are dedicated to the Holy Saints John (Evangelist and the Baptist), but prior to 1600 it was only John the Baptist. That is why in Leonardo da Vinci's first painting of *Virgin on the Rocks*, Mary Magdalene is pointing to the child she had with John the Baptist before he was beheaded. You'll notice she is pointing using the compass-and-square hand gesture. This is because it was John the Baptist who initiated Yeshua (Jesus) and was the Grand Master of the Essenic/Ægyptian tradition at the time. Upon his death, because the

Left: *Virgin on the Rocks* by Leonardo da Vinci (1452-1519). (Internet)
Inset: This painting of Mary Magdalene by Italian painter Guido Reni (1575-1642), circa 1634, contains a wealth of esoteric symbolism. Most notably, it shows the Magdalene mourning the skull of her deceased husband John the Baptist. The angled cross is symbolic of the Baptist, as he is often seen holding it in many other artistic works of that era. (Internet)
Right: This depiction of John the Baptist was painted by another Italian artist known as Titian (Tiziano Vecellio, 1488-1576) and shows his signature staff with a cross which mirrors the Remi painting. Titian also painted the lamb at John's feet which symbolizes the Precessional Age of Aries the Ram. My Masonic brothers will notice his feet positioned in a square, symbolic of the Master Mason (3rd) degree. (Internet)

priestly line went through the feminine in that tradition, a family member was obligated to marry her. That family member was Yeshua (Jesus)

The other symbolism to note is that it is John the Baptist's skull that Mary Magdalene is so often depicted with in works of art. The Magdalene is often depicted in great sorrow with his skull as she is mourning the tragic beheading of her first husband. The most important penal sign in Freemasonry has to do with John's death (I'm not at liberty to share it, but it has something to do with the hand and neck). In the final Knights Templar degree in the York Rite, John's head plays a key role. I cannot share that secret either as I have taken vows not to, but I think you get the idea. There are many Templar orders, both Masonic and non-Masonic, but the true tradition had Leonardo da Vinci as one of the past Grand Masters and you can be sure he knew ALL the secrets. Those secrets are now being revealed as was mandated at the end of the Age of Pisces and the beginning of the Age of Aquarius which we are now all living through.

September 27, 1367

We leave this day for Scottish Parliament.

Today we leave for Scottish Parliament.

May 3, 1368

We leave this day to travel to Norway to meet with King Magnus concerning my duties to the crown of Norway. I travel with 10 companions and Knights who will protect me and amuse me during the long trip.

Today we leave for Norway to visit King Magnus about my duties to Norway. I go with 10 friends and knights who will protect me and entertain me on the long trip.

May 31, 1368

We have arrived in Norway in time for the Feast of the Triple Goddess. I give thanks to the Great Goddess and ask her to bless me in my life so that I may fulfill her will. We meet in the morning with King Magnus and his court.

We got to Norway at the time of the Feast of the Triple Goddesses.[21, 22] I give thanks to the Great Goddess and pray she will bless my life so I do as she wills. We will meet with King Magnus in the morning.

June 1, 1368

This day while we supped with the King's court, we listened to a seaman who has returned from the Western Lands and tells us of the abundance of land and game past the ice banks of Groenland [Greenland]. It makes me anxious to travel to the Western Banks again as I did when I was a child. He tells of the journey and how he was forced to stay for many years before he was allowed to return. He makes me wonder of the 30 men who had left Norway in the Spring of 1358. I pray that they are well, and they will return soon.

Today we had dinner with the King's court, and we listened to a sailor who came back from the Western shores and talks about the expanse of land and deer past the ice shores of Greenland. It makes me anxious to go to the Western shores as I did when I was small. He talks of the trip and how they forced him to stay for many years before allowing him to return. He causes me to ask of the 30 men who left Norway in the spring of 1358. I hope they are well and will return soon.

This is the first mention of the "30 men" who left Norway for the Western Lands in the spring of 1358. Henry will soon learn more about this party which seems to be connected to the party that carved and buried the Kensington Rune Stone land claim in the center of the North American continent only four years later in 1362. The details Henry is soon to share only adds weight to the argument this is indeed the Kensington party and the same party, with Father Richardus and the seven new acolytes, which he inadvertently mentions in the fall of 1357.

21. https://myemail.constantcontact.com/Three-Marys-Celebration--Virgin--Magdalene--Mary-Salome.html?soid=1101794525968&aid=Z4ZQEzZ-ySM

22. http://catholicsaints.mobi/calendar/31-may.htm

July 24, 1368

We have returned to Scotland. Tomorrow there is a Freemans court which I must preside over. There is a meeting of the Craft this evening and I must remember to ask them of the brethren who have now been gone for 10 years.

We have returned to Scotland. There is a freed man's court I must preside over tomorrow and a meeting of the Order this evening and I must remember to ask the of the brothers who have been gone for 10 years now.

Henry mentions the 1358 party again and it is clear they were on an important mission he needs to learn more about.

July 26, 1368

I have spoken with the brethren regarding my concerns for the men who had traveled to the Western Banks in the spring of 1358. No word has been received from them, but Brother Cameron has said that none is expected. They were instructed to find suitable land for settlement and that more would follow. He acknowledged that they were men of the Craft and included monks with herbal knowledge. Because of the political unrest in Scotland no additional Brethren have been sent. It might be several years before another journey can be planned.

I have talked with the brothers about my concern for the men who went to Western Shores in the spring of 1358. No word has been heard of them, but Brother Cameron has said they don't expect any. They were told to find good land for settling and that others would follow. He agreed they were men of the Order and included priests with knowledge of medicines. No other men have been sent because of war in Scotland. It will be several years before another trip can be financed.

Historically, this could be one of the most important entries in all of Henry's writings. It confirms my own years-long thesis that the Kensington party buried the inscribed stone as a land claim, and the party planned to stay and not return to Europe. This entry also described the 1358 party as Freemasons and Knights Templar ("*...men of the Craft...*") and initiated

Cistercian monks ("*...monks with herbal knowledge.*"). Based upon my 2016 discovery of the Cryptic Code —initially called the Ritual Code—within the Kensington Rune Stone inscription,[23] it is clear the term "herbal knowledge" included the author of the inscription (Father Richardus perhaps?) being versed in the details of the Book of Enoch and the Secret Vault.[24]

September 27, 1368

Today we celebrate the Day of the Willows in respect to Artemis and Aherrah.[25] *I will leave this next day for Parliament in Perth. I hope to return within the month.*

We celebrate today the Day of the Willows to respect Artemus and Aherrah. I will go to Parliament in Perth tomorrow. I will return during the month.

December 22, 1370

"I have met Lady Jean Halyburton this day. She is a beauty and would be a good marriage for my family. She is well trained in womanly arts and herbs and knows her duty to her Lord and house."

"I met Lady of Haliburton today. She is beautiful and is a good alliance for our family. She is well instructed in what women need to know and know how to take care of a house and her husband."

February 25, 1371

King David has died, and his nephew Robert is to be crowned King. Sir Robert and I must attend his coronation. Upon return I will be married at Dirleton Castle to Lady Jean Halyburton on the 31st day of March. Lady Jean is the daughter of Sir John Halyburton. She is a beauty, young and of marriageable age and we should have many children. Sir John Halyburton has arranged the marriage contract, and we will live at

23. https://scottfwolter.com/wp-content/uploads/2024/08/Ritual-Code-on-the-KRS-web.pdf

24. https://skirret.com/archive/misc/misc-l/legendofenoch.html#:~:text=The%20Legend%20of%20Enoch%2C%20seventh%20of%20the%20biblical,other%20and%20entered%20through%20holes%20in%20the%20arches.

25. https://druidry.org/druid-way/teaching-and-practice/druid-tree-lore/willow

Rosslin where I must manage my estates. My children will be brought up to appreciate both their Scottish and Orkney Heritage.

King David is dead, and his nephew Robert is to be crowned King. Sir Robert and I must attend his coronation. When I return, I will be married to Lady Jean Haliburton at Dirleton on March 31st. Lady Jean is the daughter of Sir John Haliburton. She is beautiful, young and the age to be married and we should have many children. Sir John Haliburton has arranged the contract of marriage, and we will live at Rosslyn where I need to be to manage my land. My children will be raised to know both their Scottish and Orkney heritage.

March 18, 1371

I was married this day to Lady Jean Halyburton of Dirleton. She brings a dowry of much gold and lands in Dirleton.

I was married today to Lady Jean Haliburton of Dirleton. She has a dowry of a lot of gold and lands in Direlton.

June 1, 1371

We begin this day building a home for my future family. They must have a fine home according to their status where my new wife will feel safe. I will leave in seven days hence to collect the rents and inspect the farms.

Today we begin building for my future family. They need a fine home because of their rank where my wife will feel safe. I leave in a week (to) collect the rents and to inspect the farms.

October 30, 1371

Word has been received that a Franco Scottish alliance has been created through the Treaty of Vincennes.[26] *Orkney is still apart from the alliance and must determine where we lie in this alliance. I travel to Edinburgh to speak with my elders and confidants. My lady is with child and will deliver in the spring. She is attended by three of her ladies and eagerly awaits my return with news of her brothers.*

26. https://en.wikipedia.org/wiki/Treaty_of_Vincennes-Edinburgh

Word has arrived that an alliance between France and Scotland by the treaty of Vincennes has been made. I will travel to Edinburgh to talk to others about this. My lady is with child and in spring will give birth. Three of her ladies will wait over her and she is eager for news of her brothers upon my return.

November 22, 1371

I have returned from Edinburgh to find that my lady has lost our child. She cries all day and night, but I reassure her that this is common for a first child and that we will have many other children. She is glad that I have returned and looks forward to the holiday season.

I return from Edinburgh to learn my lady has miscarried. I tell her this is common with a first born and that we will have many more children. She is happy I am home and is looking forward to the holiday celebrations.

December 1, 1371

I was raised this day by the Craft as a sublime Knight and have been given instruction and obligated to the duties of the Sublime Knights Elected.

I have been raised by the order today as an exalted Knight and have been instructed in the obligation and duties of an elected exalted knight.

It appears Sir Henry has been raised/knighted to the status of a Knights Templar in a Masonic tradition versus a cultural position of high status within Scottish society. To be knighted in both traditions indicates he was a very powerful person in Scotland and elsewhere around the world.

March 3, 1372

My wife is preparing to visit her brothers and father this month and shall leave this next day. She is excited to tell him of her new life in Rosslin and the progress of the new home where she will live. She hopes to return with tapestries and cloth to decorate her new home.

My lady prepares to visit her family this month and will leave tomorrow. She wants to tell them about her new life at Rosslyn and the new home where she lives. She wants to return with cloth and tapestries to use in her new home.

April 5, 1372

I return this day from collecting rents and have spent much time deciding arguments between crofters who both claim the same goats and their get. It pleases me that they accept my judgment but distresses me that such petty things should need to be decided at all. I must create a counsel who can deal with local problems so as not to bother others with trivial things.

I have spent the day collecting money and have spent a lot of time deciding arguments between tenants who claim the same goats and kids. I am glad they accept my judgment but sad that such little things need to be solved at all. I should create a council to deal with local issues so others are not troubled by such small things.

May 5, 1372

My lady has returned from Dirleton Castle with news of her brothers Walter and Henry who are becoming fine men. She has also brought tapestries and looms to make cloth for our new home and seems happy in her duties.

My lady has returned from Dirleton Castle and tells of her brothers Walter and Henry who are growing to be good men. She has also brought tapestries and looms to make cloth for her new home and appears to be happy with her new role.

October 17, 1372

My lady tells me she is once again with child and will deliver before summer next. She hopes for a healthy boy so that we might have an heir. We celebrate with a feast during which we receive the first snow of the season. My lady calls it a blessing from the Holy Mother to blanket us with love.

My lady says she is expecting a child before summer next. She hopes for a healthy boy so we will have an heir. We celebrate with a feast, and it snows for the first time this winter. My lady calls it a blessing from the Holy Mother to cover with love.

November 22, 1372

A council of my counselors has been called to discuss the raids of the Norsemen on our shores and outlying islands. We must devise a plan to protect our neighbors and plan to build more boats to support our plan.

A councilor of my advisors has convened to talk about the raids of the pirates on our shores and neighboring isles. We need a plan to protect our neighbors and will plan to build more boats to do our plan.

March 30, 1373

The winter months have been kind, and we have been able to finish 5 small fishing craft which will be used to patrol the northern isles. With advance notice and an improved presence, we hope to discourage raids during the winter months.

Winter has been good to us and we have completed 5 small fishing boats that will patrol the north islands. If we have notice and a bigger presence, we hope raids during the winter months will be discouraged.

April 18, 1373

The Brethren of the Craft have met this day to discuss the needs of the Templari [Templars] *who have requested our assistance in Midlothian. We meet again next seventh day to conclude this matter.*

The brothers of the Order met today to talk about the Templars who have asked for our help in Midlothian. We will meet again next week to finish the matter.

This is the first mention of the descendants of the Knights Templar who served at Bannockburn and who fled France, which we will soon learn from

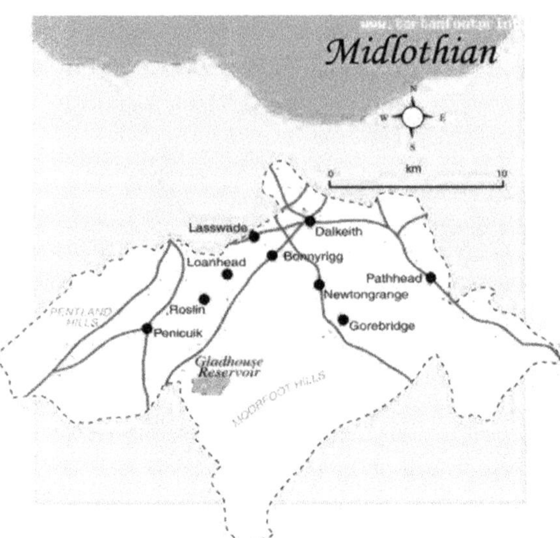

The Midlothian region in Scotland, where some of the fugitive Knights Templar and their descendants were living under the protection of the Sinclair clan in 1373. (Internet)

Henry. These knights were living near Rosslyn, and we will soon learn others were living in Wemyss Caves for several decades. Because of the fugitive knights' service at Bannockburn, the prominent Scottish clans, such as the Sinclairs and Wemyss, were obligated to protect them and eventually bring the survivors to the Western Lands. This previously unknown detail begins to answer the long-debated question of what happened to the Templars who disappeared after that fateful day on October 13, 1307.

April 25, 1373

The Brethren of the Craft met this day and discussed the needs of the Templari in Midlothian. While their order persists, and they are well provisioned, they have been outlawed in the land. They are seeking a new home in the Western Lands where their brethren are to have prepared a home for them. Plans begin to assist in their departure."

The brothers of the Order met today and talked about the Templar's needs in Midlothian. Their order still exists but has been outlawed in this land. They search for a new home in the western land where their brothers have prepared a home for them. We plan to assist their departure.

This entry begins to flesh out the plan they called the "Covenant." The mission was to bring the remaining descendants of the fugitive Knights Templar, and the treasures secreted from their headquarters in France, to the Western Lands to be used to help establish a new home. The "bretheren" in North America Henry mentions are likely the Kensington party from 1358 who had been there fifteen years by this time.

May 24, 1373

A son Henry was born this day. He is named after his father and if he lives will become heir to our estates. He is a lusty boy and howls continually.

A son Henry was born today. We have named him after his father and if he survives will become my heir to my estates. He is a loud boy and cries all day.

This son did indeed survive and would grow up to become the next generation to write in journals connected to the Covenant.

June 24, 1373

Today we celebrate St. John's Day with a feast. My daughter Margaret has joined us in Rosslin for several weeks. She is now 7 years old and adores her little brother. She will return to Strathearn shortly after Assumption of Our Lady Mary.

Today we celebrate St. John's Day with a feast. My daughter Margaret joins us for several weeks. She is 7 years old and loves her little brother. She will return to Strathearn after the Assumption of our Lady Mary.

September 29, 1373

My lady tells me she is expecting another child. She is most happy.

My lady says she is expecting another child. She is very happy.

May 15, 1374

Today my son John was born at Kirkton. He is named after my Lady's father and looks to be a healthy child. Unlike his brother who insists on holding him, he is a quiet child and seems happy and content.

Today my son John was born at Kirkton. He is named after my Lady's father. He seems a healthy child. He is a quiet and happy child. Not like his older brother who wants to hold him.

June 1, 1374

I learned this day that 4 fishing boats from Orknades were lost at sea after being driven off course while traveling to Iceland. I must make reparations to their families and see that they are cared for.

I was told today of 4 fishing boats from Orkney were lost to the sea on the way to Iceland. I need to make payments to their families and know that they are cared for.

August 1, 1374

Our new home in Rosslin is near completion and this coming season will be ready for the upcoming winter. Lady Jean has been working valiantly on the tapestries with her ladies and prepare readily for Michaelmas.

Our home in Rosslin is almost done and ready for winter and the upcoming season. Lady Jean has been working on wall coverings with her ladies and will be ready for Michaelmas.

January 2, 1375

Today is celebrated the Advent of Isis as the people prepare for a new sowing season. The old religion is still practiced in parts of Scotland even though the people claim to be good Christians.

Today we celebrate the Advent of Isis as tenants prepare for the sowing season. The old religion is still practiced in parts of Scotland although people say they are good Christians.

It is interesting how many of the Scottish people at this time were celebrating both Pagan traditions along with Christian traditions. I suspect the old rituals were practiced largely in private as crypto-Pagans so as not to draw attention of the Roman Church.

July 1, 1375

King Haakon of Norway has appointed Alexander de Ard, my cousin as administrator of Orkney. In return he has resigned all ownership to land in Scotland which he inherited from my mother's sister, Matilda de Strathearn.

King Hakon of Norway has appointed Alexander de Ard my cousin as Orkney's administrator. He has given up all ownership in Scotland in return that he received from Matilda de Strathearn, my mother's sister.

St John's Day, 1376 (June 24th)

Alexander de Ard was terminated as commissioner of Orkney this day. I must campaign for my own appointment.

Alexander de Ard was released as commissioner of Orkney today. I must campaign for my own appointment.

March 23, 1377

I must settle a dispute between the crofters of Rosslin who are unable to agree on the border of their farms. I will try to find a solution that satisfies both as I collect the rents for Rosslin.

I must settle an argument between the farmers of Rosslyn who disagree on their farm borders. I will find a solution that makes them happy as I collect rents for Rosslyn.

December 16, 1377

Today a daughter Elizabeth is born in Kirkwall. She is a comely child and does not cry. She and her mother both do well.

A daughter Elizabeth is born today in Kirkwall. She is a pretty child and doesn't cry. Both she and her mother are doing well.

July 5, 1379

Alexander de Ard, Malise Sperra, and myself leave for Norway, each to plead with the King for an appointment as Earl of Orkney. I hope that he is open to my pleas above those of my cousins.

Alexander de Ard, Malise Sperra and I go to Norway to each ask to be Earl of Orkney. I hope he will listen to my argument instead of my cousins.

August 2, 1379

A Charter was given by King Hakon today at Marstand to install me as the Earl of Orkney. I have also been given the Lordship of Hjatland [Shetland]. I will do my best to govern these lands and pray that the mother and father bless me. I have made promises I hope to keep but know they will be difficult. To keep these promises, I must find 100 good men to defend Orkney in the King's name and pay to the King or his official at the festival of St Martin, 1000 gold pieces of English coin. My cousin Malise Sparre has promised to cease his claim to the earldom, and we have made peace with my cousin Alexander de Ard. We move forward in the best interests of the people of Orkney.

King Hakon gave a charter today at Marstand to appoint me as the new Earl of Orkney. I was also given the Lordship of Shetland. I will strive to govern them and pray that mother father will bless me. I have made difficult promises I will do my best to keep. To do this I must find 100 good men to defend Orkney in name of the King and pay 1000 gold pieces of English coin to the King's official at the festival of Saint Martin. My cousin Malese Sparre has said he will stop his claim to the Earldom, and we make with Alexander de Ard. We look forward in the best interest of Orkney's people.

August 28, 1379

My brother John St. Clair was married this day to Ingeborg, the base-born daughter of King Waldemar. Her mother is Jova Little who is the daughter of Sir John Little, the Commissioner of Rugen.

My German brother John St. Clair was married today to Ingeborg the illegitimate daughter of King Waldemar. Jova Little is the mother and is the daughter of Sir John Little the Rugen Commissioner.

September 1, 1379

At King Hakon's request I must pledge my faithfulness to Norway over the country of Scotland. I take this pledge although I know in my heart that Scotland and Orkney will always be first in my thoughts. I must do my best to please the King and still make the people of Orkney happy.

King Hakon requests I pledge my loyalty to Norway over the country of Scotland. I do this pledge but know in my heart that I will always think first of Scotland and Orkney. I must do my best to make the King and the people of Orkney happy.

February 3, 1380

King Hakon has insisted that I not to enter into friendship with the bishop of Kirkwall, William IV. He is a most contentious man and finds any excuse to argue and take offense. He has taken lands which are not his and the people of Orkney fear his judgment. This past month he has excommunicated many in Orkney for non-compliance to his dictates, including several of my kinsmen. He thinks himself above the King.

King Hakon has said I should not be friends with William IV Bishop of Kirkwall. He is a of fighting man and will always argue and be offended. He has taken over land and the people of Orkneys are afraid of him. He has excommunicated many this former month in Orkney for not following his rules, including many of my family. He thinks he is more powerful than the king.

May 15, 1380

We begin this day to build a fortified house in Kirkwall for myself and my family. We must be able to defend against William IV and his followers as they constantly argue against my decisions. King Hakon has forbidden this but I am certain that I can convince him of the necessity. The people of Orkney take comfort in the fact that I will be able to defend them against the bishop and his men. We build on the edge of the bay not far from the bishop's palace to best monitor his comings and goings.

Today we start to build a strong house for my family in Kirkwall. We must be able to defend against Bishop William IV and his followers who always fight against my dictates. King Hakon has told me not to build but I think I can convince him it is necessary. The Orkney people are comforted by the fact that I can defend them against the bishop's men build on the bay's edge close to the bishop's palace to watch him coming and going.

September 9, 1380

King Hakon has required a bond of me with the Bishop of Bergen to pay 20 earls. He also requires that I reside in Orkney for the majority of the year. I will use this time to learn about my people and to solve their grievances. I must also build a fleet to stave off the pirates and English invaders that plague our shores.

King Hakon requires a bond of me with Bishop of Bergen to pay 20 Earls. He also demands that I live in Orkney for most of the year. I will spend the time learning about my people and fixing their grievances. I must also build a fleet of ships to hold off pirates and English invaders that trouble our shores.

April 15, 1381

Today the brethren have met to discuss the ideas of Nicole Oresme, the Dean of Rouen Cathedral. Brother Alynton recently heard him speak in Paris and has agreed to tell us his thoughts. More than 40 Brethren attended in the chapel.

The brothers have met today to debate the ideas of Nicole Oresme, Dean of Rouen Cathedral. Brother Alynton heard him talk in Paris recently and has agreed to tell us his thoughts. More than 40 brothers came to the chapel.

March 25, 1382

Bishop William was slain this day in Kirkwall when he openly challenged my authority with the people of Orkney. He was burned to death in his church hall by the people. He will not be missed.

Bishop William challenged my rule in the open and was killed in Kirkwall today. The people burned the church, and he was in it. I will not miss him.

September 7, 1382

Sixty of the brethren has gathered to hear John Wycliffe speak today on his views towards the Catholic Church at the Bishop's Cathedral. With no bishop presiding there is none to stop him from purporting his views. I look forward to discussion with him after the meeting.

60 of the brothers have gathered to hear the views of John Wycliffe against the Catholic Church at the Bishop's Cathedral. Because no Bishop is installed, no one can stop him from speaking. I look forward to talking to him after his talk.

September 9, 1382

We received word today that Nicole Oresme of Rouen France has died. While he is now gone his words stay with us forever.[27]

Today we were told Nicole Oresme of Rouen in France has died. His words will remain forever even though he is gone.

February 2, 1383

I have met with the Templari near the cliffs of Wemyss and have delivered provisions to them for the rest of the winter. They seem in good spirits and make good use of their time.

I met today with the Templari at the cliffs of Wemyss and delivered goods to them for the remainder of the winter. Then are in good spirits and keep busy.

Here we learn of the descendants of the fugitive Templars from 1307 are living in Wemyss Caves on the north side of the Firth of Forth seventy-six years later. It is unclear if the Midlothian Templars moved into Wemyss Caves or if they were a separate group.

27. https://todayinsci.com/O/Oresme_Nicole/OresmeNicole-Forerunner.htm

This entry is also significant as there is archaeological evidence to support the assertion the Templars were not only living in the Wemyss Caves in the fourteenth century, but making swords and other metallic objects, which means they must have made a forge. During a tour in Scotland in 2022, a local tour guide explained how evidence of a forge had been recently discovered by archaeologists. Carbon-14 dating has yet to be done, but I'd bet a large sum of money if correct dates are ever documented they will be from the fourteenth century.

April 18, 1383

Today a daughter Jean was born in Corstorphine while her mother was visiting. She is a weak and tiny child, but her mother insists she will survive. I pray for them both. They return home as soon as they are strong enough.

A daughter Jean was born in Corstorphine today where her mother was visiting. The child is weak, but the mother says she will live. I pray for both of them. As soon as they are well enough, they will come back home.

June 12, 1383

Robert Sinclair, my cousin and Dean of Moray, has been appointed as Bishop to Orkney. The people are most happy as am I. It will be good to know that we can argue in peace without wanting to kill each other.

My cousin, Robert Sinclair the Dean of Moray, has been appointed Bishop of Orkney. The people and I celebrate. It will be good to know we can argue in peace without wishing harm to each other.

May 19, 1384

Sir William Douglas has died leaving a widow and two children. His widow is my niece Margaret, and she grieves for her husband. I have promised to watch over them and give her my advice when needed.

Sir William Douglas has died leaving a wife and 2 children. My niece Margaret is his widow, and she grieves for her husband. I will look over them and will give counsel when needed.

June 22, 1384

I am back at Rosslin and must preside over the Freeman's court. I feel I have been negligent in my duties to Rosslin and plan a feast to share my thoughts with the local lords. In the presence of Thomas Erksine, George Abernethy, Walter Halyburton and John Halyburton I have given to Jacob Santo Claro [St Clair] *dominum* [governance] *of Longfurdmakhuse and adjoining lands."*

I am returned to Rosslyn and must preside over the Freed Man's court. I have *[been]* slow in my duties to Rosslyn and will host a feast to share ideas with local lords. Present, are Thomas Erskine, George Abernathy, Walter Haliburton and John Haliburton. I have given Jacob St. Clair lordship of Longfurdmakuse and adjacent lands.

September 29, 1384

We celebrate Michaelmas this day at Rosslin. My wife and family are excited to meet my niece Margaret and her family. We must discuss the education of her young children and the possibility of remarriage.

Today we celebrate Michaelmas at Rosslyn. My lady and family are excited to greet my niece Margaret and her family. We must talk about the children's education and her possible remarriage.

April 18, 1385

Walter Halyburton, John Halyburton, Robert Stewart and myself have met this day with the Templari. They have asked for additional food stuffs and will trade with swords they have manufactured over the winter months. They continue in good spirits as three children have been born this past year and four of their youth have taken the vows of the Templars.

Walter and John Haliburton, Robert Stewart and I have met with the Templars. They ask for more food and trade us swords they have made over the winter months. They are happy and 3 children were born this past year, and 4 youths have taken Templar vows.

This entry confirms the Templar tradition continued through the survivors long after the suppression in 1307. However, the values of the tradition must have evolved from what they once were when the order was beholden to the Roman Catholic Church. No longer was it just the leadership who understood the true gnostic traditions and veneration of the Goddess–who was much more ancient and real than the "Virgin" Mary they outwardly were obligated to venerate. The truth about Mary Magdalene, and the Essenic tradition the survivors were the descendants of, no longer had to be veiled. They were crypto-Essene no more and could outwardly practice the teachings of Templarism and learn their historical origins going back to the first-century royal family.

September 29, 1385

We celebrated Michaelmas this day by sharing a feast with the people of Kirkwall. They seem appreciative of the gesture and the remnants have been given to the bishop to share with the poor.

We celebrated Michaelmas today and shared a feast with the people of Kirkwall. They appreciate the feast, and remainders are given to the bishop to give to the poor.

May 15, 1386

The weather is fine and once again I must collect rents amongst the people of Orkney. I look forward to visiting each of the islands and seeing the progress my people have made.

The good weather allows me to collect rents from the people of Orkney. I like to see each of the islands and to see the progress my people make.

November 2, 1386

Brother Mair has returned from London and gives report that Geoffrey Chaucer has been made to retire from London. Brother Mair brings with him the latest in his writings for the purview of my Lady.

Brother Nairy has returned from London and says that Geoffrey has been forced to retire in London. Brother Nairy brings his latest writings for my Lady to read.

Geoffrey Chaucer (1343-1400) was a famous British poet and writer. That Early Henry and his wife were fans speaks to their high intellect and knowledge of culture of the time.

February 15, 1387

My brother and I have completed a visit to the Templari and have discovered that they are need of medical assistance. Many of them are ill with fever and spots. We have dispatched three women with herbal knowledge to assist them and have asked Lord of Wemyss to send fresh food stuffs and warm blankets. Winter has been harsh on them although their numbers increase. We must repair to Kirkwall.

My brother and I visited the Templars and have seen they need medical attention. Many are ill with fever and have spots. We have sent 3 women who know herbs to help them and have asked the Lord of Wemyss to send fresh food and warm blankets. Winter has been hard on them even though many have joined them. We must now go to Kirkwall.

May 25, 1387

The hirdmen have met this day and have brought the matters of the people to be attended to. They have done an excellent job in helping us to learn what happens in the islands. Several men have been involved in a murder and must be dealt with, as well as permissions for several to marry. I am beginning to feel as if they trust my judgment and know that I have chosen well in my hirdmen.

The hirdman have met today and have brought matters of the people to attend to. They have done a remarkable job in helping to know what happens in the islands. Several men who committed murder must be dealt with as well as permissions for many to marry. I begin to think they trust my judgment and I know I have chosen good hirdman.

"Hirdman" is a member of a Norwegian royal household, functioning as steward, guard, military personnel, and administrator.

September 9, 1387

A daughter Marjorie was born this morn. She is a screaming child and has a red face. Her mother does fine, and Elizabeth helps to care for her.

A daughter named Marjorie was born this morning. She is a screaming babe and red in the face. Her mother is doing well, and Elizabeth is helpful taking care of the babe.

November 8, 1387

I have visited Edinburg where my cousin Malise Sparre complains of harm to him and his tenants. I have agreed to pay him for damages and have ordered my councilmen to restrain those who argue against him. He is a threat to my earldom, and I cannot abide his irritation. Winter approaches and I must return to Orkney before the ice sets in.

I am back from Edinburgh where Malise Sparre, my cousin complains that my tenants have done harm to him and his tenants. I agree to pay for damages and have told my hirdman to stop those who argue with him. He threatens my rule, and I dislike his agitation. Winter comes and I must go to Orkney before the ice comes.

February 3, 1388

I have attended the council meeting in Norway and have acknowledged Margaret as the Queen and her great-nephew Eric of Pomerania as the true heir to the throne. He is but 5 years old, but she will guide him with a firm hand. The Queen is as beautiful as she was at her marriage and gives us her blessing in the governing of Orkney and Shetland. I must return to Orkney to collect rents and attend to my family.

I attended the Kings council meeting in Norway and have acknowledged Queen Margaret as my Queen and her great nephew as legal heir to the throne. He is only 5 years old but she will raise him firmly. The Queen is still beautiful as when married and she has given us her blessing in ruling Orkney and Shetland. I must go home to Orkney to attend to my family and collect rents.

August 24, 1388

The battle at Otterburn has been won in the name of Scotland and honors the Earl of Douglas who died before the battle was spent. My kinsmen Sir John Sinclair bore the banner into battle, but I did not participate, still being in Kirkwall.

Scotland has won the battle of Otterburn and honors to Earl of Douglas who died before the battle ended.[28,29] My family man Sir John Sinclair carried the banner into battle, but I did not participate because I was in Kirkwall.

September 29, 1388

Michaelmas was celebrated this day, and we had as guests 30 of the Templari and their families who come from the eastern caves. They have brought 6 children to be baptized and blessed and four of them were married this day at chapel by proper authority.

We celebrated Michaelmas with 30 Templar guests and their kin from the Eastern caves. They have 6 children to be baptized and blessed and 4 of them were married in the Chapel St. Michael by the proper authority.

July 3, 1389

At Helsingborg, Sweden I am required to bond myself to Haakon Jonsson, the royal bailiff of Norway and to pay him 140 pounds of gold beginning with 40 pounds St Lawrence's Day at the chapel of St Magnus in Tingwall in Hjatland in 1390, 40 pounds more in 1391, 40 pounds in 1392, and 20 pounds in 1393. If we should fail to meet his terms the rents we collect are forfeit. This will require that I gain and maintain control over Hjatland now that we have prepared a fleet."

I am required to make bond to Haakon Jonsson at Helsingborg in Sweden, the royal bailiff of Norway and to pay him 140 pounds gold starting with 40 pounds on St. Lawrence's Day at the church of St. Magnus in Tingwall in Shetland in 1390, 40 pounds gold in 1391, 40 pounds in 1392,

28. https://en.wikipedia.org/wiki/Battle_of_Otterburn

29. https://www.britishbattles.com/one-hundred-years-war/battle-of-otterburn/

and 20 pounds in 1393. If I fail to meet the terms the rents we collect are forfeit. This will require that I gain and continue control over Shetland now that we have built a fleet.

September 18, 1389

I have travelled to Oslo to be present with my cousin Sir Malise Sparre at the accession of King Eric of Pomerania. He succeeds Queen Margaret who adopted him when he was a child.

I have gone to Oslo with my cousin Sir Malise Sparre for the coronation of King Eric of Pomerania. He follows Queen Margaret who adopted him as a child.

October 23, 1389

Before we could attend the Althing to be held at Scalloway in Shetland, I was forced to take my cousin Malise Sperra captive. He has attempted to take over Hjatland in opposition to my reign and has threatened the people I am sworn to the King to protect. My cousin irritates me no more as he and 7 others are now dead. Others have escaped but I will deal with them when necessary. I return to Rosslin to secure my cousins holdings.

Before we go to the Althing held at Scalloway in Shetland I am forced to make my cousin Malise Sparre captive. He has tried to take over Shetland in opposition to my rule and has threatened the [people?] I have sworn to protect. My cousin and 7 others are now dead and irritate me no more. Some have escaped but I will catch them when necessary. I now go to Rosslyn to take over my cousin's land.

Although he doesn't give details about Malise Sparre's death, Sinclair and Me write that Earl Henry killed him and his seven followers, "*Their animosity climaxed on the return voyage, when Earl Henry slew Malise and seven of his followers at the standing stone at Scalloway on Shetland.*"[30] This stone is called the Murder Stone.[31]

30. Sinclair and Me, Page 343, 2018.
31. https://www.megalithic.co.uk/article.php?sid=22190

November 2, 1389

A son William is born this morn in Rosslin. He is a thick child and quite large. His mother is doing well, and the older children help to care for him.

A son William is born this morning in Rosslyn. He is a fat child and very big. His mother does well, and the older children help to take care of him.

April 19, 1390

King Robert II of Scotland has died, and his son John Stewart is now King Robert III, but has no power to rule. He is a quiet and reflective man and was hurt by a horse years ago. Until he is considered able to rule his brother Robert will rule from Fifeshire.

King Robert II of Scotland has died, and his son John Stewart is now King Robert III but he cannot rule. He is a quiet and thoughtful man who was injured by a horse years ago. Until able to rule his brother Robert will rule from Fifeshire.[32]

The so-called Murder Stone where the treacherous Malise Sparre and seven of his colleagues were put to death by Earl Henry Sinclair at Scalloway on Shetland in 1389. (Internet)

32. https://www.scotlandmag.com/robert-iii-biography/

May 15, 1390

We have set out with a fleet of 10 ships for Hjatland where we will patrol the shores against pirates and interlopers. I will also collect rents when visiting the shores before we move on to the Faroe Islands.

We have left with a fleet of 10 ships for Shetland where we will patrol for pirates along the shoreline before we go to the Faroe Islands.

May 31, 1390

We have word that an Italian ship has wrecked off the shores of Balta Island in the Shetlands and have been put upon by the people from the mainland who hope to subdue them and loot their stores. The shores there are rocky and hazardous and are the resting place of many wrecks. I will take three of my ships in the morrow and rescue them. Perhaps they will have news of Paris and Venice.

We have received word that an Italian ship has been wrecked off the shore of Balta Island in the Shetlands and have been attacked by the island folk who want to capture them and loot their ship. The shore there is wicked and rocky and have many wrecks sleeping there. I will take 3 ships tomorrow and get them. Maybe they have news of Paris and Venice.

This entry is where the story of Nicolo and Antonio Zeno and their interactions with Earl Henry Sinclair begins. Much has been written about the Zeno's activities in the North Atlantic with a man named Zichmni, who is believed to be Earl Henry Sinclair.[33] In the forthcoming entries it will become obvious the legendary Zichmni is in fact Earl Henry Sinclair.

June 1, 1390

We have rescued the captain and crew of the Italian ship which has floundered and been broken apart by the waves upon the shore. The captain is Nicolo Zeno of Venice, whom I've heard much about. We are able to converse in Latin and I have befriended him and hope that he can teach us how to be more effective at sea battle.

---

33. https://en.wikipedia.org/wiki/Voyage_of_the_Zeno_brothers

I have rescued the Captain and Italian ship's crew which had sunk and was broken apart by the waves on the shore. The captain is Nicolo Zeno of Venice who I've heard a lot about. We can talk in Latin, and I have made him my friend and hope he will teach us how to fight at sea better.

From the very beginning after the rescue of Nicolo Zeno and his men, he and Earl Henry develop a friendship based on mutual respect. Their friendship would continue to develop and thrive, culminating in their trip to the Western Lands in 1395.

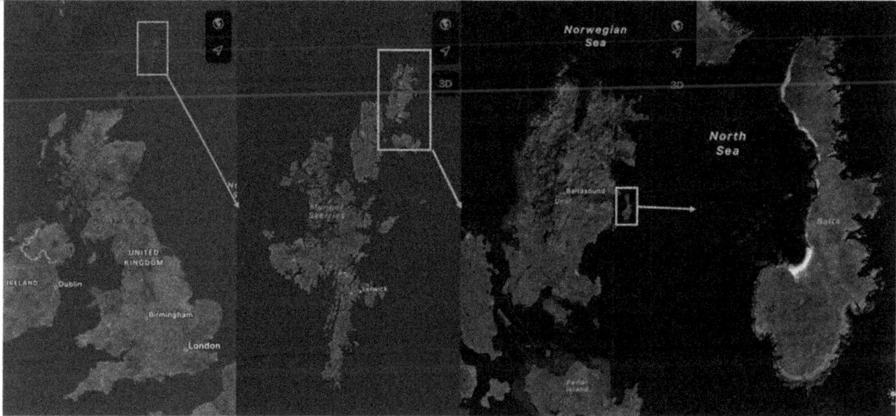

Balta Island is an extremely remote island where Captain Nicolo Zeno's ship ran aground in the Shetland Islands in 1390.

June 3, 1390

At my request, Captain Nicolo Zeno and his men have participated in a brief battle against the followers of Malise Sperra who escaped my vengeance last year. They have now been subdued and we should hear no further of them as they flee back to Norway whence they came. I learn more each day as I speak with Captain Zeno. I have asked him to stay for the summer and to help us prepare our fleet and my men for a voyage of discovery and exploration. He is most apt to do this as he has visited Groenland before and wishes to return to complete his mapping of the northern shorelines.

Captain Zeno and his men have taken part in a sea skirmish at my urging against Malise Sperra and his men who escaped last year from my fury. They are now silenced, and we should hear nothing of them as they have fled to Norway where they came from. Captain Zeno teaches me more each time we talk. I asked him to remain for the summer to help us ready the ships and men for a voyage of exploration and discovery. He has visited Greenland before and is eager to accompany us to complete his map of the north shore.

August 15, 1390

This day I have knighted Captain Nicolo Zeno in recognition of his bravery and given him command of my fleet. He has shared information on weaponry and rigging that is greatly appreciated and knows more about navigation and sea battles than all of my captains. There is no ill will amongst them as they are familiar with his reputation as a fair and experienced Captain. He has written to his son in Venice asking him to join us and a ship heading for Venice will deliver it this fall. There will be no answer till Spring as the ships only traverse during the spring and the fall. Until then his men and he will stay the winter with us.

To my surprise, I discover he and his brother and son are familiar with the vows of the brethren as their grandfather was also a Templar. This pleases me as he understands my plan to visit the Western Lands.

I knighted Captain Nicolo Zeno today to recognize his courage and gave him command of my fleet. He shared rigging and weaponry information that is greatly needed and knows more about sea battles and navigating than all of my captains. They are all familiar with his reputation as an experienced and good captain so there is no angst among them. He wrote to his son in Venice to join us in the spring. A ship going to Venice will deliver this fall. No one will answer till spring because ships only come in spring and fall. He and his men will stay through the winter with us. I have discovered as a surprise that both he and his son and his brother know the vows of the brethren as their grandfather was a Templar. I am pleased as he now understands why I visit the western lands.

The importance of this entry cannot be overstated when considering what is believed to be known about the Zeno families' history with Earl Henry Sinclair. Not only was there a deep respect between Nicolo and Earl Henry—as evidenced by Henry giving Zeno command of his fleet of ships—but there was also a deep respect for Zeno and his rescued men by Sinclair's men.

Nicolo has also summoned his son, Antonio, who will arrive in the spring. It has long been believed the Zeno brothers traveled to Scotland, spending years serving alongside Earl Henry. However, while Nicolò Zeno did have a brother named Antonio, it was his son, also named Antonio, who joined his father in Scotland in April of 1395. This is a new fact previously unknown to historians.

Nicolò Zeno the Younger was a child when he tore up the five letters his ancestor Antonio Zeno had written to a brother about his adventures in the North Atlantic circa 1400. As a remorseful adult, he had the remaining documents compiled into what is now known as the Zeno Narrative that was published in 1558. (Internet)

It should also be pointed out there are numerous details in the entries that conform to events described in the historical document first published in 1558 called, *The Zeno Narrative*.[34] This document was created by a descendant of Nicolo and Antonio Zeno named Nicolò Zeno the Younger (1515-1565). As a young boy, Nicolò found five long letters written by Antonio about their experiences in the North Atlantic in the late fourteenth century and tore them up around 1520.[35] Upon reaching adulthood, he realized the damage he had done and tried to recreate the content of what remained of the letters, and the map found with the original letters.

Historians have debated the events described in the narrative, with many calling the whole story a hoax, claiming the names of land masses on the map were incorrect and therefore fraudulent. Other scholars claim the map is genuine, and these entries of Earl Henry Sinclair provide strong

34. Cooper, Foreword Page 1, 2004.

35. https://www.ancient-origins.net/history/zeno-map-0014659

support for the narrative, as well as incredible new details. Masonic Brother Robert Cooper published a book in 2004 that translated the original narrative from Italian into English. Upon reading the narrative, I was struck by how many specific points matched with the journal entries by Earl Henry. In fact, nearly everything matches, with one big exception: Nicolò and Antonio were not brothers, according to the journals they were father and son. While this detail is an important deviation from the original narrative, essentially everything else does match. It appears both documents provide independent corroboration of the other.

February 4, 1391

A daughter whom we named Anne was born this morn at Kirkwall. She has long silver hair and waves her tiny arms as if welcoming the world. She will be a happy child.

A daughter was born this morning at Kirkwall. We named her Anne. She has long white hair and welcomed the world by waving her tiny arms. She is a happy child.

March 10, 1391

We have been granted safe passage by King Richard II of England for 25 persons.

King Richard the 2nd of England has granted safe passage for 25 people.

April 23, 1391

I have given by charter to my brother David of St Clair [son of Isabella] *the lands of Newburgh and Auchdale in Aberdeenshire to rule and protect. Witnessed by many of the brethren we met to discuss a voyage of discovery to the Western Lands. All agree that it is time.*

I have given a charter to my brother David St. Clair, the son of Isabella to govern and protect the lands of Newburgh and Auchdale in Aberdeenshire. Many of the brethren were witness and we met to discuss a voyage of discovery to the western lands. All agree it is time to go.

September 3, 1391

We have completed the fort in Bressay and I have left Sir Nicolo with several small ships, men and stores for the coming winter. They will complete the remaining work on the fort and the docks in preparation for spring fishing.

The fort in Bressay has been finished today and I left Sir Nicolo with several small ships and men and supplies for the winter coming. His men will complete the work remaining on the Fort and docks to prepare for spring fishing.

March 25, 1392

I return home from parliament which was held in Perth. Those present at the killing of Sir Walter de Ogilvy have been condemned and I have no reason to object. The senseless killing of our brethren is horrific, and the offenders should be caught and punished. They will have no quarter in the lands of Rosslin, Orkney, Shetland, or the Faroes.

Parliament was held in Perth, and I am now home. Those who participated in killing of Sir Walter de Ogilvy have been sentenced and I do not object. The meaningless killing of our brothers is terrible and those who did it should be found and punished. There is no safe haven for them in Rosslyn, Orkney, Shetland, or the Faroes.

September 27, 1392

We return from England where we were granted safe conduct for 28 men. Captain Zeno has assisted in procuring 7 ships at Queen Margaret's request for the Orkney fleet. He has also sent missives to his brother Carlos Zeno of Venice and has told him of the progress we have made in the Orkneys.

We have returned from England where we obtained safe passage for 28 men. Captain Zeno has helped in securing 7 ships for Queen Margaret required for the Orkney fleet. He has also sent letters to Carlos Zeno, his brother in Venice to tell him of progress being made in Orkney.

March 23, 1393

Eight ships have sailed to the Faroes to subdue attacks of pirates from England and Norway. A late snow came upon us and 4 ships were wrecked off the shores of Mykines in the blinding storm. We have departed for Iceland to repair the ships before we return to Orkney.

Eight ships have gone to the Faroes to answer attacks from pirates from England and go to Norway. Four ships crashed off the shore of Mykines due to a blinding snowstorm. We will depart for Iceland to repair the ships before we return to Orkney.

October 24, 1393

I have attended Parliament in Perth where the coin of the realm was discussed and agreed upon. Until it becomes a reality we will continue to deal in gold and silver.

I have been to Perth for Parliament where we have talked about the coin of the country that we agreed on. We will still use gold and silver until it becomes real.

March 8, 1394

I have attended the Scottish Parliament in Scone. I spoke with Sir Robert Stewart about the proceedings, and we have agreed to meet with the brethren to discuss another visit to the Western Lands.

I have gone to Scone for Parliament. I spoke with Sir Robert Stewart about the discussion, and we decide to meet with the brothers to talk about another visit to the western lands.

July 3, 1394

Captain Nicolo has written to his brother Carlos Zeno in Venice about a voyage of discovery he wishes to make. His ship being destroyed he requests that Carlos send Antonio, the son of Nicolo, to Orkney on another ship. He should arrive in the spring. Captain Nicolo has now left for Groenland to explore the western coastline and will return in 2 months.

Captain Nicolo has written to Carlos Zeno, his brother in Venice about the voyage of discovery he wants to make. His ship was destroyed, and he requests that Carlos send his son Antonio and another ship to Orkney. He should arrive in the spring. Captain Nicolo has gone to Greenland and will return in 2 months.

August 31, 1394

I have attended the Scottish Parliament in Edinburgh. I spoke once again with Sir Robert and the brethren. Plans continue for a journey to the Western Lands once Antonio has arrived in the spring.

I attended Scottish Parliament in Edinburgh. I talked again to Sir Robert and the brothers. We continue to plan for a trip to the western lands when Antonio arrives in the spring.

February 28, 1395

A daughter whom we named Cecilia was born this morn and died the same day. Her mother grieves at her loss. The babe will be buried in the bishop's churchyard in the morrow. My wife is weak but is in the care of her ladies."

A daughter we named Cecilia was born this morning and died the same day. Her mother grieves at the loss. We will bury the child in the bishop church yard tomorrow. My wife is weak and is in the care of her ladies.

April 15, 1395

My wife has recovered, and Captain Zeno and I make plans to travel to Groenland to exchange Bishops. My lady assures me she will be well with her ladies and the children to keep her busy.

Captain Nicolo's brother arrived three days ago and has brought with him 2 galleys from Venice and many men. The galleys are appointed with the newest in canon weaponry and are an amazement to behold. His father Nicolo is pleased to see him and has spent much time in his company discussing family and political matters. He too feels it imperative that the brethren move quickly. Both Captain Nicolo and his son are members of the Craft and understand the necessity of finding a suitable place for the Templars to settle and flourish. Many of the men in Antonio's crew are also members of the Craft or are descendants of Templars who flourished in France and Italy. They are skilled and good men, and I welcome their assistance.

My wife is well, and Captain Zeno and I plan to travel to Greenland to trade bishops. My wife tells me she is well with her ladies and children to keep her busy. Captain Nicolo's son came 3 days ago and brought 2 galleys with him and many men from Venice. The galleys are an amazement to see and have the newest in canon weaponry installed. Antonio's father is happy to see him and spends a lot of time with him talking about family and politics. He also thinks it is important that the brothers move fast. He and Captain Zeno are both members of the Craft and know the need to find a suitable place for the Templars to live and prosper. Many of Antonio's men are also members of the Craft or are descended from Templars who flowered in France and Italy. I welcome their help as they are skilled and good men.

The arrival of Antonio Zeno—indicated in multiple entries that he is Nicolo's son—is called into question in this entry. Diana's translation has the following, *"Captain Nicolo's brother arrived three days ago..."* However, later in the entry it is clear Antonio is Nicolo's son. Sister Harkin's translation does not contain confusion about the relationship, so it appears the mistake was likely made by Diana who appears to have subconsciously assumed Antonio was Nicolo's brother, because this has become the narrative of modern historians. After this speculation I called Diana (September 2, 2024) to ask her if she could have made a mistake. She said she remembered there being a conflict on this point in her translation and said it was almost certainly her mistake.

5

Journals of Earl Henry Sinclair

Book 2

Earl Henry Sinclair
1345–1404

Translated from Latin

May 1, 1395

Diana's Translation (Italics): *We leave this daybreak from Kirkwall for the western banks with the blessing of King Robert and with the support of the hirdmen who will oversee my obligations in Orknades while I am gone. My brother David Sinclair, son of Isabella, and my eldest son Henry will govern in Rosslin with the assistance of my very capable wife and her brother John who oversees Hjatland.*

Our goal is to find a better route to the empires of China further south than the ice-covered lakes and suitable land for settlement beyond the boundaries of Groenland which we visit on our journey. We also travel with 120 remaining Knights Templars, descendants of those at Bannockburn under my grandfather's rule in search of a free Templar state. We will search for suitable places to transfer the Templar treasure hidden in Scotland. The weather is exceptional this day and we assembled a fleet of 8 ships, 4 galleys and 4 barques. As we visit Groenland and Reykjavik we will gather additional fishing vessels. Among our retinue is Nicolo and Antonio Zeno from Venice who are experts in navigating these seas. We intend to stop at Reykjavik to speak with the Althing[36] to gain their support for our journey in the name of Queen Margaret, as well as stores for our journey. Then we will visit the settlement in Groenland and the monastery there. I will miss my family while gone but trust in God and the King to protect them in my absence.

36. Old Norse name for the Icelandic Parliament.

Sister Harkin's Translation (plain): We leave Kirkwall this morn for the Western Lands with King Robert's blessing and with the hirdman who will oversee my events in Orkney while I travel. David Sinclair, Isabella's son and my brother, will rule in Rosslyn with help from my good wife and John her brother who rules Hjatland

We hope to locate a good way to China more south than the icey seas and good land for settling beyond the land of Greenland that we will visit in our travels. We travel with Knights Templars remaining in 120 numbers, descended from Templars at Bannockburn that my grandfather led to search for a free Templar State. We also look for good places to bring the treasure of the Templars still hidden in Scotland. The weather is best today, and we have put together a fleet of 8 ships which are 4 galleons and 4 barke. We will get more fishing vessels when we visit Greenland and Iceland. Nicolo and Antonio Zena from Venice are going with us and are expert sea navigators. We will stop at Reykjavik to talk with the Althing to get support from Queen Margaret for our travels as well as supplies for our trip. We will then get to the people and monastery in Greenland. While I am gone, I will miss my family but will trust in God and King to watch over them while I am gone."

Author's Commentary (shaded box): Any ambiguity about the mission of the Covenant is removed with this entry. It also brings clarity to the persistent legend of the fugitive Knights Templar fighting alongside King Robert the Bruce and his troops in their defeat of the English at Bannockburn. Because of this, the Scottish King and most prominent Scottish clans were obligated to protect the Templars and their descendants. It took nearly ninety years but the plan to bring treasures to be hidden for some day—and the physical bloodline—to North America was finally put in motion.

May 8, 1395

We have spent 7 days in Groenland taking on supplies and stores. We will continue on to [the] *Western Lands with 8 ships to relocate the remaining Templars who came in 1358. Bad weather continues and Nicolo has taken ill due to the coldness of the weather. Captain Nicolo returns to Orkney, but Captain Antonio and his men will journey with us to the Western Lands.*

We have stayed 7 days receiving supplies and corn[37] in Greenland. We will go on to the Western Lands to search for the Templars who came before us in 1358. It continues to be stormy weather and Nicolo is sick because of the cold weather. Captain [Nicolo] will return to Orkney, but Captain Antonio and his men will continue with us to the Western Lands.

There appears to be an error with the May 8 date. The party couldn't have left Orkney on May 1 and arrived at Greenland in one day to have spent seven days taking on supplies by the 8th.

The plan to find the thirty brethren who came to North America in 1358 is interesting as we will learn they do not find them. Instead, they find out the party went west, which is consistent with the Kensington party who traveled to what is now Minnesota to place the land claim stone and establish a settlement by 1362.

We also learn about Nicolò Zeno falling ill in Greenland. Because Earl Henry and the rest of the fleet continued to Nova Scotia they would not learn of the elder Zeno's death for several months. *The Zeno Narrative* describes the unfortunate event this way: "At length Messire Nicolò, not being accustomed to such severe cold, fell ill, and a little while after returned to Frislandia [Scotland], where he died."[38]

May 22,1395

We have arrived at the Isle of the White Stag but see no evidence of the native people. We will rest for 2 days and then head south along the coast to find evidence of our brethren and to map the coastline.

We arrive at the Island of the White Deer but don't see any Indians. We will stay for 2 days and then to travel south on the coast to map the coastline and search for our brothers.

May 26, 1395

We have searched four different inlets but still see no signs of our brethren. The few natives we've seen on shore remain out of sight.

37. In the UK "corn" can mean any type of grain. While it is possible corn originating from the Americas could have made its way to Greenland by the 1300s, it most likely refers to wheat.

38. Cooper, Page 18, 2004.

We have searched in four different estuaries but there are no signs of our brothers. The Indians we see on shore stay there.

May 28, 1395

A terrific storm has beset us and both the Repostus and Persephone have (been) driven out to sea and lost. As soon as the storm abates, we must begin a search for our brethren.

A horrible storm has come upon us and the *Repostus* and *Persephone* have been forced to open sea and lost. As soon as the storm ends, we will search for them.

May 30, 1395

The seas are much calmer this day and we begin our search for our brethren continuing south along the coast.

The water is calm today and we have begun to search for our brothers as we continue south on the coast.

May 31, 1395

We have found the remains of the Repostus *in the middle of a large bay just to the south of where the storm has deposited us. There are no signs of survivors, and the mast of the ship is floating broken on the sea. Several bodies have washed up on a nearby island and we can only suppose that the remainder of our brethren have drowned. We continue on to search for the Persephone. We ask the Holy Father to accept these poor souls into Heaven.*

The place we arrived at is a large bay with hundreds of small islands. There are also several larger ones that are suitable for settlement and securing the cargo we wish to bring. We must visit each of the islands looking for survivors and determine which are best suited for our future needs. We must also explore the inlets and nearby shores to learn if there are native people and adequate game before returning home.

We found the debris of the *Repostus* in the center of a large bay just to the south of where the storm put us. The main is broken and floating on the water. There are no signs of survivors. Many bodies have washed up on an island near us and we think the rest of our brothers have drowned. We will move on to find the *Persephone*. We plead Heavenly Father to welcome these poor men into Heaven.

We have come to a small bay hundreds of small islands. Several larger ones are suitable for settling and depositing the cargo we want to bring. We will visit all the islands looking for survivors and to decide those that are suitable for our need in the years to come. We will also explore rivers and nearby shores to see if there are Indians and animals before sailing home.

The horrific storm that took the *Repostus* illustrates how dangerous life on the seas can be, especially across the vast uncharted waters of the Atlantic Ocean at that time.

July 1, 1395

A smoke signal to the southeast tells us that some of our brethren survive. The Ortus will continue in that direction with hope in our hearts. The other ships wait for our return in the safety of the bay which we have named after Queen Margaret of Norway.

Southeast smoke signals tell us some of our brothers survive. With hopefulness in our safe breasts the *Ortus* will go in that direction. The rest of the fleet waits for us to return in the bay we have named for Queen Margaret of Norway.

July 2, 1395

We have arrived at a sand island in the shape of the waning moon where 23 men await their rescue. Captain Zeno survives and tells us of how the ship was grounded on the reef and after a week was broken apart by the waves. Six men have drowned but the rest of his men have salvaged the supplies from the ship and have awaited rescue. We are happy that we are able to find them. They are hungry but happy to be found and together we head back to the center of the bay where the other ships await us.

We have gotten to an island made of sand in the shape of the passing moon with 23 men awaiting their rescue. Captain Zeno has survived and tells the story of how the ship was pushed onto the reef and after seven days broke apart. Six are drowned but others of his men have gotten supplies from the ship and have waited for rescue. We are glad we were able to find them. They are happy to be found and hungry. Together we go back to the middle of the bay where the other ships wait for us.

July 15, 1395

We encountered the native people for the first time and were welcomed as friends. They live on the mainland near the center of the bay in small, wooded huts. They are fair skinned with black hair and slightly shorter than my men. They wear no clothing and seem not ashamed of their nakedness. They carry spears and seem to be experts at spear fishing in the waters of the bay.

Their leader's name is Keloah and by drawing signs in the sand related that they have seen white men from the East before. He drew a picture of many men with tunics and swords in the sand and then pointed to the southwest. He also drew a picture of a boat that had crashed on the rocks indicating that the men were now on foot. After an evening meal we exchanged gifts, and they assisted us in tethering our boats against the evening tide. We leave in the morning to travel in the direction he pointed knowing that we have made new friends.

Natives have met us for the first time and call us friends. They live near the bay center in small wooden huts on the mainland. They have light skin and dark hair and are shorter than my men. Keloah is their sachem and draws signs in the sand of men from the East they saw before. He draws many men swords and blouses with swords and pointed his hand to the southwest. He drew a ship in the broken on the rocks and men walking on the sand. They helped us to tie our boats against high water after a supper meal and we gave each other gifts. In the morning he pointed the direction to go and we knew we had made new friends.

The bond formed between the indigenous people and Earl Henry and his men would prove to be invaluable in the eventual success of the Covenant mission.

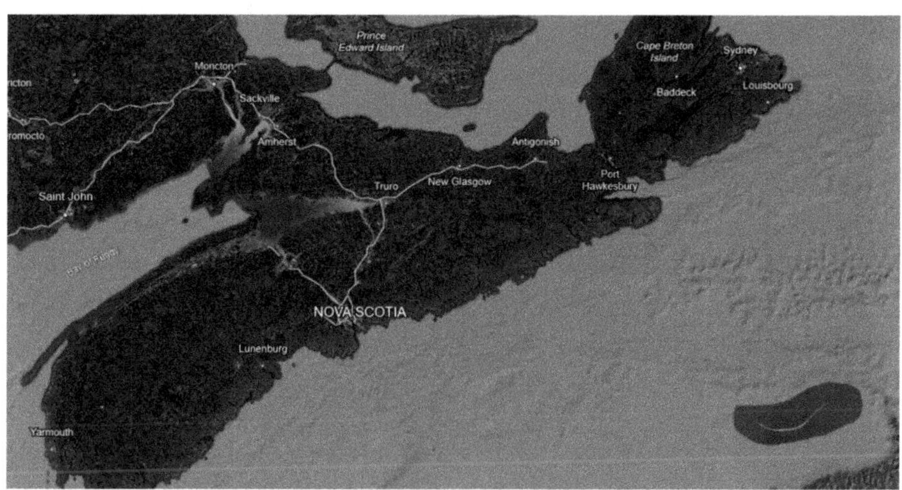

It took two days for Earl Henry to find the survivors of the *Persephone* who sent smoke signals into the air. They had been blown to Sable Island in the lower right corner of this map. (Internet)

July 30, 1395

This day we found a large boulder at the entrance to a large inlet at the southern edge of the bay with the sign of the Templari we left behind many years before. A cross and an arrow signify that they have headed inland to the southwest. I suspect this is where their ship went ashore but see no signs of wreckage. Unwilling to leave the ships I sent a group of 6 knights on foot to follow the direction of the arrow. I assure them we will return to the same place in two weeks' time. We wish them good luck and pray that the Holy Mother will guide them and protect them in their search.

We found a big rock at the beginning of a large river at the southern edge of the bay with a Templar sign from years ago. A cross and an arrow show they went to the southwest away from the sea. There are no signs of wreckage, but I think this is where their ship came on shore. I am unwilling to abandon the ships but send 6 knights on foot in the direction the arrow points. I tell them we will return in 2 weeks and wish them well and pray the Holy Mother will protect and guide them on their way."

The description of the *"big rock"* with *"a cross and an arrow"* is reminiscent of the carvings of the Westford Boat Stone with a large arrow, medieval-era boat, and three symbols which are deeply weathered indicating significant age. To me, the mysterious carved boulder is a Templar artifact that likely dates to this period and could be directly connected to either this expedition or the one in 1398.

August 4, 1395

We have concluded our survey of the bay and have identified at least 10 islands that are suitable for our plans. Captain Zeno has finished mapping the islands that we have chosen and has assured me that he will be able to find them again when we return. We will pick up the 6 men we left behind at the southern point of the bay. I look forward to their report.

Our survey of the bay is complete and we have noted 10 isles suitable for our plans. Captain Zeno has mapped the islands we have found and tells me he can locate them when we come back. We now go to find the 6 men we left behind at the bay's south point. I look forward to their reports.

August 7, 1395

We have sailed southward along the shore and have made note of the richness of the western shores and the abundance of lumber for ship building. A small group of Templars under the command of Sir Humphrey Dennison has asked to stay behind and establish a small colony off the shores of the southernmost point of our journey. We will stay for a week to help them establish their camp and then will begin northward once again.

We write about the richness of the western shores and the large amount of trees to build ships. Sir Humphrey Dennison and a small group of Templars have asked to stay and build a small colony on the southernmost point of our travels. We stay a week to help build the camp and then we will go north again.

The southernmost point of their journey was most likely Narragansett Bay where we know the Newport Tower was constructed and a settlement established at about this time.

The carvings described by Earl Henry are reminiscent of the Westford Boat Stone and the Templar cross carved on a boulder along the shore of the Hudson River. (Wolter, 2007/2021)

August 17, 1395

The men we left behind at the southern shore have returned and report that they have found 2 more stones two days march distance apart indicating that the brethren continued inland to the southwest. Because of this, almost half of the brethren have requested to stay behind to continue the search. This place is marked on Antonio's map as the embarkation point and they have promised to leave markers as they proceed, two days distant. When we return, we will begin our search here.

The men left behind have returned to the southern shore and say they found 2 more rocks 2 days walk apart showing the brothers continued southwest inland. Due to this half of the brothers have asked to stay behind to keep searching. We have marked the place of embarking on Antonio's map, and they promised to leave markers every 2 days as they go. We will begin our search here when we return.

The mention of carvings as signposts and maps recalls one of the most interesting carvings I have seen on the East coast that could be related to the Earl Henry expeditions. The Tyngsboro Map Stone in Massachusetts is a deeply carved map of the Merrimack River that sits on the south bank

The Tyngsboro Map Stone has a deeply carved and heavily weathered map of the Merrimack River that includes Lake Winnipesauke. It is found on the south side of the Merrimack—the border between New Hampshire and Massachusetts—near the mouth of the river. It's very possible the map was carved by a member of the Earl Henry Sinclair expedition in either 1395 or 1398. (Wolter, 2006)

One of over a dozen rounded, triangular stone holes cut with a straight chisel and hammer into large glacial boulders on the eastern end of the Ohman farm near Kensington, Minnesota. The association of the stone holes with the Kensington Rune Stone was confirmed in 2005 when Janet Wolter theorized the holes could triangulate the discovery site. (Wolter, 2016)

A large piece of the Tyngsboro Map Stone sits on the ground that includes part of the river system and a rounded, triangular, hand-carved stone hole that is commonly associated with pre-Columbian Knights Templar activity in North America. (Wolter, 2006)

near the mouth that empties into the Atlantic. The carving also includes a one-inch diameter, rounded-triangular stone hole made with a hammer and straight chisel which is a tell-tale sign of Templar travels.

August 19, 1395

We leave this day to return to Groenland and then home to Orknades.

Today we leave for Greenland and then go home to Orkney.

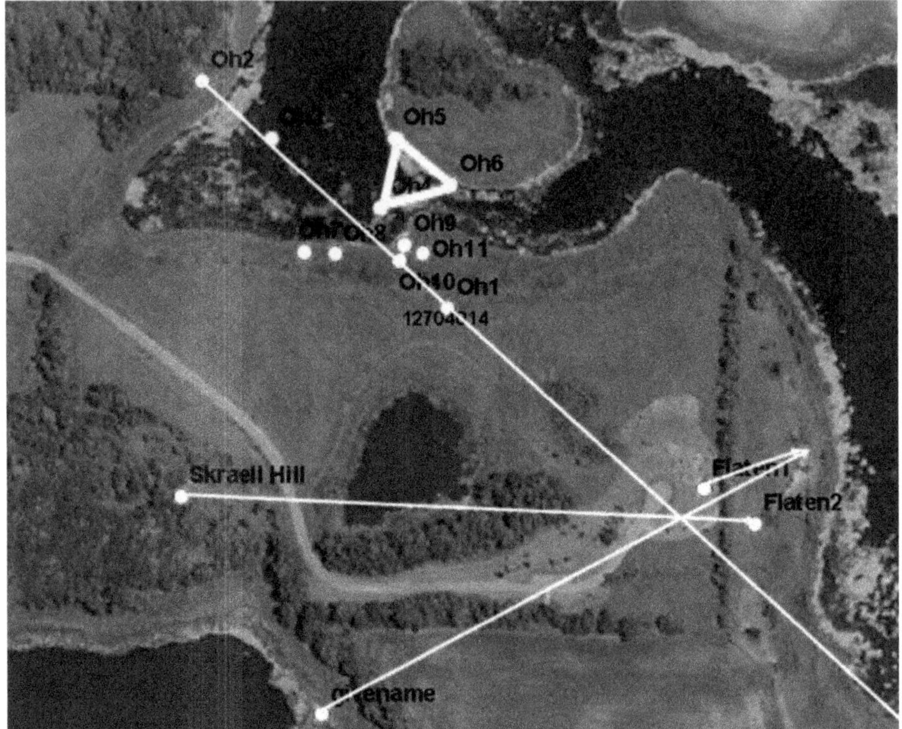

Eight stone holes cut in glacial boulders on the Ohman Farm triangulate exactly where the Kensington Rune Stone was discovered in 1898. The four stone hole boulders along the north side of the field are believed to have been moved by Ohman and his sons in the early twentieth century. The three stone holes that form an equilateral triangle—a symbol of Deity—was left by the party who carved the Kensington Stone land claim. (Wolter, 2005)

October 23, 1395

We have returned from the Western Lands with 5 ships, having left 65 Templari and 2 ships in the New World. One will explore the northern passage to the inner seas and the other has been given the mission of exploring the eastern coast of the Western Lands and establishing a small colony. Needing to return to my duties, I have requested Antonio Zeno to stay on as Admiral of the Orkney fleet.

We have come back from the western lands with 5 ships because we left 2 ships and 65 of the Templars in the New World. One ship will explore the northern route to the inland seas and other is tasked with exploring the eastern shore of the Western lands and starting a small colony. I need to return to my obligations and ask Antonio Zeno to become Admiral of the Orkney fleet.

September 4, 1397

Plans continue for a second trip to the Western Lands to determine the progress of the men left behind. Will meet with the brethren to ascertain the men to accompany me.

We continue to make plans for a second [trip] to know the progress of the men we left behind in the Western Lands. I will meet with the brothers to decide which men to take with me.

SHIPS' CREW LISTS: 1395

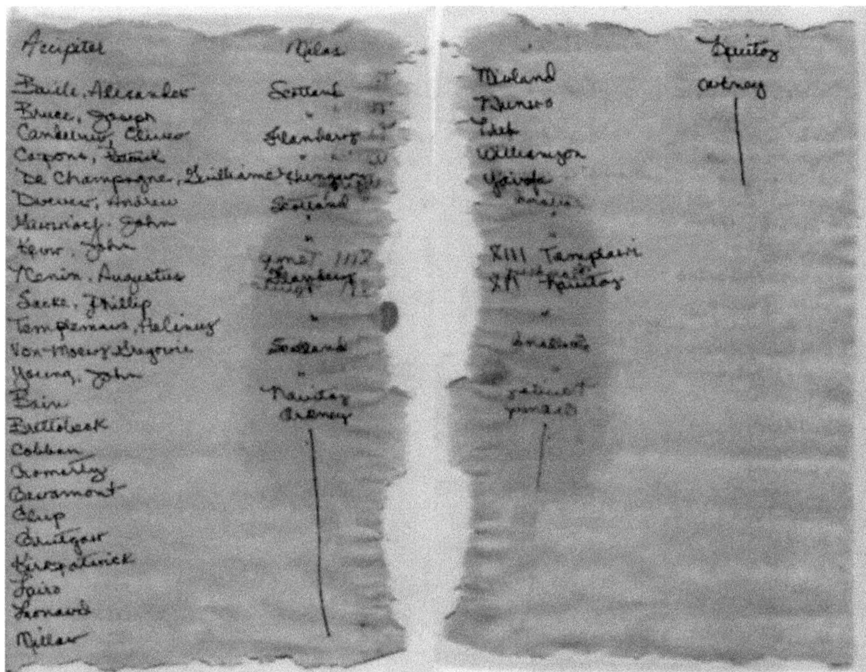

Left: Diana texted me six low-resolution photos of crew lists for three of the fleet of eight ships that sailed to the Western Lands in 1395. This page contains the names of thirteen Templar Knights and sixteen crew members.
Right: The back side also contains the Hooked X symbols within the "x" in the name Alexander, and in the Roman numeral ten in the number "13 Templari" and "16 Navitoy." (Wolter, 2016)

SHIP NAME: *ACCIPITER*

Type and Cargo: Barque, Supplies. Used in 1395.
Carrying 29 men total: 13 Templars, and 16 Seamen.

Ship: *Accipiter*			
Origin Country	**Surname**	**First Name**	**Title**
Scotland	Baillie	Alexander	Sir Knight/Templar
Scotland	Bruce	Joseph	Sir Knight/Templar
Flanders	Candebur	Oliver	Sir Knight/Templar
Flanders	Capons	Patrick	Sir Knight/Templar
Hungary	De Champagne	Guilliame	Sir Knight/Templar
Scotland	Drever	Andrew	Sir Knight/Templar
Scotland	Garrioch	John	Sir Knight/Templar
Scotland	Kerr	David	Sir Knight/Templar
Flanders	Menin	Augustus	Sir Knight/Templar
Flanders	Sacke	Philip	Sir Knight/Templar
Flanders	Templemars	Helinus	Sir Knight/Templar
Scotland	Von Moers	Gregorie	Sir Knight/Templar
Scotland	Young	John	Sir Knight/Templar
Orkney	Bain		Seaman
Orkney	Brettobreck		Seaman
Orkney	Cobban		Seaman
Orkney	Cromarty		Seaman
Orkney	Garamont	Cullen	Captain
Orkney	Glup		Seaman
Orkney	Grutgar		Seaman
Orkney	Kirkpatrick		Seaman
Orkney	Lairo		Seaman
Orkney	Leonard		Seaman
Orkney	Millar		Seaman
Orkney	Mirland		Seaman
Orkney	Munro		Seaman
Orkney	Treb		Seaman
Orkney	Williamson		Seaman
Orkney	Yairfa		Seaman

Ship Name: *Itienere*

Type and cargo: Barque, supplies. Used in 1395.
Carrying 29 men total: 13 Templars and 26 Seamen.

Ship: *Itienere*			
Origin Country	**Surname**	**First Name**	**Title**
Flanders	Ardenhort	Henri	Sir Knight/Templar
Flanders	Breman	Jacque	Sir Knight/Templar
Flanders	Campanels	Henricus	Sir Knight/Templar
Scotland	Cunningham	Alexander	Sir Knight/Templar
Flanders	Doual	Guilermo	Sir Knight/Templar
Flanders	Ferno	Johannes	Sir Knight/Templar
Flanders	Izenberge	Henri	Sir Knight/Templar
Flanders	Marion	Philippe	Sir Knight/Templar
Flanders	Olgilvie	Denis	Sir Knight/Templar
Flanders	Reppe	Nicolai	Sir Knight/Templar
Scotland	Stanger	Robertus	Sir Knight/Templar
Flanders	Versqui	Nicolas	Sir Knight/Templar
Scotland	Work	Hugh	Sir Knight/Templar
Orkney	Banks		Seaman
Orkney	Curcum		Seaman
Orkney	Garson		Seaman
Orkney	Gyre		Seaman
Orkney	Halkland		Seaman
Orkney	Hammer	Georgi	Captain
Orkney	Harper		Seaman
Orkney	Housebie		Seaman
Orkney	Kennedy		Seaman
Orkney	Marykirk		Seaman
Orkney	Mathieson		Seaman
Orkney	Nicholson		Seaman
Orkney	Porteous		Seaman
Orkney	Tulloch		Seaman
Orkney	Wards		Seaman
Orkney	Yule		Seaman

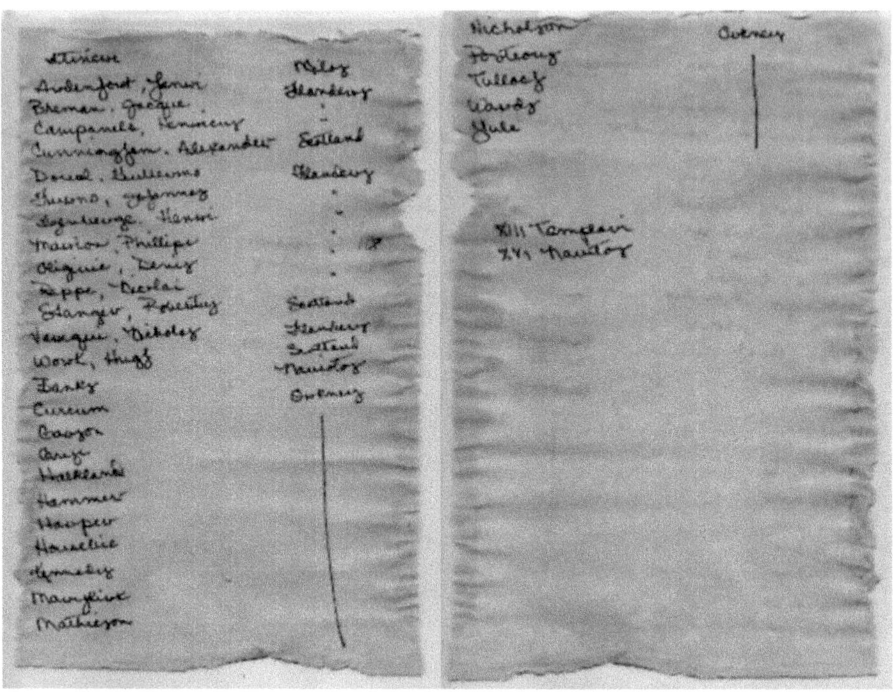

Left: This page also contains the names of thirteen Templar Knights and sixteen crew members on the *Itienere*. The front side contains a Hooked X symbol in the "x" in the name Alexander.
Right: The back side of the page has two Hooked Xs in the Roman numeral ten used to make up "13 Templari" and "16 Navitoy." (Wolter, 2016)

SHIP'S NAME: *PEREQUIN*

Ship Type and Cargo: Galley, used in 1395.
Supplies, ballast, 6 barrels of acorns.
Carrying 41 men: 21 Templars and 20 Seamen.

This is most likely the ship and crew that stayed behind in the Westford, Massachusetts area. Notice that their ballast is acorns. They could have used these acorns for foodstuff in an emergency, or to plant oak groves.

Ship: *Perequin*			
Origin Country	**Surname**	**First Name**	**Title**
Flanders	Andre	Bethune	Sir Knight/ Templar
Flanders	Biersi	Joannes	Sir Knight/ Templar
Flanders	Bruges	Guiscard	Sir Knight/ Templar
Flanders	Caestree	Jean	Sir Knight/ Templar
Scotland	Cauper	William	Sir Knight/ Templar
France	de Blois	Thibault	Sir Knight/ Templar
Scotland	Dennison	Humphrey	Sir Knight/ Templar
Scotland	Dunlop	William	Sir Knight/ Templar
Flanders	Geneffe	Geofrey	Sir Knight/ Templar
Scotland	Gunn	James	Sir Knight/ Templar
Flanders	Lamingi	Gilbertus	Sir Knight/ Templar
Spain	Merrett	Francisco	Sir Knight/ Templar
Scotland	Netherskail	James	Sir Knight/ Templar
Flanders	Podiebrand	Boczeck	Sir Knight/ Templar
Flanders	Shirley	Sir Hugh	Sir Knight/ Templar
Scotland	Sinclair	Henricus	Sir Knight/ Templar
Flanders	Slijpe	Johannes	Sir Knight/ Templar
Scotland	Thomson	Alastair	Sir Knight/ Templar
Scotland	Watt	William	Sir Knight/ Templar
Scotland	Winghtmane	Harold	Sir Knight/ Templar
Scotland	Yule	John	Sir Knight/ Templar
Orkney	Anderson	Humphry	Captain
Orkney	Cooper		Seaman
Orkney	Corse		Seaman

Ship: *Perequin*			
Origin Country	**Surname**	**First Name**	**Title**
Orkney	Duncan		Seaman
Orkney	Estaquoy		Seaman
Orkney	Flattay		Seaman
Orkney	Gorrie		Seaman
Orkney	Grind		Seaman
Orkney	Hewison		Seaman
Orkney	Hunter		Seaman
Orkney	Hutchison		Seaman
Orkney	Ingrow		Seaman
Orkney	Irvine		Seaman
Orkney	Kirk		Seaman
Orkney	Laughton		Seaman
Orkney	Pratt		Seaman
Orkney	Ring		Seaman
Orkney	Rorie		Seaman
Orkney	Rousay		Seaman
Orkney	Ruthquoy		Seaman

Here is the crew list where we find the mysterious name of Sir James Gunn, the knight the legend of the Westford Sword has been attached to for as long as people in the town of Westford, Massachusetts can remember. The legend goes that Gunn was the personal bodyguard of Earl Henry Sinclair, and accompanied him on the expedition to the Western Lands in 1395. This appears to be confirmed by his name on the crew list of the *Perequin*. His name also appears on a separate list of names with the comment "dead". Curiously, his is the only name on this lengthy list that has "dead" next to it.[39] There are fourteen names that have the word "west" next to them, presumably meaning they stayed in the Western Lands and did not return to Scotland.

Like most urban legends there is usually at least some kernel of truth to them, and the Sinclair/Wemyss journals injects powerful evidence the legend of the Westford Sword (Knight) is likely true. If so, the question

39. It should be noted the list of names referred to with Sir James Gunn listed as "dead" was written by Sister Agnes Harkin in 1885. The Diana Muir copy of the journals does not have a similar list.

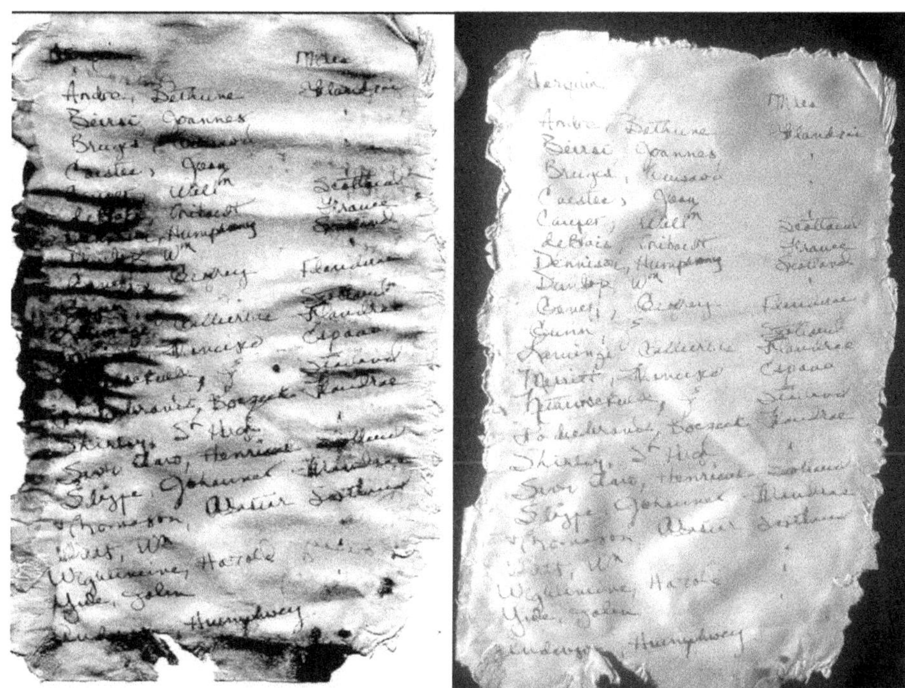

Two very different looking pictures of the same list of names aboard the *Perequin* as taken by Diana Muir (**left**) and Jeffrey Irving (**right**). While the pictures look to be the same piece of paper as the raveled edges appear to match, the Muir image appears to have undergone alteration. (Muir, 2016/Courtesy of Jeffrey Irving, 2016)

becomes how did Sir Gunn die? Many speculate he was killed by natives during a conflict, but given the close ties the local indigenous people had with the Templars–made clear from the journal entries–this seems unlikely. Since the crew lists do not list his death by drowning, as so many others were who died when the *Ortis* sunk off the southern coast of Nova Scotia during a violent storm during the 1395 expedition, he must have died some other way. The most likely cause was either by accident or natural causes. Regardless of how he died, the carving of the Westford Sword (Knight) provides compelling evidence to support the veracity of the Sinclair/Wemyss journals.

The Westford Knight is actually only a sword created using a pecking technique for the handle and hilt. The blade of the sword incorporates parallel glacial striations gouged into the mica-schist bedrock during the last ice age. Legend says the sword was carved by mourning colleagues to honor fallen Templar Knight Sir James Gunn in the late fourteenth century. (Wolter, 2014)

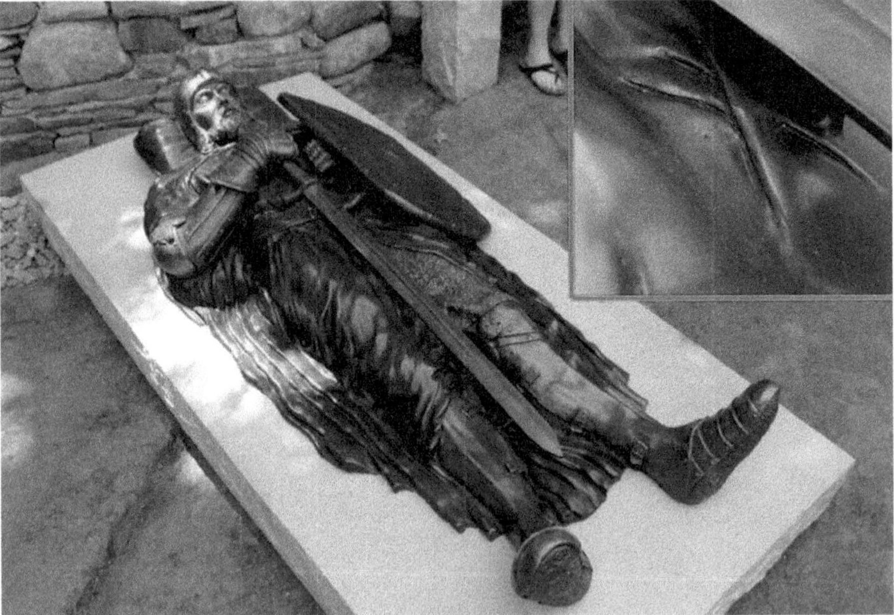

On June 13, 2015, a life-size bronze statue of Sir James Gunn made by David Christiana, was dedicated at the site of the Westford Knight in Westford, Massachusetts. Below the sword, Christiana cast a Hooked X, the secret and sacred symbol of the Templars. (Wolter, 2015)

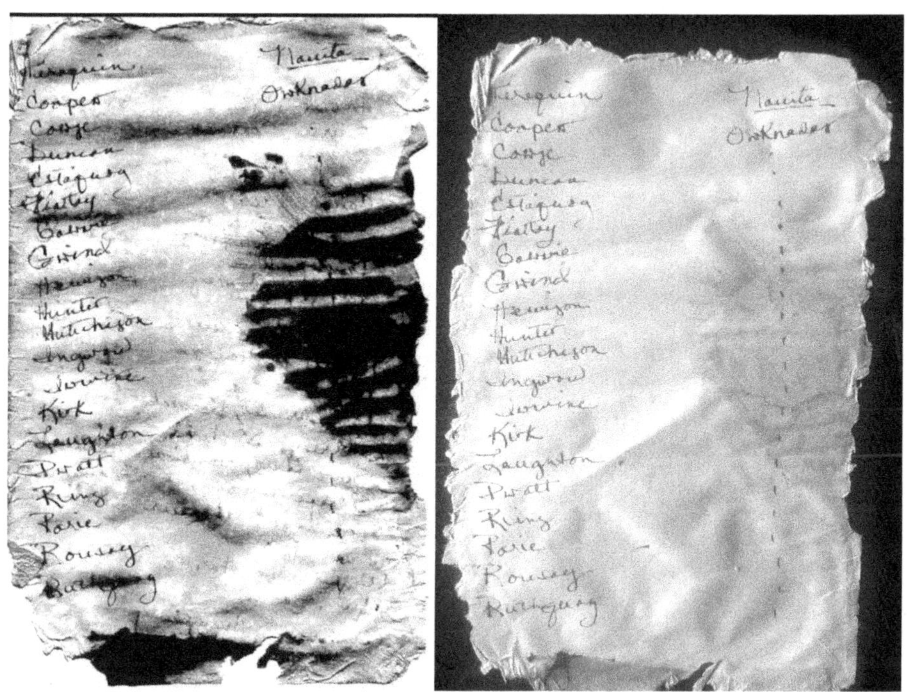

Two pictures of the back side of the crew list of the *Perequin* which shows only the surnames of the crew, who were all from Ornades (Orkney Islands). The photo on the left provided by Diana Muir is obviously electronically altered. (Muir, 2016/Courtesy of Jeffrey Irving, 2016)

SHIP NAME: *REPOSTUS*

Ship Type and Cargo: Barque, used in 1395.
Carrying 29 men: 13 Templars and 16 Seamen.

Ship: *Repostus*			
Origin Country	**Surname**	**First Name**	**Title**
Scotland	Aytoun	John	Sir Knight/Templar
Flanders	Bremers	Sir James	Sir Knight/Templar
Flanders	Candeb Cadeleta	Jacobus	Sir Knight/Templar
Flanders	Dampierre	Robert	Sir Knight/Templar
Scotland	Douglas	Robert	Sir Knight/Templar
Flanders	Garneys	Robert	Sir Knight/Templar
Scotland	Kennedy	Alan	Sir Knight/Templar
Scotland	Maxwell	Alexander	Sir Knight/Templar
Flanders	Osqueriis	Haniad	Sir Knight/Templar
Scotland	Rollo	Angus	Sir Knight/Templar
Scotland	Stewart	Andrew	Sir Knight/Templar
Flanders	Versinara	Joannes	Sir Knight/Templar
Scotland	Wylie	Alick	Sir Knight/Templar
Orkney	Alexander		Sir Knight/Templar
Orkney	Bichan		Seaman
Orkney	Borwick		Seaman
Orkney	Brown		Seaman
Orkney	Burness		Seaman
Orkney	Gray		Seaman
Orkney	Hourie		Seaman
Orkney	Kelday		Seaman
Orkney	Learmonth		Seaman
Orkney	Northskaill	Archibald	Seaman
Orkney	Ockilsetter		Captain
Orkney	Omand		Seaman
Orkney	Quoybanks		Seaman
Orkney	Westerholland		Seaman
Orkney	Whitelaw		Seaman

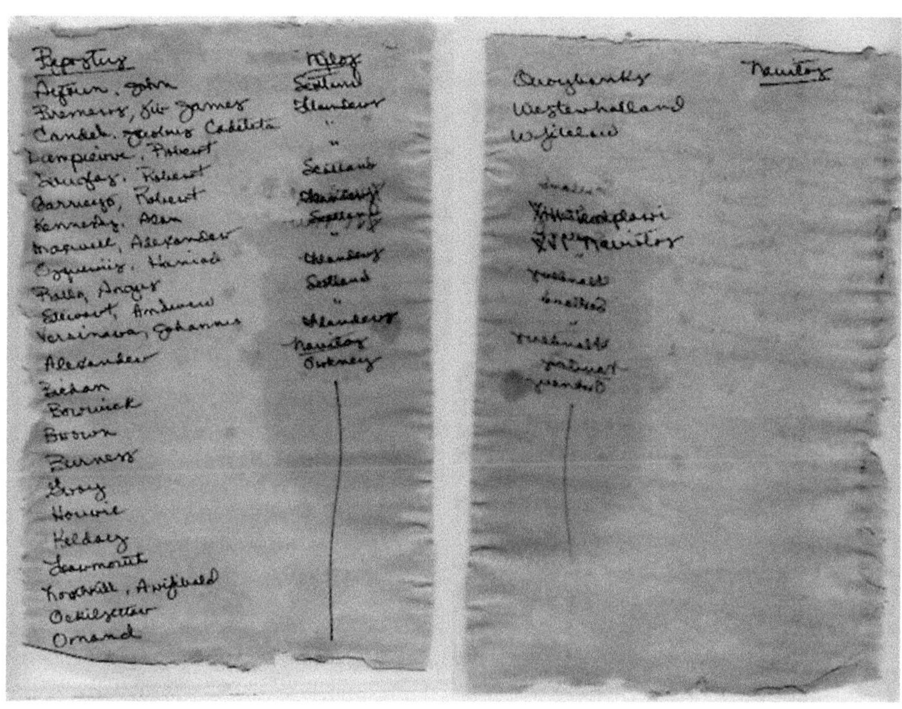

Here again on the *Repostus* list of names we find thirteen Templar Knights and sixteen crew members. The front side contains a Hooked X symbol in the "x" in the name Alexander and two Hooked Xs on the back side in the Roman numeral ten in the number "13 Templari" and "16 Navitoy." (Wolter, 2016)

SHIP NAME: *SOMNIUM*

Ship Type: Galley, used in 1395.
Carrying 42 men: 20 Templars and 22 Seamen.

Ship: *Somnium*			
Origin Country	**Surname**	**First Name**	**Title**
Flanders	Arbia	Hendrik	Sir Knight/Templar
Flanders	Brabant	Aeaneas	Sir Knight/Templar
Scotland	Budge	Robert	Sir Knight/Templar
Flanders	Caestree	Gerard	Sir Knight/Templar
Flanders	Clouttying	Thomas	Sir Knight/Templar
France	de Blois	Philip	Sir Knight/Templar
Hungary	Deponthieu	Guillaume	Sir Knight/Templar
Flanders	Flamingi	Robert	Sir Knight/Templar
Scotland	Ghent	Gossin of Ghent	Sir Knight/Templar
Scotland	Hamilton	Georgei	Sir Knight/Templar
Scotland	Laughton	Cullen	Sir Knight/Templar
Scotland	Muir	Sir John	Sir Knight/Templar
Flanders	Nevers	Philip	Sir Knight/Templar
Scotland	Reid	Geordie	Sir Knight/Templar
Scotland	Simison	Ervin	Sir Knight/Templar
Scotland	Spence	Payton	Sir Knight/Templar
Flanders	Valera	Wiliam	Sir Knight/Templar
Scotland	Wemyss	Michael	Sir Knight/Templar
Flanders	Wingfield	John	Sir Knight/Templar
Flanders	Zacke	Milton	Sir Knight/Templar
Orkney	Aim		Seaman
Orkney	Couper		Seaman
Orkney	Doull		Seaman
Orkney	Fairwell		Seaman
Orkney	Fea		Seaman
Orkney	Fiddler		Seaman
Orkney	Fotheringham		Seaman
Orkney	Gaudie		Seaman
Orkney	Gruthay		Seaman

Ship: *Somnium*			
Origin Country	**Surname**	**First Name**	**Title**
Orkney	Leean		Seaman
Orkney	Mackay		Seaman
Orkney	Mair		Seaman
Orkney	Mooney	Geoffrey	Captain
Orkney	Neagar		Seaman
Orkney	Netherhunclett		Seaman
Orkney	Paplay		Seaman
Orkney	Peace		Seaman
Orkney	Rainbister		Seaman
Orkney	Roberston		Seaman
Orkney	Sandison		Seaman
Orkney	Winksetter		Seaman
Orkney	Work		Seaman

SHIP NAME: *SPECULATOR*

Ship Type: Barque, used in 1395.
Carrying 26 men: 13 Templars and 13 Seamen.

Ship: *Speculator*			
Origin Country	**Surname**	**First Name**	**Title**
Flanders	Ardenbourg	John	Sir Knight/Templar
France	Braybrooke	Humphrey	Sir Knight/Templar
Flanders	Cambrai	Henri	Sir Knight/Templar
Scotland	Corston	William	Sir Knight/Templar
Flanders	DeRoet	Andre'	Sir Knight/Templar
Scotland	Forsyth	James	Sir Knight/Templar
Scotland	Hunter	John	Sir Knight/Templar
Flanders	Maile	Bernard	Sir Knight/Templar
Flanders	Nivelles	Arnau	Sir Knight/Templar
Flanders	Rendall	Patrick	Sir Knight/Templar
Flanders	St. Veerle	Francisco	Sir Knight/Templar
Flanders	Varsenacre	Philippe	Sir Knight/Templar
Scotland	Wood	Archibald	Sir Knight/Templar
Orkney	Scambester		Seaman
Orkney	Sclater		Seaman
Orkney	Seatter		Seaman
Orkney	Shearer		Seaman
Orkney	Sinclair		Seaman
Orkney	Skebister		Seaman
Orkney	Smyddie		Seaman
Orkney	Stennesgord	Johannes	Captain
Orkney	Stockan		Seaman
Orkney	Surquoy		Seaman
Orkney	Swanson		Seaman
Orkney	Tait		Seaman
Orkney	Thomson		Seaman

Ship Name: *Ortus*

Ship Type: Barque, used in 1395
Carrying 44 men: 21 Templars and 23 Seamen

Ship: *Ortus*				
Origin	**Surname**	**First Name**	**Title**	**Status**
Scotland	Beaton	James	Sir Knight/Templar	
Flanders	Brueria	Johannes	Sir Knight/Templar	Stayed Behind
Flanders	Cadeleta	Jacob	Sir Knight/Templar	Stayed Behind
Flanders	Capons	Enricus	Sir Knight/Templar	Stayed Behind
Hungary	de Tinj	Theobold	Sir Knight/Templar	Stayed Behind
Flanders	Denis	Le Mesureur	Sir Knight/Templar	Stayed Behind
Hungary	Destpol	Entienne Henri	Sir Knight/Templar	Stayed Behind
Scotland	Dunlop	Alexander	Sir Knight/Templar	
Flanders	Geneffe	Egidius	Sir Knight/Templar	Stayed Behind
Scotland	Groat	Angus	Sir Knight/Templar	
Scotland	Kerrie	Archibald	Sir Knight/Templar	
Spain	Merret	Garcia	Sir Knight/Templar	
France	Navarre	Humbert	Sir Knight/Templar	Stayed Behind
Flanders	Perbone	Guilliame	Sir Knight/Templar	Stayed Behind
Scotland	Scott	Hugh	Sir Knight/Templar	
Scotland	Sinclair	Henri	Sir Knight/Templar	
Scotland	Skinner	Ode (Otto)	Sir Knight/Templar	
Flanders	Templemars	Michael	Sir Knight/Templar	Stayed Behind
Flanders	Von Sacke	Christoph	Sir Knight/Templar	Stayed Behind
Scotland	Westerholland	Aurthur	Sir Knight/Templar	
Flanders	Ypres	Louis	Sir Knight/Templar	Stayed Behind
Orkney	Beatton	Guilliame	Captain	
Orkney	Burgar		Seaman	
Orkney	Byres		Seaman	
Orkney	Chalmers		Seaman	Drowned
Orkney	Costie		Seaman	
Orkney	Cutt		Seaman	
Orkney	Davie		Seaman	
Orkney	Dennison		Seaman	

Ship: *Ortus*				
Origin	**Surname**	**First Name**	**Title**	**Status**
Orkney	Ellibister		Seaman	
Orkney	Goodsir		Seaman	
Orkney	Harrold		Seaman	
Orkney	Heddle		Seaman	
Orkney	Holm		Seaman	Drowned
Orkney	Howan		Seaman	
Orkney	Kilpatrick		Seaman	
Orkney	Liddle		Seaman	
Orkney	Logie		Seaman	
Orkney	Lyall		Seaman	
Orkney	Meaness		Seaman	
Orkney	Renaland		Seaman	
Orkney	Twatt		Seaman	Drowned
Orkney	Voy		Seaman	
Orkney	Wassie		Seaman	

Ship Name: *Persephone*

This was the ship captained by Antonio Zeno
and which crashed on Sable Island.

Ship: *Persephone*				
Origin	**Surname**	**First Name**	**Title**	**Status**
Spain	Adres	Didacus	Seaman	Dead
Italy	Aebli	Heinrich	Seaman	
Italy	Brunner	Jacob	Seaman	
Italy	Castell	Alexander Frederick Von Faber	Sir Knight	Dead
England	Collier	Wignmund	Seaman	
Spain	Garsea	Julius	Seaman	
China	Huagau	Liu	Navigator	
Hungary	Mstislawna	Bronislav	Sir Knight/Templar	
Italy	Netstaler	Fridolin	Seaman	Dead
Italy	Netstaker	Gilg	Seaman	Dead
Spain	Ranft	Aloys	Seaman	
Switzerland	Simon	Jakob	Seaman	
Italy	Sontag	Jost	Seaman	
Italy	Stauffacher	Uli	Seaman	
Italy	Steinmann	Balthaser	Seaman	
Italy	Tscudi	Josh	Seaman	
Italy	Vogel	Jakob	Seaman	
Italy	Von Buerglen	Konrad	Seaman	
Italy	Von Diesbach	Rudolf	Sir Knight/Templar	Dead
Italy	Von Hoyen	Baskardt	Sir Knight/Templar	
Italy	Von Schaepfer	Ermo	Sir Knight/Templar	
Italy	Von Schudi	Chevalier Heinrich	Sir Knight/Templar	
Italy	Von Seedorf	Ulrich	Sir Knight/Templar	
Italy	Von Vennen	Wilken	Captain	
Italy	Von Windegg	Roland	Sir Knight/Templar	
Hungary	Wullinger	Bratomil	Seaman	
Italy	Zeno	Antonio	Captain	
Italy	Zwiefel	Hans	Seaman	

Book 3

Journals of Earl Henry Sinclair Continued

(1345-1404)

June 4, 1398

Diana Muir's Translation (italics): *We have arrived at the Isle of the White Stag and were greeted by the natives who saw our ships from a distance and came to meet us with knives and spears and painted faces. Many of my men were frightened at their sight as they are naked, light skinned with dark hair and fiercely appointed with bird feathers and bones. Their leader approached me with his outstretched hand and head bowed and I knew my old friend instantly from the whale bone knife he held in his hand. I gratefully greeted Askoosh and the men were put at ease when I explained that he was known to me.*

We will stay here for 2 or 3 days to plan our investigation of the western shores and to replenish stores perched on the top of the cliff and a prayer of protection with the brethren. Askoosh and his men prepare a feast for us this eve and the weather remains fair.

Sister Harkin's Translation (plain): We landed at the island of the White Deer and were met by natives who came with knives and painted faces and spears after seeing our ships sail in. The leader held his hand to me with his head bowed and my whale bone knife in his hand I knew my old friend Askoosh immediately. I happily greeted him and told the men he was known to me making them at ease.

We will stay here for 2 to 3 days to consider our searching the western lands and to rebuild our stores. Most men have come on land, and we have remembered our trip on a stone lying on the cliff top with the brother's prayer for protection. Askoosh make a meal tonight for us and the weather remains good.

Author's Commentary (shaded box): One cannot read this entry without being emotionally moved. For Earl Henry and Askoosh to be reunited after forty-two years is remarkable and fortuitous, and sets the table for the 400-years-long cooperation between the Templars and their indigenous brothers, who bonded through ritual, mutual respect, and intermarriage. As will be seen in forthcoming entries, the natives promised to guard the treasures for their Templar brothers and did so until the treasures were recovered in 1769 and 1770. As Americans, when celebrate the founding of our country and give praise to our brave Founding Fathers who put their lives on the line for our republic, we cannot forget about our indigenous brothers. They stood with our Templar Brethren, the Founders, and the Sinclair and Wemyss clans for four centuries until the job was finished. Despite the genocide that occurred during settlement of North America, it is never too late to acknowledge and honor the commitment they made to help in the founding of the United States of America.

June 7, 1398

I have sent 100 men to cross this new found land to find a waterway to the inner seas. Askoosh has assured us that it is several days journey on foot but that the weather on the western shore is fairer than the coast we now perch on, being not affected by the great storms of the northern seas. I have also sent 20 men northward to a bay near Askoosh's home to establish a home for the monastery. Askoosh has given them bones of passage so that those they meet will know they are welcome visitors.

I will send 100 men to go across this newly found country to find a water way to the inside seas. Askoosh told us it is many days passage on foot but says weather on the western shore is better than the shore where we are now because the northern sea storms do not affect them. I will also send 20 men to the north to a lake near Askoosh's village to build a monastery. Askoosh has given bones of passage so their people will know they are greeted visitors.

"Bones of passage" is reminiscent of a tradition of indigenous travel that was shared with me by an Ojibwe medicine man many years ago. He explained how, when traveling, it was customary to have a small leather bag with stones and bones that were used to make symbols when meeting with other tribes. The bones must be placed in a specific sequence and shape to allow friendly passage. Not surprisingly this is obviously an ancient tradition.

June 15, 1398

We have spent this past week restocking the ships and resting for our journey southward. During this time Askoosh's men have taught us much about the raging tides and the people who live here. He has heard little about the men who stayed behind years before when we were both children. He knows that they traveled southward and now live in the mountains far to the south along the great inner seas.

My men have made many friendships, and the people have taught us much about their worship of the Great Goddess which is similar to the old religion of Orknades and Scotland. We share many common beliefs and Father Nicolas is making a record of their beliefs and rituals. Together we celebrated the initiation of his youngest son into manhood as he celebrates his 18th year.

This past week we have rested for our passage to the south and restocking our ships. Askoosh's men have taught us about the big tides and the people who live here during this time. He says he has little knowledge about the men who stayed here years ago when we were children. He knows they traveled southwest and now live far to the south in the mountains near the big inner seas.

My men have made good friendships, and the people have taught us a lot about their great Goddess worship which is like the old religion of Orkney and Scotland. We have many similar beliefs and Father Nicolas is keeping a record of their rituals and beliefs. We all celebrate the manhood initiation of Askoosh's youngest son when he celebrates his 18th birthday.

This must be a reference to the Kensington party of 1358. Askoosh says they live in the mountains near the inner seas. The "mountains" could be along the north shore of Lake Superior, but it is not clear. In any case, this provides another clue the 1358 party is connected to the Kensington Rune Stone Knights Templar land claim.

The mention of their veneration of the Great Goddess is also noteworthy. This is consistent with our thesis the Templars were not the good Catholics historians claim. Their true ideology was a reverence for the sacred feminine, and served as the foundation of their deep spiritual bond with the indigenous people. This was why they were able to travel freely across the continent with the assistance of their indigenous brothers.

June 21, 1398

The men I sent to cross this land have returned with good news. The inner seas are only 4 days march along plentiful streams and are wide enough to allow the passage of 2 to 3 ships. There are several wide beaches where we can winter, and the hills are rich with deer and birds. Lumber is readily available to build shelter, and the hills shelter against the wind. They spent 5 days exploring the western shores both north and south and reported no incidents with the natives who gave them a wide berth. Askoosh has assured us that we can reach the inner bay by traveling southward around the rocky peninsula. We leave tomorrow to travel south.

The men I sent to cross this land have returned with good news; it is a 4 day walk along well filled streams and are wide enough for 2 or three small ships to pass. Several big beaches are there where we can stay for the winter and hills to shields us against the wind. They explored north and south along the western shores for 5 days and said the natives stayed away and there no accidents. Askoosh says we can travel south around the rocky peninsula and reach the inner bay. We will travel south tomorrow.

June 22, 1398

At daybreak we have taken leave of our new friends and begin our journey southward. Askoosh has promised to watch over our friends who have traveled northward to make a home near his tribe. We plan to visit with them before we return home to Orknades to assess their progress.

In the morning, we say goodbye to our friends and begin to journey. Askoosh promises to watch over the priests who travel north to make a home near his village. We hope to visit them before we return home to Orkney to see their progress.

June 23, 1398

Disaster has visited our journey, and we are lucky to have survived a horrific violent storm this past night. Once leaving the Isle of the White Stag we headed south-southeast in search of a protected harbor large enough for 8 ships which we had visited on our prior voyage. Instead, we were driven further to sea by a sudden violent storm which came from the North in the midday hours. As darkness approached the thunderous rain, and lightning struck the mast of one of the ships to our starboard bow and I watched in horror as it was driven south with the current of the sea.

Two other ships were driven off course and I could see them making for land with the promise of regrouping after the storm. The Katherine *under my command was driven onshore a small island of about 1 and a half leagues by a rogue wave at midnight. It was not till this morning that we were able to ascertain our position of latitude 44.51° N with a slight variance. With still cloudy skies it is difficult to be exact. Our rendezvous point of 44.65 is many leagues distant and unapproachable in our condition.*

The mast of the Katherine *has been torn asunder and as we were pushed onto this small island the hull was pierced by a tree stump spilling our ballast of acorns and supplies all around us. We are wedged between trees and appear to have been lifted halfway across this small island. Our cargo remains intact midship, but it will take weeks of labor to free and repair the ship.*

"Our journey is met with disaster and luck has saved us from a terrible storm last night. We left the Island of the White Deer and went south-southeast to find a harbor that was big enough for 8 boats we had visited on our last trip that is protected from the wind. We were instead driven out to sea by a sudden violent hurricane that came at midday from the north. When it got dark the loud thunder, rain and lightning cut the mast of a ship off starboard bow and it was forced to the south as I watched it pitch and roll.

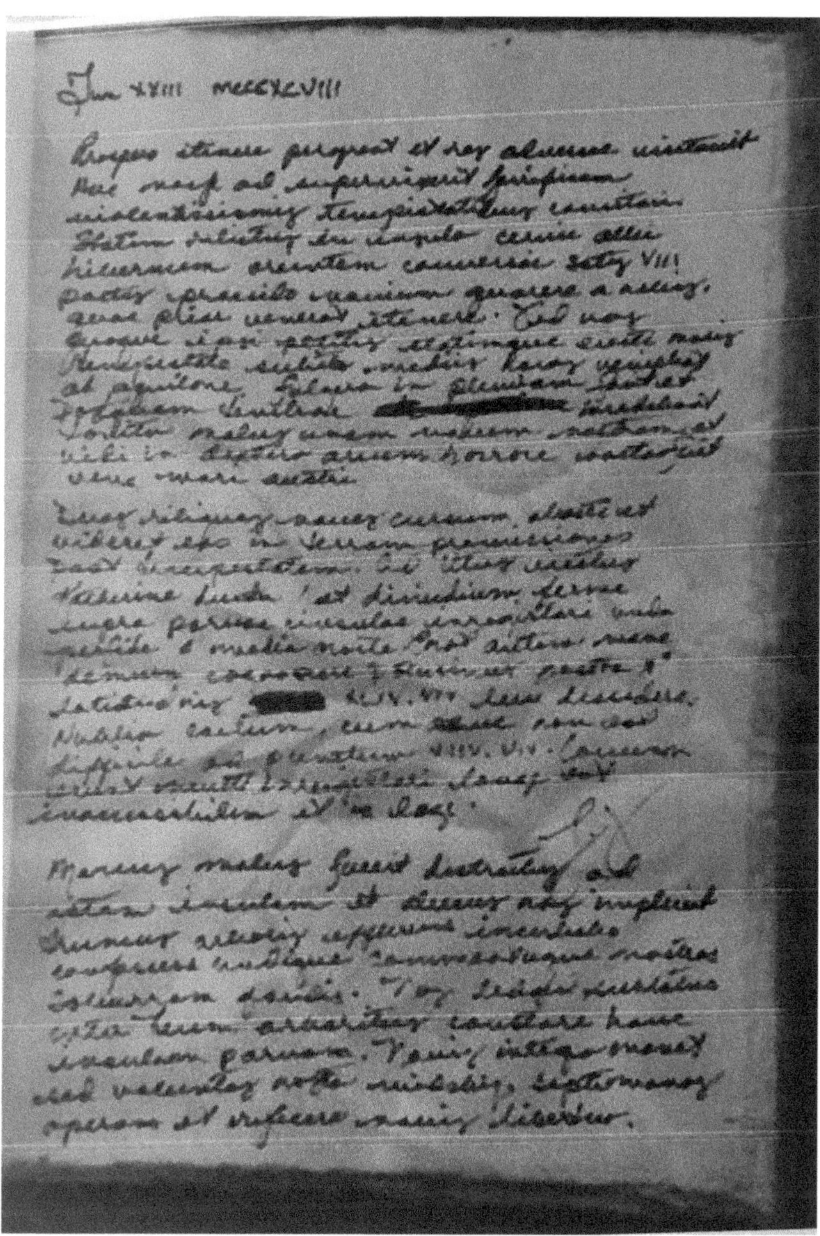

A rather poor-quality photograph of the journal page with the June 23, 1398, entry made by Earl Henry Sinclair in Latin. The page includes three examples of "fish" symbols which are encoded marks of authenticity. One is found in the stylized letter "j" in "June" at the top left and opposing, vertically aligned fish symbols in the area between the second and third paragraphs. (Muir, 2016)

Two more boats were forced to sea, and I saw them trying to make it to land and come together later. My ship the *Katherine* which I command was pushed onshore on a small island about 1-½ leagues by a wild wave during the middle of the night. In the morn we able to determine our location of 44.51 degrees north with a little error. It was still cloudy and hard to be correct. The meeting place of 44.65 is far distant and impossible to reach in our state.

The mast of the *Katherine* was broken and split and when we landed on this tiny island our ship was punched by a tree root and our ballast of acorns and cargo was spilled all round us! We are perched between several trees and looks to be halfway into the small isle. Some of our cargo is intact in the ships middle but it will be weeks before we repair and free the ship."

Reading this entry sent chills up my spine the first time I read it. It was so unexpected and felt so real. It reminds me of one of the dangers of traveling at sea even when close to the coastline. Death can come out of nowhere in an instant.

August 1, 1398

We have labored for many weeks to free the Katherine *and are unable to do so while her cargo is onboard. We have felled trees to the west and have attempted to dig a ditch filled with water that she might slide into the harbor on the other side of the island which we have named "Dog Island". The island is uninhabited and has no evidence of having been visited by the native people recently. At this time five other ships have been located and lodge in the harbor which we have named for Queen Margaret, Margaret's Bay. In our search for the other ships, we have located the wreck of the* Ortus *midway across the bay and are still Searching for survivors, two of my own kinsmen amongst them.*

After many weeks of work, we have failed to loosen the *Katherine* while the cargo is still on ship. We cut trees to the west and have dug a water filled ditch so the ship could slide into the harbor on the opposite side of the isle we have called Dog Island. There are no people here and the natives appear not to have visited soon past. We have 5 other ships and now anchor in the harbor we named for Queen Margaret: Margaret's Bay. While searching for the other boats we found the wreck of the *Ortus* halfway across the bay and continue to search for survivors. Two of my kin were on the ship.

<u>*August 2, 1398*</u>

It has been decided amongst the captains to bury the treasure that each ship carries in its predetermined location – found during our voyage 3 years past with the assistance of the Knights Templars left behind. The treasure of the Katherine *will be offloaded and buried here on Dog Island in two different places. The bulk of the treasure will be buried approximately* ████ *off the beach on the* ████ *end of the island at* ████. *It should be known that the spot was paced off by Sir Robert Sutherland whose legs are exceptionally long. The 2nd half of the treasure gold and silver coin will be buried in* ████ *of the island at* ████. *Three Knights will stay on the island once the treasure is buried to make certain it is marked and kept safe until our return. The cargo of the* Ortus *also gold and silver coin lies at the bottom of the bay and will be their priority to retrieve. We leave behind one small fishing vessel so they may continue their search.*

Once the treasure is buried the Katherine *will be burned or the wood used to build a shelter for the men left behind. There is no hope of her ever sailing again and the crew will be transferred among the other ships. It is with great sadness that I transfer my belongings to the* Somnium *with Captain Zeno. Once our labor is complete, we will sail south to find the colony that was to be founded to our south where we left a group of Templars under the command of Sir Humphrey Dennison at* ████. *We hope for news of our friends who traveled north at that time. It has been three years, and we hope they have fared well.*

The captains have decided to bury the treasure on each ship in the places we found 3 years before with the help of the Knights Templars who stayed behind. The treasure of the *Katherine* will be taken off and buried in 2 different spots on Dog Island. Most of the treasure will be placed about ████ off the beach from ████ of the isle at latitude ████. Sir Robert Sutherland walked it, and he has very long legs. The second half of the treasure, which is gold and silver coins is buried in buried in a [redacted] of the island at [redacted] [redacted]. Three Templar Knights will stay here after it is buried to mark it and keep it safe till we come back. The cargo from the *Ortis* is also gold and silver coins, is at the [redacted] and will be their responsibility to find. We will leave a small fishing boat to help them as they search.

Once the treasure is secured the *Katherine* will be scuttled and burned. The men we leave behind will use some of the wood to build a shack. The ship will never float again, and the crew has reassigned to another ship. I am saddened to move my kit to Captain Zeno's ship the *Somnium*. Once our efforts are done, we sail south to find Sir Humphrey Dennison and the Templars we left to found a colony to the south at [redacted]. It has been three years, and we hope for news of our friends who traveled north. We hope they are well.

We now know Dog Island became known as McNab Island, where the two treasures from the *Katherine* ship were buried. We also now know one of the treasures was recovered in the mid-seventeenth century to fund the building of the first church in Montreal, for which the first foundation stone was laid in 1656. This information came to Donald Ruh in the form of an original letter written by the French Catholic Priest and missionary Jean-Louis Le Loutre. Le Loutre has an interesting history. He first arrived in Nova Scotia in 1738 and, after leading revolts and numerous battles and skirmishes that failed to wrest control of Acadia from the British, he realized he was a marked man and boarded a ship for France in 1755. After the ship was seized, Le Loutre was captured and imprisoned for eight years until his release in 1763. While it is possible Le Loutre could have written the letter after 1763 and before his death 1772, it seems more likely it was written between 1749 and 1755. This interesting letter was translated into English as follows:

> *My master, the engraver François de Poilly in collaboration with Claude de François, known as Brother Luc, gave Marguerite Bourgeoys for the chapel of Notre-Dame du Bon [Secuors]* [...illegible...] *the map at the back of this letter. He shows the location of the treasure brought there by the descendant of Knights Templar of 1422 and is composed of*

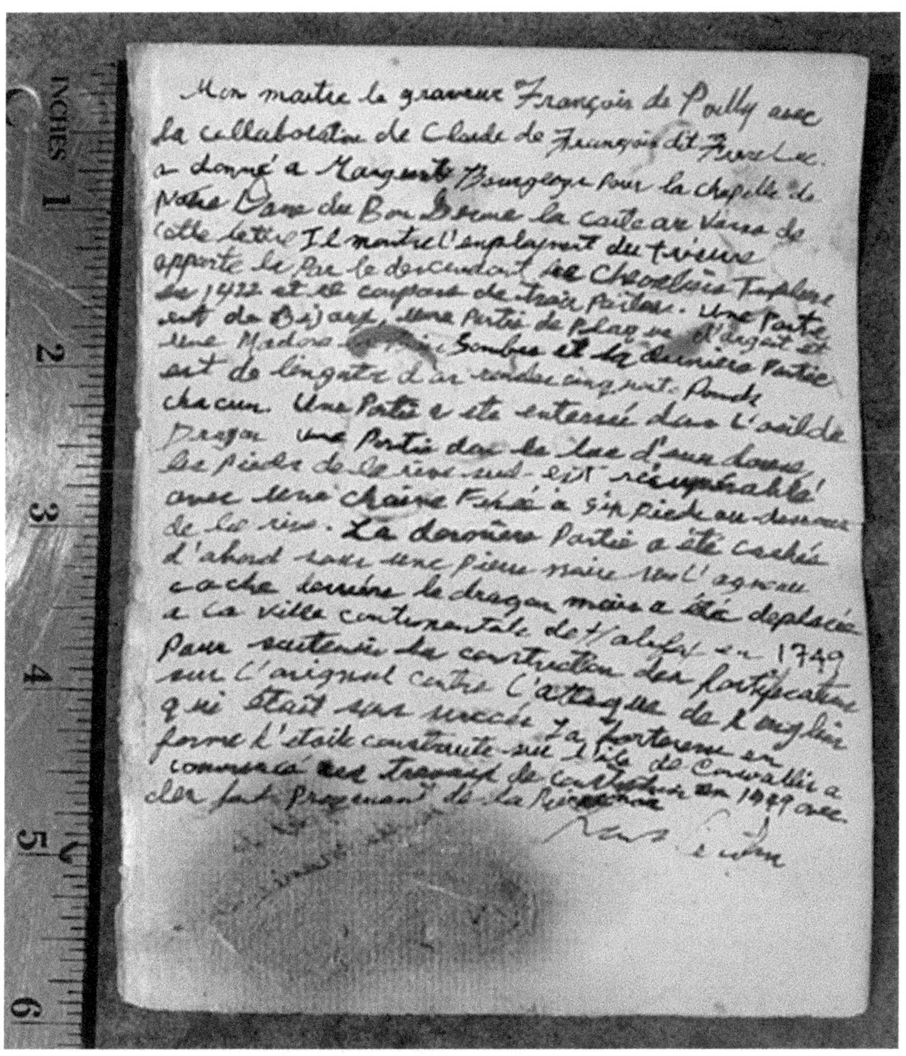
Mon maître le graveur François de Poilly avec
la collaboration de Claude de François dit Frère Luc
a donné a Marguerite Bourgeoys pour la chapelle de
Notre Dame du Bon Secours la carte au verso de
cette lettre. Il montre l'emplacement du trésor
apporté [illegible] le descendant les Chevaliers Templiers
de 1422 et se composé de trois parties. Une partie
est de [illegible], une partie de plaques d'argent et
une Madone [illegible] sombre et la dernière partie
est de lingots d'or [illegible] cinquante pounds
chacun. Une partie a été enterrée dans l'oeil de
dragon une partie dans le lac d'eau douce
[illegible] récupérable!
avec une chaîne fixée à six pieds au-dessous
de la rive. La dernière partie a été cachée
d'abord sous une pierre noire [illegible] l'agneau
caché derrière le dragon mais a été déplacée
à la ville continentale de Halifax en 1749
pour soutenir la construction des fortifications
sur l'original contre l'attaque de l'anglais
qui était sans succès. La forteresse en
forme d'étoile construite sur l'île de Cornwallis a
commencé ses travaux de construction en 1749 avec
des fonds provenant de la Réserve
[illegible]

(This page and next) This letter was given to Donald Ruh by Bill Jackson upon his death in 2019, via the estate of their mutual friend John Drake. Written by French Catholic Priest and missionary Jean-Louis Le Loutre, who led French, Acadian, and Mi'kmaq militia groups against the British. He was ultimately unsuccessful and was captured and imprisoned in 1755, and held until his release in 1763. Exactly when he wrote the letter with the treasure maps on the opposite (next page) side is unknown, but it is believed to have been sometime between 1749 and 1755, or as late as 1772 when he died. (Courtesy of Donald Ruh)

three parts. One part is jewels. One part is a silver plaque and a black stone Madonna. And the last part is gold ingots worth fifty pounds each. One part has been buried in the eye of the Dragon. One part in the lake (…illegible…) at the feet of the southeastern shore is recoverable with a chain attached six feet below the shore. The last part had been hidden at first under a black stone on the lamb hidden behind the dragon but was moved to the continental city of Halifax in 1749 to support construction of fortifications on the Moose River against the attack of the English which was unsuccessful. The star-shaped fortress built on Cornwallis Island started the construction work in 1749 with funds originating from the Renaissance.

The letter tells of what happened to one of the two treasures Earl Henry and his men left on McNab Island. That treasure was used to build the first church in Montreal, called Notre Dame de Bon Secours Chapel, which was dedicated to the Virgin Mary—or more likely, Mary Magdalene.[40] The timing of the building of this church in 1655/1656 led by Marguerite Bourgeoys, who obviously was a member of the Covenant mission—was not a coincidence. In 2021 Don Ruh received another letter from the Spartan Box, this one written by Lionel de Walderne XXI in 1656, in which he notes settlers moving into the area of the Temple of the Goddess on Hunter Mountain in the Catskills. He also tells how the remaining scrolls that were not recovered by Sir Ralf de Sudeley in 1778-80, needed to be moved to "...the place of the Sulpicians beyond the great river to the north." The full letter translated in 2021 is here:

My dear Robert,

You'll see your friend's father shall receive this message the way you have previously done it for me. You shall keep this secret between us. This day is our last in the temple of the Goddess on the mountain in the Manitou.

The flat landers and the Halandus [Hollanders?] *are every day in a hurry and these people are much dreaded. I'll be with my mother's people in the South, at the water shore. I placed a message in a stone and another one in the Priestess Altomara's cave to tell of our passing.*

I received a missive from Father Olier to go to his place of the Sulpicians to the north, above the large river. 26 soldiers and Imogène and all the true-hearted people are also going to the north.

I am sending 4 attached boxes with the 13 Adoniram's rolls, 26 pharax's ones, 129 Euripid's ones, 9 Cohan's ones, 16 of ours,

40. https://en.wikipedia.org/wiki/Notre-Dame-de-Bon-Secours_Chapel

8 Yeshua's ones and the Celt's story. I also sent the Lord's war book.

Also, our Lord's secret teachings. All are going to the north."

These letters are significant as they relay the details about who was involved, what a particular treasure was used for, and where the money was spent. It is an interesting coincidence the founder of Notre Dame de Bon Secor Church, Marguerite Bourgeoys– a highly celebrated historical figure in Montreal–was a French nun born in Troyes, France. It was at the Council of Troyes, convened by Bernard de Clairvaux at Troyes Cathedral, where the Knights Templar became an official order when Pope Honorius II signed a papal bull on January 13, 1129. These documents tell an important yet small part of the incredible story of the eventual founding of the United States of America.

August 17, 1398

We have arrived at the colony which was established 3 years before and have found 23 Knights remaining. They are happy to see us and report that 16 Knights have traveled southwest into the hills and mountains, and one has died. We plan to stay with them for 2 weeks to help repair the small stockade that they have created which shelters them from the weather and encloses a small garden.

Sir Dennison reports that they have befriended the natives and that they trade venison with them for fish they catch off the small harbor to the east. They have learned to harvest their own vegetables and have gathered grains to make bread with the help of the natives. Several of the men have taken native wives and others plan to in the near future.

We have found 25 knights at the colony that was established 3 years ago. They say 16 knights have gone to the hills and mountains in the southwest and that only 1 has been killed. We will stay for 2 weeks with them to rebuild the fence that keeps them from storms and circles a small garden.

Sir Denison says they have made friends with the natives and catch fish in the small bay eastward and they trade for deer meat. They know how to grow

8 Jour Mai 1656

Robert

Ce qui est notre dernier dans le Temple de la déesse
sur la montagne de Manitou
Les habitants forts et les Scalandere empiètent
quotidiennement et les gens sont tres agitées.
J'ai mis un message en pierre et un dans la grotte
de la Prêtresse Altemona pour parler de notre décision.
Je vais chez les gens de ma mère au sud par l'eau.
De Fathe Olier a réussi à aller à sa place des
Sulpiciens dans le Nord, au-delà de la grande
rivière du Nord. Vingt-six soldiers et Iroquis et
tous les fidèles vont aussi au nord. J'envoie quatre
boites reliées avec treize rouleaux d'Adoniram,
vingt-six des défilés de Pharos, cent vingt neuf
d'Euripodes, neuf du Cahen, seize de notre saint
de Yeshua et son histoire parmi les Celtes.
J'ai également envoyé le Livre de Guérison du
Seigneur. Tous vont au nord.

M. Frank de Valdene XXI

16 42

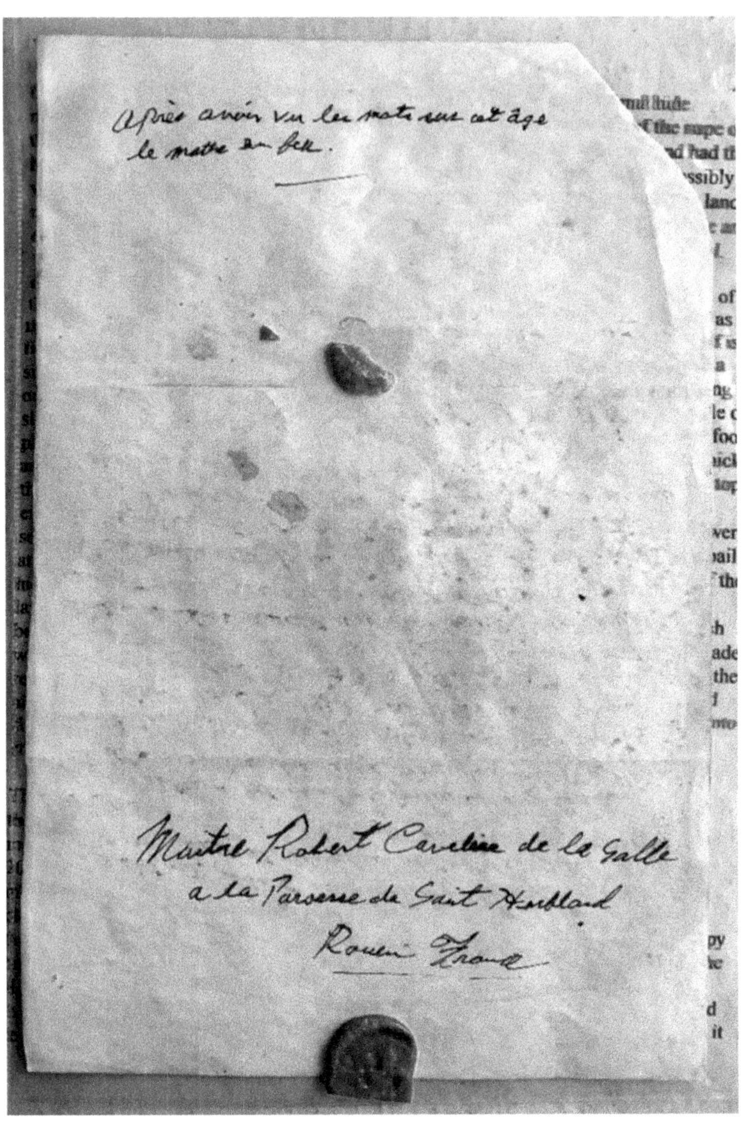

Après avoir vu les mots sur cet âge
le mettre en feu.

Maitre Robert Cavelier de la Salle
a la Paroisse de Saint Herbland
Rouen France

This letter, written by Lionel De Walderne XXI to Robert De La Salle on May 8, 1656, details the list of documents remaining at the Temple of the Goddess on Hunter Mountain in the Catskills of New York. Because of encroaching settlement, De Walderne wrote the remaining documents were to be taken to the "...place of the Sulpicians..." in Montreal. At that time, it was Notre Dame de Bon Secor Chapel that would be built, in part, using money from a Templar treasure given to Marguerite Bourgeoys, a celebrated French nun who was born in Troyes, France—the same French city where the Knights Templar were officially founded on January 13, 1129. (Wolter, 2021) their own vegetables and natives have taught them to make bread from grains they gather. Some men have married native women and others plan to shortly.

August 31, 1398

Our two weeks with our brethren have been most enlightening. They have remained strong in their faith and have learned a lot about surviving in the wilderness. Several days after we arrived the natives visited to trade, and I was surprised to learn that many of them had learned Latin words to communicate. They related that they have had many encounters with white men from the eastern lands in the mountains to the west. They report there are at least 30 men who wear white tunics with red crosses and pray to the sun God. The natives have traded venison and fish to them in exchange for silver and copper and have shared many meals and rituals with them. The eldest of the natives, called Kaholii, has spent more than one year with them learning their language. The leader of the men is called Mu'ro and is now gray haired and wise. He says most of the other men have married and they now have children who are young adults with children of their own. It was then that I realized the men he had encountered were from the group of Brethren who had stayed behind when I was a child. Only they could have children as old as mine own. It pleases me to know that they are safe and happy. Kaholii says he sees them at least every three months and has promised to take a message to them if I so request. I must fashion a message before we leave and Kaholii has promised to fashion a map so that we might find them if needed. Kaholii and his men left a few days later and I hoped my message would reach the men of the mountains and the man called Mu'ro. We must now return north to the island.

We have learned a lot from our brothers in the past two weeks. They have learned to survive in the woods and are still faithful. I was surprised to learn many natives have learned Latin words to trade three days after we came. They told us they have seen white men from the east in the mountains to the west. They say there are at least 30 men who pray to the sun god and wear white tunics with red crosses. They have received white and gold metal for deer meat and fish. They have shared many meals and rites with the natives.

Kaholi is the Chief of the natives and has learned their words after spending 1 year with them. The white leader is named Munro and is now old and gray haired and very wise. Kaholi says most are married to native women and have children who are young adults also with children. I remembered then that the men they met were the men who stayed behind when I was a child. Their children would be as old as mine. I am happy to know they are happy and safe. Kaholi says he sees them about each three months and will take a message if I

This hand-drawn map, redrawn from Kaholi, was found inside the journal at the end of the June 23, 1398 entry. However, this must be a copy of the map Earl Henry referenced in his August 31, 1398 entry. He wrote that the native, named Kaholi, told him about older white men who had married native women and had children. This led him to a realization about the party that left Norway, never to return, in 1358. I believe this group were the Templar Knights who carved and placed the Kensington Rune Stone as a land claim in the geographic center of the continent in 1362. The right (east) side of the map shows what must be the diagnostic hook of Cape Cod with a close approximation of the shoreline north to the Merrimac River. Here it appears a ship(s) traveled up the Merrimac River to the west. However, to reach what is now central Minnesota, the ships would have needed to travel up the St. Lawrence River, then up the Ottawa River to the Great Lakes and eventually to the western end of Lake Superior. From there the party would likely have traveled up the St. Louis River to the headwaters of the Red and Mississippi rivers where the Kensington stone was found. (Wolter, 2022)

like. I must create a message before we go. Kaholi promises to make a map so we can find them if we want. Kaholi left 2 days later, and I hoped that my message to Munro would reach the men in the mountains. Now we return to the northern bay where Askoosh says we should stay the winter in the bay island.

Here again we have a reference to the "30 men" who must be the Kensington party. Yet another reference to the "mountains in the west" seems to indicate lands as far away as modern-day Minnesota is bolstered by additional information not seen before in the entries. Earl Henry's mention of trading gold and silver (sister Harkin's wrote "white and gold metal" which is the same thing) indicates the 30 men are as far west as the mid-continent region in North America, because the only place on earth where, geologically, native copper and silver occur in abundance is the western Lake Superior region, including the Upper Peninsula of Michigan, Isle Royale, and Northern Minnesota.

September 23, 1398

We have taken our time sailing north to the bay which lies on the west coast of the peninsula where the Bay of Margaret lies. We have stopped at several places to replenish our stores and have made note of the inlets and rivers we have passed, leaving several markings behind us to mark our passage. Upon reaching the southern peninsula many of the men argue that they want to return home even though the season grows late. With regrets I allow them to take the ships with sail and more than 2/3 of the men return home via the northern route. They leave us with enough sail cloth and rope to outfit a boat and two small boats with oars. We will need to build another boat in order to go home in the spring and so we begin to search for a suitable place to winter. The beach we have chosen is wide and lies between two bluffs giving us shelter from the winds. We plan to build a shelter at the top of the bluff on the south side and use the beach for building an additional ship to return home. There is abundant lumber for both, and the 26 men left behind begin to build a forge to assist with making the necessary items. Father Nicolas has remained behind, and he continues his studies of local flora and animals.

We do not hurry north to the bay on the other side of the peninsula from the Bay of Margaret. We have made note of bays and rivers when stopping to refill our supplies and have left several stone markers to show our way. When we arrive at the southern peninsula many men say they want to go home even though the season is changing. I allow them to take 2 ships with sailcloth and 2/3 of the men leave by the northern route to my regrets. Enough rope and sailcloth is left to build another ship and two small oar boats. In order to go home we began to search for a good winter berth and to build another boat. The beach we choose is between 2 cliffs and gives us shelter from the wind. We will build a shelter on top of the south cliff and can use the beach to build another ship to go home. There is lots of timber for ship building and for the 26 men who stayed behind to build a forge and needed things. Father Nicolas has stayed behind to do his continued studies of plants and animals.

This entry struck me as particularly interesting, as staying on the other side of an ocean would be risky and daunting to say the least, but Earl Henry and his 26 men seem mentally steady and ready to accept the challenge. Here again, we see the significance of sacred numbers. Like Sir Ralf de Sudeley did when he traveled with 26 men to the Temple of the Goddess over two centuries earlier, Earl Henry had the same 2 x 13 (the sacred number of the Goddess) men stay behind to build a boat while surviving the winter of 1398/99.

October 15, 1398

We have completed our shelter and stocked it with food and wood for the upcoming winter. We are now prepared for any bad weather which may come. The forge is complete, and the men have felled more than enough lumber to complete a small barque. We have seen the natives at a distance, but they have not come to the beach. They do not hide their presence, and we have made no advances on them. We do not wish them to be afraid and concentrate on small forages into the hills for deer and meat while fishing for cod in the frigid bay.

Our shelter is done, and we have stocked it with wood and food for the new winter. Now we are ready for any coming bad weather. The forge is done, and enough timber has been cut by the men to build a small barque. Natives stay distant and do not come to the beach. They do not hide, and we don't approach them. We do small trips in the hills for deer and meat and fish for white fish in the icy bay, so we don't make the natives afraid.

November 13, 1398

The first large storm has arrived and after three days the snow reaches my chest. The men have done their best to clear a path to the beach and the bay is frozen for a distance. Still, they are good-hearted and continue with their work on the boat which provides our only transportation home. The logs have been split and it begins to take shape as the weather freezes and thaws repeatedly. We rejoice that the natives have finally made contact. This day a small group of 3 natives appeared on the beach and we greeted them with outstretched arms. They were clothed in animal pelts and had feathers in their hair, giving them a colorful look. They wore pelts on their feet wound with woven cords to protect their feet and seem accustomed to the cold. One of them, called Gray Moose, spoke Latin words and said that he knew of Askoosh and had been informed of our presence. He asked if we were well. We replied yes and I felt as if they were watching over us. They traded some deer pelts for some fish and after sharing a meal in the long house we parted ways as friends. They said they would return every 10 days or so to make certain we were well. I am glad that we have finally been accepted as friends.

Our first big storm has come, and snow reaches my breast after 3 days. My men do their best to keep a path to the beach clear and the water is frozen for short way. The men are in good spirits, and they still work on the boat to take us home. The planks have been cut and the boat begins to look like a boat as the weather thaws and freezes in a cycle. We are excited that the natives have finally contacted us. Today a small group of 3 natives came to the beach and we stretched our arms to welcome them. They wear animal skins and have feathers in their hair making them colorful. Their feet are wound in skins and woven cords and they look used to the cold weather. One of them was called Grey Moose and he spoke words in Latin and said he knew Askoosh who told him we were here. Gray Moose asked if we were well and I felt that they had been watching over us and I replied yes. We traded deer skins for fish and shared a meal in the shelter before we said goodbye as friends. Gray Moose said they would be back in 10 days to check on us if well. I was happy we had been accepted as friends.

November 25, 1398

Gray Moose has returned with four of his fellow men and together we shared a meal while they told me the history of their people. His ancestors had been here for thousands of years, and he could recite the genealogy of his people for many generations. He asked about my ancestors, and I told him of the great kings and nobles from Scotland and Norway who had been coming to the Western Lands for generations. He stated he had 6 sons and 3 daughters, and I replied that I had 2 sons and 3 daughters all with red hair. He laughed and told me that red hair rarely appeared in his people and when it did, they were considered blessed by the Great Goddess.

Gray Moose returns with 4 men, and he told us his people's history as we shared a meal. His grandfathers have been here for thousands of years, and he knew them by name for generations. He asked about my grandfathers, and I told him about grand kings and noble men from Scotland and Norway who had come to the fishing lands for generations. He said he had 6 sons and 3 daughters, and I said I had 2 sons and 3 daughters all with ginger hair. He laughed and told me that ginger hair in his people was rare and was thought to be blessed by the Great Goddess.

December 31, 1398

We have celebrated winter solstice and invited the natives to a feast to join with us in friendship. Gray Moose has brought his wife and children with him and four others and their families. Together we ate and smoked the pipe to send our prayers to heaven.

We celebrated winter solstice and invited the natives to feast us as friends. Gray Moose has come with his wife and children and 4 others and their families. We ate and smoked the pipe to lift our prayers to heaven.

January 15, 1399

I begin to lose count of the days but watch the stars overhead to know when we should return home. The boat is almost done although the cold weather has made it difficult to bend the planks to our liking. As soon as the bay is free of ice, we must test its sea worthiness. The men stay good hearted but have begun to talk more and more of home. I know they are eager to leave in the spring and try to find things for them to do while we huddle inside against the cold during the long nights. The natives have taught us to trap small animals and how to build caves of ice to keep the fish and game fresh. Our beards grow long as we wait for spring and the men take pride in the rituals of welcoming the new year and purification.

I have lost count of the days but use the stars over head to know when we are to go home. The cold weather has been difficult, but the boat is almost done but the boards have been difficult to bend as we like. We will test it on the sea when the bay is freed from the ice. The men talk constantly of home and stay happy. They are eager to go in the spring and we find tasks for them to do inside as we surround the fire trying to keep warm. The natives teach us to trap small animals and to keep them fresh in the ice caves they taught us to build. Our hair grows lengthy as spring approaches and the men are proud of new year purity rituals to welcome the new year.

February 22, 1399

Another large storm has left us buried in snow. As soon as the wind stops howling, we must dig ourselves free. The men sing songs to brighten their spirits and take turns teaching the others about their chosen crafts. When the natives visit, they tell us stories of their people and the men reciprocate with stories of Orkney, sea monsters and little people. I begin to think that they will miss their friends when the bay finally melts, and we return home.

We are buried in snow from another big storm. We must dig ourselves free as soon as the wind stops. The men sing songs to uplift their spirits and teach others their craft by taking turns. The natives tell us stories of their ancestors when they visit, and the men tell stories of sea monsters, trolls, and Orkney in return. I think they will miss their new friends when the bay melts and we can finally return home.

March 15, 1399

The weather has suddenly become warm and the snow begins to melt. The men's mood brightens and we are anxious to finish the boat. Some of the men have begun to fashion the mast and others continue to hunt for meat and dry it over the forge fire for our return trip.

The weather begins to warm, and the snow has begun to melt. The men are in a hurry to finish the boat, and they are happier. Some men begin to sew the sail and to build the mast while others hunt for meat to dry in the forge for our journey home.

March 29, 1399

The bay is partially melted, and we are able to test the boat in the water. It leaks and we must take time to make it seaworthy.

The bay has melted halfway, and we can test the boat in the water. There are leaks and we must fix it for the sea.

April 15, 1399

The boat at last floats on its own without taking on water with the extra weight of men and goods. Several men have taken it into the bay and have decided it is seaworthy. We begin to make plans to leave and hope to make our way down the bay before the 1st of May.

The boat finally floats even with men and supplies and does not leak. Many men have taken the boat into the bay and declared it seaworthy. Plans are made to leave and on the first day of May we hope to make our way south on the bay."

May 6, 1399

We have now said goodbye to Gray Moose and his family and tell him of our appreciation for his assistance and friendship over the winter. We have learned so much from him and his men and hope that they have learned as much from us. We begin our journey south and hope to meet up again with Askoosh before traveling east across the northern seas.

We say goodbye to Gray Moose and his family and tell him we appreciated his help and friendship during the winter. We have learned so much from him and his men and pray [we] have taught them much. We hope to visit Askoo[sh] as we journey east and north before we cross the northern sea to the east.

May 15, 1399

Askoosh and his men await us at the Isle of the White Stag and greet us as we disembark our small boat that we have named the Hanna. We will spend a day or two with them before we leave for the east.

Askoosh and his men wait for us at the Isle of the White Deer and meet us as we leave our small boat we call the *Hanna*. We will spend two days with them before we leave to the east.

May 18, 1399

We leave this morn to go east to Groenland. There is still ice on the seas, but our small boat is easily navigated. Askoosh raised his hand from the shore until I could see him no more and I wondered if we should ever meet again. We plan to return in a few years but the political unrest in Scotland often interferes. May we both remain healthy and happy until we meet again.

This morning we leave to go east to Greenland. Ice is still on the sea, but our small boat is easy to maneuver if we stay close to land. Askoosh raised his hand until I could see him no more on the shore. I wondered if we would meet again. I plan to return in a few years, but Scotland politics often changes our plans. I pray we both stay healthy and happy until we meet again.

June 12, 1399

We have arrived safely on the shores of Caithness and are glad to be in Scotland. I must remove myself to Rosslin and give the men leave to return to Kirkwall.

We arrive safely on Caithness shores and are happy to be in Scotland. I must go to Rosslyn and tell the men to go home to Kirkwall.

SHIPS' CREW LISTS: 1398-1399

SHIP NAME: *KATHERINE*

Ship grounded on McNab Island.
Cargo offloaded and buried. Ship burnt.

Ship: *Katherine*				
Origin	**Surname**	**First Name**	**Title**	**Status**
Hjatland	Balfour	Laurens	Sir Knight/Templar	Stayed Behind
Scotland	Blair	David	Sir Knight/Templar	
Orkney	Buchanan	Walter	Sir Knight/Templar	Stayed Behind
Scotland	Chricton	Robert	Sir Knight/Templar	[41]
Scotland	De Brox-mouth	Gary	Sir Knight/Templar	Stayed Behind
Scotland	De Gremi-slaw	Christian	Sir Knight/Templar	Stayed Behind
Scotland	De Wynton	Robert	Sir Knight/Templar	Stayed Behind
Scotland	Edmonstone	John	Sir Knight/Templar	[42]
Scotland	Glendonwyn	Adam	Sir Knight/Templar	
Scotland	Hay	Thomas	Sir Knight/Templar	
Scotland	Irvine	Alexander	Sir Knight/Templar	Stayed Behind
Scotland	Longantach	John	Sir Knight/Templar	
Scotland	MacDonald	Godfrey	Sir Knight/Templar	
Scotland	Magerton	Alexander	Sir Knight/Templar	Stayed Behind
Scotland	Maule	William	Sir Knight/Templar	
Scotland	Ochtery	John	Sir Knight/Templar	Stayed Behind
Scotland	Ogilvy	Walter	Sir Knight/Templar	Stayed Behind
Orkney	Ross	William	Sir Knight/Templar	
Scotland	Shuldham	Alexander	Sir Knight/Templar	
Scotland	Sinclair	Henricus	Sir Knight/Templar	
Scotland	Sutherland	Robert	Sir Knight/Templar	
Hjatland	Thompson	James	Sir Knight/Templar	
Orkney	Bacon		Seaman	

41. Related to James II, Lord of Chricton, near Edinburgh, Midlothia, Scotland.

42. Listed on 1391 charter to David Sinclair, possibly collaborated with Henry Sinclair on planning the trip.

Ship: *Katherine*				
Origin	**Surname**	**First Name**	**Title**	**Status**
Scotland	Bassett		Seaman	
Scotland	Bertram		Seaman	
Hjatland	Bruce		Seaman	
Orkney	Butler		Seaman	
Orkney	Eden		Seaman	
Orkney	Edrington	Bertran	Captain	
Scotland	Flavesley		Seaman	
Orkney	Graham		Seaman	
Orkney	Grandson		Seaman	
Hjatland	Latimer		Seaman	Stayed Behind
Scotland	Leyburn		Seaman	
Hjatland	Lindsay		Seaman	
Hjatland	Martin		Seaman	
Scotland	Orreby		Seaman	
Orkney	Plessets		Seaman	
Hjatland	Ramsay		Seaman	Stayed Behind
Orkney	Schumberg		Seaman	

Ship: *Perequin*
Went to Halifax

Ship: *Perequin*				
Origin	**Surname**	**First Name**	**Title**	**Status**
Scotland	Abercrombie	Alexander	Sir Knight/Templar	Stayed behind, went to Halifax
Scotland	Barclay	Christian	Sir Knight/Templar	Stayed Behind
Scotland	Burnard	Robert	Sir Knight/Templar	
Scotland	Borthwick	William	Sir Knight/Templar	
Scotland	Colville	Thomas	Sir Knight/Templar	
Scotland	de Houston	John	Sir Knight/Templar	Stayed Behind
Scotland	De La Hay	Thomas	Sir Knight/Templar	
Scotland	Douglas	John	Sir Knight/Templar	
Scotland	Erksine	William	Sir Knight/Templar	Stayed Behind

Ship: *Perequin*				
Origin	**Surname**	**First Name**	**Title**	**Status**
Scotland	Gordon	John	Sir Knight/Templar	
Scotland	Haya	Thomas	Sir Knight/Templar	
Scotland	Johnstone	Adam	Sir Knight/Templar	
Orkney	Audley		Seaman	Stayed Behind
Orkney	Bard		Seaman	
Orkney	Beatton	Johanni	Captain	
Orkney	Beauchamp		Seaman	
Orkney	Blair		Seaman	
Orkney	Blount		Seaman	
Orkney	Butler		Seaman	
Hjatland	Craufoord		Seaman	
Orkney	Daubeney		Seaman	
Orkney	Felton		Seaman	
Orkney	Foliot		Seaman	
Hjatland	Grey		Seaman	
Hjatland	Macdonald		Seaman	
Scotland	Meinhill		Seaman	
Scotland	Montfiet		Seaman	
Scotland	Romare		Seaman	
Scotland	Sackville		Seaman	
Scotland	Vere		Seaman	
St. Andrews	Father Nicolas		Cleric	

Ship: Somnium
Went to Cambellton Island

Ship: Somnium				
Origin	**Surname**	**First Name**	**Title**	**Status**
Scotland	Abernethy	David and George	Sir Knight/Templar	
Scotland	Barthwick	William	Sir Knight/Templar	
Scotland	Boswell	John Rodger	Sir Knight/Templar	
Scotland	Calder	Andrew	Sir Knight/Templar	

Ship: Somnium				
Origin	**Surname**	**First Name**	**Title**	**Status**
Scotland	Coupare	Symon	Sir Knight/Templar	
Scotland	de Lidsay	James	Sir Knight/Templar	
Scotland	Douglas	Thomas	Sir Knight/Templar	Stayed Behind
Scotland	Faslane	Duncan	Sir Knight/Templar	
Scotland	Gordon	Roger	Sir Knight/Templar	
Scotland	Haylburton	Walter	Sir Knight/Templar	
Scotland	Keith	Rober	Sir Knight/Templar	
Scotland	MacGregor	Iain	Sir Knight/Templar	Stayed Behind
Scotland	Melville	John Rodger	Sir Knight/Templar	
Scotland	Munro	Christian	Sir Knight/Templar	Stayed Behind
Scotland	Oliphant	John	Sir Knight/Templar	
Scotland	Seton	Christian	Sir Knight/Templar	
Scotland	Urquhart	Adam	Sir Knight/Templar	Stayed Behind
Italia	Zeno	Antonio	Captain	
Orkney	Albini		Seaman	
Orkney	Aungier		Seaman	
Orkney	Beche		Seaman	
Orkney	Bohun		Seaman	
Hjatland	Boteler		Seaman	
Orkney	Bourchier		Seaman	
Orkney	Dacre		Seaman	
Orkney	deErville		Seaman	
Hjatland	Douglas		Seaman	
Orkney	Hacche		Seaman	
Orkney	Heris		Seaman	
Orkney	Lucy		Seaman	
Orkney	Mechines		Seaman	
Hjatland	Monk		Seaman	
Orkney	Multon		Seaman	
Orkney	Paynell		Seaman	
Hjatland	Sinclair		Seaman	
Orkney	Sydney		Seaman	
Hjatland	Wilson		Seaman	

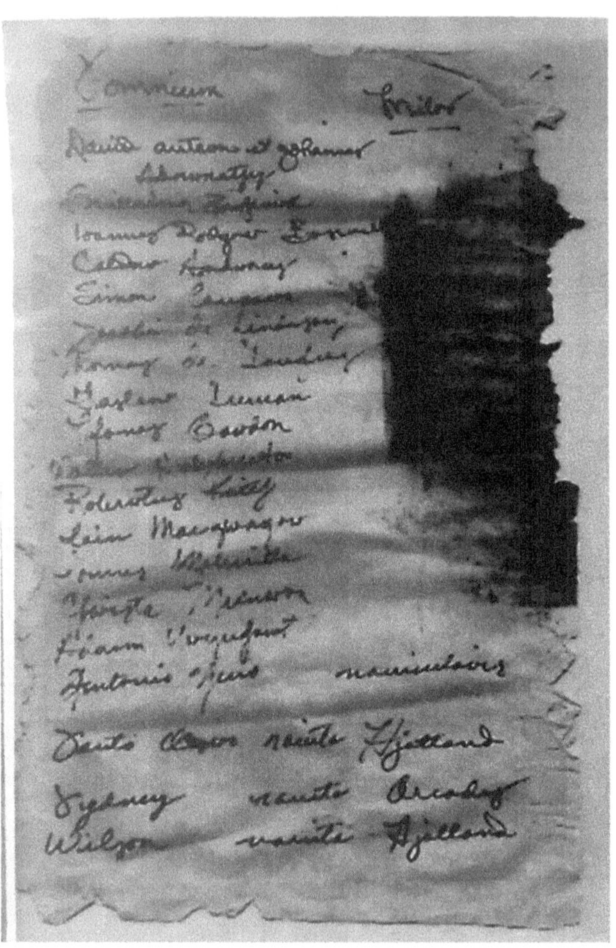

This picture is the crew list of the *Somnium* from the 1398 trip to the Western Lands. There also appear to be three vertically aligned "fish" symbols being used for the letter "s" in three names, "Somnium", "Sauts" and "Sydney." (Muir, 2016)

Ship: *Orknades*
Went to East Ironbound Island

Ship: *Orknades*				
Origin	**Surname**	**First Name**	**Title**	**Status**
Scotland	Atheyn	Eachann	Knight	
Orkney	Berkeley	William	Knight	Stayed Behind
Scotland	Boyd	William	Knight	
Orkney	Campbell	George	Knight	
Hjatland	Cruickshanks	David	Squire	
Scotland	DeErkskine	Thomas	Knight	Stayed Behind
Hjatland	Denniston	Robert	Hird	
Hjatland	Drummond	John	Squire	Stayed Behind
Scotland	Forrester	Adam	Knight	
Hjatland	Gray	Andrew	Squire	
Scotland	Herries	John	Knight	Stayed Behind
Scotland	Leighton	William	Knight	
Scotland	MacKinnon	John	Knight	
Orkney	Mure	Godfrey	Knight	Stayed Behind
Hjatland	Ross	William	Hird	
Scotland	Somerville	William	Knight	
Orkney	Allington		Seaman	Stayed Behind
Orkney	Benhale		Seaman	Stayed Behind
Orkney	Cantilupe		Seaman	
Orkney	DeLorraine		Seaman	
Scotland	Douglas		Seaman	
Scotland	Douglas		Seaman	
Orkney	Dunbar		Seaman	
Orkney	Gant		Seaman	
Orkney	Harington	Alexander	Captain	
Scotland	Kerdeston		Seaman	
Orkney	Labourchere		Seaman	
Scotland	Montacute		Seaman	
Scotland	Montalt		Seaman	
Orkney	Powlett		Seaman	

Ship: *Orknades*				
Origin	**Surname**	**First Name**	**Title**	**Status**
Orkney	Roper		Seaman	
Hjatland	Sutton		Seaman	
Orkney	Wyndham		Seaman	

SHIP: *ORTUS*

Went down halfway across Mahone Bay.

Ship: *Ortus*				
Origin	**Surname**	**First Name**	**Title**	**Status**
Scotland	Armstrong	Alexander	Knight	Lost at sea.
Scotland	Beaton	Johanni	Knight	Lost at sea.
Scotland	Boswell	Ralph	Knight	Lost at sea.
Orkney	Cameron	John	Knight	Lost at sea.
Scotland	Crichton	John	Knight	Lost at sea.
Scotland	de Barclay	Richard	Knight	Lost at sea.
Scotland	de Maxwell	Robert	Knight	Lost at sea.
Scotland	Douglas	Nicolas	Knight	Lost at sea.
Scotland	Fleming	David	Knight	Lost at sea.
Orkney	Graham	Patrick	Knight	Lost at sea.
Hjatland	Hepburn	Patrick	Hird	Lost at sea.
Scotland	Kennedy	Gilbert	Knight	Lost at sea.
Scotland	Mackenzie	Murdoch	Knight	Lost at sea.
Scotland	Mentieth	William	Knight	Lost at sea.
Scotland	Rose	Hugh	Knight	Lost at sea.
Hjatland	Spence	David	Squire	Lost at sea.
Orkney	Badlemere		Seaman	Lost at sea.
Orkney	Cumryn		Seaman	Lost at sea.
Orkney	Dernewick		Seaman	Lost at sea.
Orkney	Dunstanvil		Seaman	Lost at sea.
Orkney	Ferrers		Seaman	Lost at sea.
Orkney	Granville		Seaman	Lost at sea.
Hjatland	Holland		Seaman	Lost at sea.
Orkney	Multravers		Seaman	Lost at sea.
Hjatland	Nevill		Seaman	Lost at sea.

Ship: *Ortus*				
Origin	**Surname**	**First Name**	**Title**	**Status**
Hjatland	Nevill		Seaman	Lost at sea.
Hjatland	Plantagenet		Seaman	Lost at sea.
Hjatland	Seton		Seaman	Lost at sea.
Orkney	Sinclair		Seaman	Lost at sea.
Orkney	Sinclair		Seaman	Lost at sea.
Orkney	Smythe		Seaman	Lost at sea.
Orkney	Stratbogie	Andrew	Captain	Lost at sea.
Hjatland	Straford		Seaman	Lost at sea.
Hjatland	Vere		Seaman	Lost at sea.
Orkney	Wahull		Seaman	Lost at sea.

Ship's Name: *Apricitas*

Uncertain where it went.

Ship: *Apricitas*				
Origin	**Surname**	**First Name**	**Title**	**Status**
Scotland	Aylesbury	John	Knight	
Scotland	Bethune	John	Knight	
Scotland	Boyd	Thomas	Knight	
Scotland	Campbell	Colin	Knight	
Scotland	Cunninghame	Robert	Knight	Stayed Behind
Scotland	deGordon	Adam	Knight	
Scotland	DeSeton	William	Knight	Stayed Behind
Scotland	Dunbar	John	Hird	
Scotland	Galbraith	James	Knight	
Scotland	Grierson	Gilbert	Knight	Stayed Behind
Scotland	Herries	John	Knight	Stayed Behind
Scotland	Leslie	George	Hird	
Scotland	Macleod	William	Knight	
Scotland	Murray	David	Knight	Stayed Behind
Scotland	Ross	William	Knight	Stayed Behind

Ship: *Apricitas*				
Origin	**Surname**	**First Name**	**Title**	**Status**
Scotland	Stewart	Alexander	Knight	
Scotland	Watson	John	Squire	Stayed Behind
Scotland	Anderson		Seaman	
Italia	Arden		Seaman	
Orkney	Arden		Seaman	
Orkney	Beche		Seaman	
Orkney	Berkeley		Seaman	Stayed Behind
Orkney	Campbell	Duncan	Captain	
Hjatland	Descpencer		Seaman	
Orkney	Devereaux		Seaman	
Orkney	Ferrers		Seaman	
Orkney	Harcla		Seaman	
Hjatland	Ingbortsen		Seaman	Stayed Behind
Orkney	Ingham		Seaman	
Orkney	Kennedy		Seaman	
Orkney	Knovill		Seaman	
Orkney	Lyttleton		Seaman	
Hjatland	Monthermer		Seaman	
Orkney	Percy		Seaman	
Orkney	Sandiland		Seaman	
Hjatland	Talbot		Seaman	

Ship's Name: Fortunae

Uncertain where it went.

Ship: Fortunae				
Origin	**Surname**	**First Name**	**Title**	**Status**
Scotland	Baillie	William	Knight	
Scotland	Bissett	Walter	Knight	Stayed Behind
Hjatland	Bruce	Andrew	Hird	
Scotland	Chisholm	John	Knight	

Ship: Fortunae				
Origin	**Surname**	**First Name**	**Title**	**Status**
Scotland	Danielston	Robert	Knight	Stayed Behind
Scotland	deGray	Andrew	Knight	Stayed Behind
Scotland	deSwinton	John	Knight	Stayed Behind
Scotland	Dundas	James	Knight	
Hjatland	Gibson	William	Squire	
Scotland	Halyburton	John	Knight	
Scotland	Hunter	William	Knight	
Scotland	Livington	John	Knight	Stayed Behind
Hjatland	Mangusson	John	Knight	Stayed Behind
Hjatland	Neaves	David	Knight	
Scotland	Rutherford	Richard	Knight	Stayed Behind
Scotland	Stuart	William	Knight	
Scotland	Wallace	Adam	Knight	
Scotland	Wardlaw	William	Knight	Stayed Behind
Scotland	Wemyss of Methil	David	Knight	
Scotland	Aton		Seaman	
Orkney	Beke		Seaman	
Orkney	Brooke		Seaman	
Scotland	Bryan		Seaman	
Orkney	De Birmingham		Seaman	
Hjatland	Dundas		Seaman	
Hjatland	Everingham		Seaman	Stayed Behind
Orkney	Fitz-Payne	David	Captain	
Orkney	Gorlton		Seaman	
Orkney	Hastang		Seaman	
Hjatland	Herberet		Seaman	Stayed Behind
Orkney	Kyme		Seaman	
Hjatland	Maxwell		Seaman	
Hjatland	Morley		Seaman	
Hjatland	Obrian		Seaman	
Hjatland	Ogilvy		Seaman	
Orkney	Phipps		Seaman	

Ship: Fortunae				
Origin	**Surname**	**First Name**	**Title**	**Status**
Orkney	Pinkney		Seaman	
Orkney	Sheffield		Seaman	
Orkney	Thomson		Seaman	
Scotland	Vere		Seaman	

1395 Ship Synopsis					
Ship	**Type**	**Knights**	**Crew**	**Notes**	**Left Behind**
Accipitor	Barque	13	16	Made it to Mahone Bay, returned to Scotland.	6
Itienere	Barque	13	16	Made it to Mahone Bay, returned to Scotland.	10
Perequin	Galley	21	20	Made it to Mahone Bay, explored East Coast.	11
Repostus	Barque	13	16	Lost at sea	0
Somnium	Galley	20	22	Landed in Halifax, went N to St. Lawrence River.	8
Speculator	Barque	13	13	Made it to Mahone Bay, returned to Scotland.	12
Ortus	Galley	21	23	Made it to Mahone Bay, returned to Scotland.	12
Persephone	Galley	10	19	Sank at Sable Island, 6 men drowned	
	Totals:	124	145		65

1398-1399 Ship Synopsis					
Ship	**Type**	**Knights**	**Crew**	**Notes**	**Left Behind**
Perequin	Galley	12	18	Carried treasure, went to Halifax.	6
Katherine	Galley	22	18	Carried treasure, grounded/burnt on Oak Island.	11
Somnium	Galley	18	19	Carried treasure, went to Cambellton Island.	4
Orknades	Galley	16	19	Carried treasure, went to East Ironbound Island.	6

1398-1399 Ship Synopsis					
Ship	**Type**	**Knights**	**Crew**	**Notes**	**Left Behind**
Ortus	Galley	16	17	Carried treasure. Lost at Sea.	0
Apricitas	Galley	17	19	Carried treasure, uncertain where it went.	9
Fortunae	Galley	19	21	Carried treasure, uncertain where it went.	10
	Totals:	120	131		46

Those who stayed behind: 1395-1399					
Surname	**First Name**	**Title**	**Ship**	**Origin**	**Year**
Abercrombie	Alexander	Knight	Perequin	Scotland	1398
Allington		seaman	Orknades	Orkney	1398
Andre	Bethune	Sir Knight	Perequin	Flanders	1395
Arbia	Hendrik	Sir Knight	Somnium	Flanders	1395
Ardenbourg	John	Sir Knight	Speculator	Flanders	1395
Ardenhort	Henri	Sir Knight	Itienere	Flanders	1395
Audley		seaman	Perequin	Orkney	1398
Balfour	Laurens	Knight	Katherine	Hjatland	1398
Barclay	Christian	Knight	Perequin	Orkney	1398
Beauchamp		seaman	Perequin	Orkney	1398
Berkeley	William	Knight	Orknades	Orkney	1398
Berkeley		seaman	Apricitas	Scotland	1398
Biersi	Joannes	Sir Knight	Perequin	Flanders	1395
Bissett	Walter	Knight	Fortunae	Scotland	1398
Brabant	Aeaneas	Sir Knight	Somnium	Flanders	1395
Braybrooke	Humphrey	Sir Knight	Speculator	France	1395
Breman	Jacque	Sir Knight	Itienere	Flanders	1395
Brueria	Johannes	Sir Knight	Ortus	Flanders	1395
Bruges	Guiscard	Sir Knight	Perequin	Flanders	1395
Buchanan	Walter	Knight	Katherine	Orkney	1398
Cadeleta	Jacob	Sir Knight	Ortus	Flanders	1395
Caestree	Gerard	Sir Knight	Somnium	Flanders	1395

Those who stayed behind: 1395-1399					
Surname	**First Name**	**Title**	**Ship**	**Origin**	**Year**
Caestree	Jean	Sir Knight	Perequin	Flanders	1395
Cambrai	Henri	Sir Knight	Speculator	Flanders	1395
Campanels	Henricus	Sir Knight	Itienere	Flanders	1395
Cunninghame	Robert	Knight	Apricitas	Scotland	1398
Candebur	Oliver	Sir Knight	Accipiter	Flanders	1395
Capons	Enricus	Sir Knight	Ortus	Flanders	1395
Capons	Patrick	Sir Knight	Accipiter	Flanders	1395
Clouttying	Thomas	Sir Knight	Somnium	Flanders	1395
Danielston	Robert	Knight	Fortunae	Scotland	1398
De Broxmouth	Gary	Knight	Katherine	Scotland	1398
De Champagne	Guilliame	Sir Knight	Accipiter	Hungary	1395
de Houston	John	Knight	Perequin	Scotland	1398
de Tinj	Theobold	Sir Knight	Ortus	Hungary	1395
deBlois	Philip	Sir Knight	Somnium	France	1395
deBlois	Thibault	Sir Knight	Perequin	France	1395
DeErkskine	Thomas	Knight	Orknades	Scotland	1398
deGray	Andrew	Knight	Fortunae	Scotland	1398
DeGremislaw	Christian	Knight	Katherine	Scotland	1,398
Denis	Le Mesureur	Sir Knight	Ortus	Flanders	1395
Deponthieu	Guillaume Talvas	Sir Knight	Somnium	Hungary	1395
DeRoet	Andre'	Sir Knight	Speculator	Flanders	1395
DeSeton	William	Knight	Apricitas	Scotland	1398
Destpol	Entienne Henri	Sir Knight	Ortus	Hungary	1395
deSwinton	John	Knight	Fortunae	Scotland	1398
deWynton	Robert	Knight	Katherine	Scotland	1398
Doual	Guilermo	Sir Knight	Itienere	Flanders	1395
Douglas	Thomas	Knight	Somnium	Scotland	1398
Drummond	John	Squire	Orknades	Hjatland	1398
Erkskine	William	Knight	Perequin	Scotland	1398
Everingham		seaman	Fortunae	Hjatland	1398

Those who stayed behind: 1395-1399					
Surname	**First Name**	**Title**	**Ship**	**Origin**	**Year**
Flamingi	Robert	Sir Knight/Chap-lain	Somnium	Flanders	1395
Furno	Johannes	Sir Knight	Itienere	Flanders	1395
Geneffe	Egidius	Sir Knight	Ortus	Flanders	1395
Geneffe	Geofrey	Sir Knight	Perequin	Flanders	1395
Ghent	Gossin of	Sir Knight	Somnium	Flanders	1395
Grierson	Gilbert	Knight	Apricitas	Scotland	1398
Herberet		seaman	Fortunae	Hjatland	1398
Herries	John	Knight	Apricitas	Scotland	1398
Herries	John	Knight	Orknades	Scotland	. 1398
Ingbortsen		seaman	Apricitas	Hjatland	1398
Irvine	Alexander	Knight	Katherine	Scotland	1398
Izenberge	Henri	Sir Knight	Itienere	Flanders	1395
Lamingi	Gilbertus	Sir Knight	Perequin	Flanders	1395
Latimer		seaman	Katherine	Hjatland	1398
Livington	John	Knight	Fortunae	Scotland	1398
MacGregor	Iain	Knight	Somnium	Scotland	1398
Magnusson	John	Knight	Fortunae	Hjatland	1398
Maile	Bernard	Sir Knight	Speculator	Flanders	1395
Mangerton	Alexander	Knight	Katherine	Scotland	1398
Marion	Philippe	Sir Knight	Itienere	Flanders	1395
Menin	Augustus	Sir Knight/ Chaplain	Accipiter	Flanders	1395
Merrett	Francisco	Sir Knight	Perequin	Spain	1395
Munro	Christian	knight	Somnium	Scotland	1398
Mure	Godfrey	Knight	Orknades	Orkney	1398
Murray	David	Knight	Apricitas	Scotland	1398
Navarre	Humbert	Sir Knight	Ortus	France	1395
Nevers	Philip	Sir Knight	Somnium	Flanders	1395
Nivelles	Arnau	Sir Knight	Speculator	Flanders	1395
Ochtery	John	Knight	Katherine	Scotland	1398
Ogilvy	Walter	Knight	Katherine	Scotland	1398
Olgilvie	Denis	Sir Knight	Itienere	Flanders	1395

Those who stayed behind: 1395-1399					
Surname	**First Name**	**Title**	**Ship**	**Origin**	**Year**
Perbone	Guilliame	Sir Knight	Ortus	Flanders	1395
Podiebrand	Boczeck	Sir Knight	Perequin	Flanders	1395
Ramsay		seaman	Katherine	Hjatland	1398
Reppe	Nicolai	Sir Knight	Itienere	Flanders	1395
Ross	William	Knight	Apricitas	Scotland	1398
Rutherford	Richard	Knight	Fortunae	Scotland	1398
Sacke	Philip	Sir Knight	Accipiter	Flanders	1395
Shirley	Sir Hugh	Sir Knight	Perequin	Flanders	1395
Slijpe	Johannes	Sir Knight	Perequin	Flanders	1395
St. Veerle	Francisco	Sir Knight	Speculator	Flanders	1395
Templemars	Helinus	Sir Knight	Accipiter	Flanders	1395
Templemars	Michael	Sir Knight	Ortus	Flanders	1395
Urquhart	Adam	Knight	Somnium	Scotland	1398
Valera	William	Sir Knight	Somnium	Flanders	1395
Varsenacre	Philippe	Sir Knight	Speculator	Flanders	1395
Versequi	Nicholas	Sir Knight	Itienere	Flanders	1395
Von Sacke	Christoph	Sir Knight	Ortus	Flanders	1395
VonHoyen	Baskardt	Sir Knight	Persephone	Italian	1395
VonPort	Herman	Sir Knight	Persephone	Italian	1395
VonSchaepfer	Ermo	Sir Knight	Persephone	Italian	1395
VonSchudi	Chevalier H(einrich)	Sir Knight	Persephone	Italian	1395
VonSeedorf	Ulrich	Sir Knight	Persephone	Italian	1395
VonWindegg	Roland	Sir Knight	Persephone	Italian	1395
Wndardlaw	William	Knight	Fortunae	Scotland	1398
Watson	John	Squire	Apricitas	Hjatland	1398
Wingfield	John	Sir Knight	Somnium	Flanders	1395
Ypres	Louis	Sir Knight	Ortus	Flanders	1395
Zacke	Milton	Sir Knight	Somnium	Flanders	1395

That 111 Templars and seaman chose to stay in North America is a startling and significant part of history that was unknown until now. I heard about it firsthand after participating in an Ojibwe Mide'win (Great

Medicine Society) sweat lodge ceremony in Canada several years ago. When it was my turn to ask the medicine man questions about the Templars he interjected, "You mean our blood brothers?" We will learn much about these brave men who stayed behind in the coming entries.

6

Journals of Henry, William, William, and Henry Sinclair:

Books 4 through 7

Book 4

Henry Sinclair, 2nd Earl of Orkney

(1373-1421)

April 15, 1406

Diana Muir's Translation (italics): *I have not time to visit the Western Lands and dislike the smell of the sea. I regret that I cannot fulfill my father's request at this time. The King has been captured and I must attend to my duties to the King.*

Sister Harkin's Translation (plain): I do not have time or desire to go the western lands and hate the smell of the sea. With regret Father's request will not be fulfilled. The King has been taken prisoner and I must attend my king's duties.

BOOK 5

WILLIAM "THE BUILDER" SINCLAIR, 3RD EARL OF ORKNEY

1408 - 1480

May 1, 1432

My father's dying request this ten years past has required me to make a trip to the Western banks to find and contact the Templari who have traveled there years before. Although he never visited the Western Lands on his own accord, he has given me explicit instructions on how to find the Templari and the markers that were left behind. In preparation we gather together 3 ships and plan to bring back cod fish that are far superior to our local fish. While I am gone my uncle David Menzies of Weems will conduct business in my absence.

Ten years ago, my father's dying wish was to travel to the western lands to contact the brothers who traveled and stayed there years before. He never visited the western lands himself but has given me exact instructions on how to [find] the markers they left behind by the brethren. We prepare 3 ships for the journey and will bring back whitefish that are superior to our local fish. My uncle David Menzies of Weems will conduct business in my name while I am gone.

Author Commentary (shaded box): Unlike his father, William was ready to go to the Western Lands and honor the Covenant by checking on the treasures his grandfather had brought over from Scotland and buried in multiple places.

May 15, 1432

We leave this day for the Western Banks. We will stop first in Iceland and at the monastery in Groenland. The journey should take us approximately 5 months to complete.

Today we leave for the western lands. We will stop in Iceland first and then visit the Greenland monastery. It will take 5 months to complete this trip.

June 2, 1432

We have arrived in the Western Lands and search for the island with the large cliff face. It is here we are to anchor before traveling south.

We search for the island in the western lands with the large cliff front. We will anchor here before we go south.

June 3, 1432

The natives have greeted us as friends upon our arrival at the island they call the "Isle of the White Stag." This is so because of the rare white deer that frequent the island and whose pelt is revered above all others. They know our language and have told us of how my grandfather visited years before. They have shown us the boulder that was marked with the year of passage and have given us gifts of pelts to soften our sleep during our journey.

The friendly natives have greeted us on the island they call the Isle of the White Deer. They say it is because of the rare white deer on the island whose skin is valued more than all others. They are able to talk with us and know our words. They say my grandpere visited many years ago. They showed us the rock that was marked with the year of our voyage and have given us skins to soften our sleep during our time here."

It is interesting but not surprising Sister Harkin uses the French word for grandfather, "grandpere." Since she was educated in the French speaking city of Montreal, Canada, it's surprising she didn't have more French words slip into her translations.

June 7, 1432

The weather has been clear and fair, and we make good progress to the Bay of Margaret. The map that was given to me by my father shows clearly the islands that preserve the treasures of the Templari which was moved 35 years before. We are surprised to find that one of the three Templari left on Dog Island continues to live on the island. We have offered to take him home to Scotland, but he refuses. He says he has a wife and children here and cannot leave his home. He assures us that the islands have been undisturbed and remain guarded by the natives who befriended my grandfather years before. They take their promise seriously and visit him regularly. He speaks their language fluently and calls them his family.

The weather is good, and we are making good progress to Margaret Bay. My father gave me a map that is clear about the island where the brothers moved treasure to 35 years ago. We were surprised to find that one of the brothers left on Dog Island. He has refused our offer to take him home to Scotland. He states he has a wife and children and cannot leave the treasure. He says the isles are undisturbed and are guarded by native friends of my grandfather. They visit the brother on a regular basis and take their promise seriously. He calls them family and speaks their words.

I was heartened to read about the Templars who married, had children, and thrived still in the Western Lands 34 and 37 years after being left behind by Earl Henry in 1395 and 1398.

June 22, 1432

We have completed our survey of the treasure caches and are satisfied that all are undiscovered and secure. Lastly, we will visit the Big Stone Fort to determine if the small colony of Knights has persevered.

Our survey of the treasure is complete, and we know they are secure and not found. We will visit the Big Stone Fort last to visit the small colony of Knights if it is still there.

June 25, 1432

We have traveled inland to the Big Stone Fort and have found a small group of 8 Knights who have long since completed the fort and now maintain their homes nearby. Each has married and although now elderly, they have taught their children well and they celebrate the rituals of Christianity as well as the rituals of the Great Goddess. They crave news of Scotland and are happy to hear that their friends are safe although they had hoped to see the Earl of Orkney, my grandfather, once more. As they told me stories of the time they had spent with him, I learned to appreciate the man I had never known as he had died 4 years before I was born. We discussed the goal of establishing a free Templar state here in the new lands and they tell us they have news of the group who moved north to establish a monastery and also the 45 Knights who had traveled into the southern mountains to find their elders 34 years ago. The monastery has done well and produces 150 barrels of wine each year. The community is mostly monks who have never married and suggested we bring others to join them in their community. I promise to consider it for the next voyage.

We have found a small group of 8 knights where we have traveled inland to the Big Stone Fort. They have long finished the fort and now live nearby. Each has married and are now elderly. They have taught their children to celebrate Christian rituals and the rituals of the Goddess also. They seek news of Scotland and are glad to know their friends are safe, but they had wanted to see my grandfather the Earl of Orkney again. They told me stories of my grandfather and the time they had spent with him, and I learned to know the man I had never met as he died 4 years before I was born. We talked about the goal of creating a free Templar state in the new land and they say they [have] news of the monks who went to establish a monastery in the north and also the 45 knights who went into southern mountains to find the Templars who came 34 years ago. The monastery has done well and makes 150 barrels of grape wine each year. They [are] mostly monks who did not marry and they ask we bring others to add to their community. I promise to request it for the next voyage.

This entry was very personal, as the Big Stone Fort must be the site of the legendary castle at New Ross where I was lowered in to the "Holy Well" while filming an episode of *America Unearthed* in 2012. Numerous large boulders in the woods with what appeared to me to be man-made cleaved faces and impact fractures were consistent with the remains of a fort. Skeptical at the time the site could be related to the Templars, I was shocked upon reading this entry, realizing we had indeed been walking in the footsteps of the knights who built a fort and lived here. Further, it was shocking to know the well I had descended into, in fact, did hold Templar treasure in the past. Alas, the ideological descendants of these brave and committed knights beat me to it.

This entry is also significant as we learn from William himself that his grandfather, Earl Henry Sinclair, died in 1404. This is a fact not previously known to be found anywhere in the historical records.

Steve St. Clair and I crouch next to a drill rig boring a hole into what we hoped would be a chamber filled with Templar treasure next to the "Holy Well" at New Ross, Nova Scotia during filming of an episode of *America Unearthed* in October of 2012. (Wolter, 2015)

June 28, 1432

Satisfied that I have completed my promise to my fathers, we leave for the beach where we will sail back to the Isle of the White Stag. There we will fill the boats with cod and return home to Scotland. I return home a changed man as I now understand the reason my grandfather came here years ago. I know that the treasure is well cared for and the men left behind have thrived.

Happy that I have completed my promise to my father, and we leave to go to the beach at the Isle of the White Deer where we will sail back home to Scotland. I will return home a different man as I understand now why my grandfather came here long ago. We will fill the boats with white fish and return home. I know the treasure is taken care of and the men left behind have done well.

August 16, 1432

We arrived this morning in Caithness home from our journey to the Western Lands. I give thanks to God and the Goddess for our safe return and commit myself to building an effigy to honor my grandfather and the Knights who risked their lives for the cause of the brethren. I look forward to the day when I can share my journey with my young son William who is only 2 years of age. Hopefully he will honor his ancestors by continuing the Covenant of the brethren.

We arrived home in Caithness this morning from our trip to the Western lands. I thank God and the Goddess for our safe return and promise to build a chapel to honor my grandfather and the natives and knights who gave their lives to the cause of the brothers. I look to the day when I can share my knowledge with William, my son who is 2 years old. I hope he will honor his grandfathers by continuing the sacred covenant of the brothers.

This entry is significant for a couple of reasons. First, in the Harkin translation William states he will "*...promise to build a chapel...*" whereas in Diana's translation he says, "*...and commit myself to building an effigy...*". William's apparent intention to build a chapel is significant because a chapel is what was ultimately constructed. After I transcribed this entry and shared with my colleague, Hayley Ramsey, she made an interesting comment: "*This proves the chapel was never intended to be a cathedral as many people over the centuries have speculated.*" This is an excellent point, as the west end of the chapel appeared to have been unfinished, leading to the speculation the much larger religious structure was never completed due to a lack of funding. If William Sinclair did indeed write the word "chapel" instead of "effigy" then the debate over whether he intended to build a cathedral, or a chapel is ended.

The second important point is in this part of Harkin's entry: "*...to honor my grandfather and the natives and knights who gave their lives to the cause of the brothers.*" Diana's translation of the same passage is different: "*...to honor my*

A drone's eye view of Rosslyn Chapel taken looking from the east in 2022. (Wolter, 2022)

grandfather and the Knights who risked their lives for the cause of the brethren." The notable difference is the mention of "natives...who gave their lives" in Sister Harkin's translation which is not in Diana's. Nowhere in Diana's translated journal entries is there mention of any natives dying, let alone while guarding the treasures left behind by Earl Henry. However, in Donald Ruh's five encrypted messages concerning the underground project on what would become known as Oak Island he received in 2023, in message #5 we learn that twenty-one people died, "*XXI* [21] *have died on the project.*" We also learn in the same message at least one of those who perished was a Sakonet indigenous person who was killed when volatile gas exploded underground in Well #1.

> *Well I* [1] *finds I* [1] *natural cavity in soft rock I IV O* [140] *feet down a Sakonet goes down with a lamp. There is a loud noise. Gas, he was killed and is in pieces.*

The Sakonet are an indigenous tribe within the territory of the Wampanoag that now includes parts of Massachusetts and Rhode Island.

These facts are extremely important in providing independent corroboration supporting the veracity of both documents. Critics trying to accuse Don and Diana of conspiring together will be stymied because

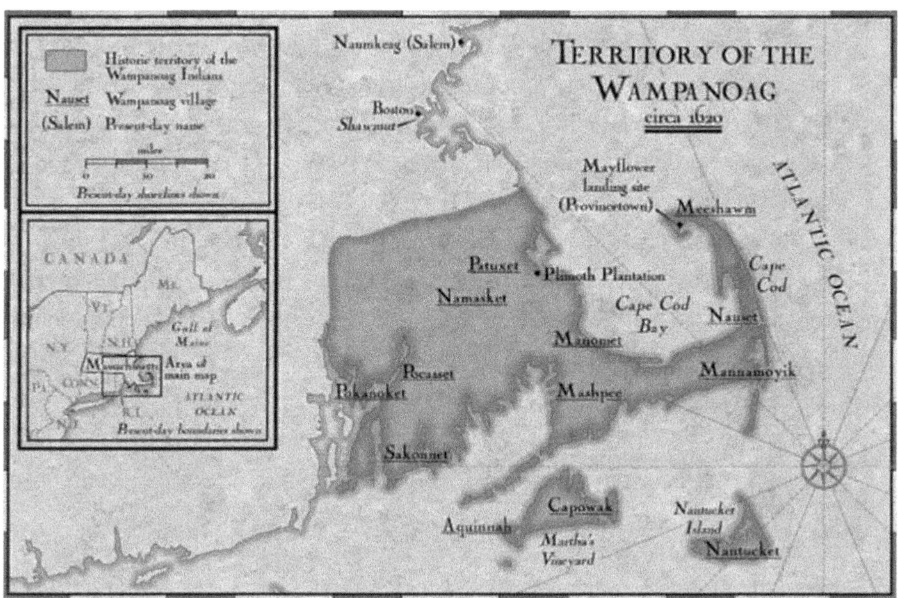

This map shows the tribes within the Wampanoag nation at the beginning of the seventeenth century. The Sakonnet (Sakonet) tribe's territory included the eastern half of Narragansett Bay and Aquidneck Island where the Newport Tower stands to this day. (Internet)

Diana received the sister Harkin copy of the translated journals in July of 2021, while the Cremona Document material concerning the activities on Oak Island came forward in February of 2023.

Book 6

William "The Waster" Sinclair

1430-1487

March 19, 1458

We leave this day to visit Iceland and the Western Lands at my father's insistence. He has given me strict instructions to find the markers left behind and has given me a map of the places to visit. I travel with 10 Brethren and a crew of 20. We hope to bring home fish from the Western Lands and furs for the upcoming winter.

Today we go to Iceland and the western lands as demanded by my father. He has written specific instructions to locate the markers left behind and a map of the places to visit. We have a crew of 20 and 10 brother Knights. We will bring fish and furs home with us for next winter.

Forgive me if I seem to dwell on the importance of the sacred numbers of the Fibonacci sequence we find so often associated with Templarism and Freemasonry, but the "Waster" doesn't seem to understand what other generations of Sinclairs did. One could argue his apparent lack of understanding and appreciation of the secrets and mysteries was due in part to his reported selfish and greedy personality. This could account, at least in part, for he and his son's lack of success in the Western Lands and with the indigenous people.

August 6, 1458

We have returned from the Western Lands. All is secure. We met no natives but are aware they were watching. I bring home a white deer pelt for my wife Christian. I hope she will be pleased.

We return from the west. Everything is safe. I bring home a white deer skin for Christian my wife. I hope she will like it.

BOOK 7

HENRY SINCLAIR

(1459-1513)

June 13, 1489

King James IV has been crowned and I now have time to fulfill my family's obligation to protect the Templar treasure. My father has told me much about the treasure and I hope to bring part of it back to help enlarge our holdings in Midlothian and Orkney.

King James the fourth is now king and now I have time to complete my family promise to protect the treasure of the Templars. My father told me a lot about the treasure, and I want to bring some back to make our lands bigger in Orkney and Scotland.

August 18, 1489

We have arrived in the Western Lands but have been driven from the shores by the natives. I am unable to find the markers given to me by my father. We must return at another time.

We were driven from the shores when we arrived. We may be lost as I cannot find any of the markers given by my father. We will come another year.

7

Journals of David, John, David, James, James, David, James, and David Wemyss:

Books 8 through 15

Book 8

The Journal of Earl David Wemyss

1494-1544

Translated from Latin

October 30, 1518

Diana Muir's Translation (italic): *Since Earl Henry's death at Flodden Field my wife, Katherine has feared for the safety of the journals which have been handed/inherited through her family. She claims her father and brother were planning on retrieving the treasure for their own use and knows that her grandfather's covenant with God should be honored. She has given me the journals which she found in the vault and asked me to read them. She fears if the journals go to her brothers that their value and the treasure they protect will be lost forever. She trusts the brethren and I do what her grandfather requested and protect the Covenant and treasure which was taken to the Western Lands long ago. I begin to plan my trip to the Western Lands and* *have asked 12 of the brethren to travel with me. In order to be best prepared I have read through the journals of Earl Henry, 1st Earl of Orkney, and am amazed that such secrets have been kept. I feel blessed and honored to be given this responsibility and consider the Covenant to now be my own.*

Sister Harkin's Translation (plain): After Earl Henry died at Flodden Field Katherine my wife fears for the safety of the books her family has inherited though her family. She overheard her father and brother who planned to get the Templar treasure for themselves. She knew her covenant with God should be kept. Katherine has found the books in the scriptorium[43] and has told me to read them. If the books go to her brothers, she is afraid the Templar treasure they protect will be gone always. She trusts me and the brothers to honor her grandfather and to always protect the treasure taken to the western lands long ago. I start to plan a trip to the lands in the west and have asked 12 of the brothers to accompany me. I have read the books of Earl Henry the first Earl of Orkney to prepare myself and are astounded at the secrets they hold. I feel honored and blessed to be given this Covenant which I now think of as my own."

Author's Commentary (shaded box): It is ironic the journals transferred from the Sinclairs to the Wemyss clan via Katherine Sinclair, as if a Goddess were watching over the Covenant literally as much as she did spiritually.

May 15, 1520

We leave in the morrow for the Western Lands. Twelve of the brethren travel with me aboard the Elizabeth. We plan to visit Iceland and Groenland to bring back furs and corn. I have the map of Captain Zenn [Zeno?] *and believe I understand their significance. I hope to be able to find the markers and make contact with the Native people to request their help.*

We leave tomorrow for the western lands. Twelve of the brothers travel on the *Elizabeth* of with me. We will visit Iceland and Greenland to bring home furs and maize. I have the map Captain Zenn [Zeno?] and know their worth. I hope to make contact with the local people and to request their assistance to find the markers.

43. Indeed, there was a scriptorium at Roslin Castle at the time mentioned in the journals. https://en.wikipedia.org/wiki/Roslin_Castle#:~:text=The%20castle%20contained%20a%20scriptorium,a%20window%20by%20his%20chaplain.

October 3, 1520

We have returned from the Western Lands without incident. The natives were friendly and helpful and took us to the sites to show that they have fulfilled their promise of protection to their and my ancestors and the Great Goddess. We have shared stories, food, and smoke and return to Scotland knowing that all is safe and undisturbed.

We have returned from the western lands without problems. The natives were friendly and helped to take us to the places we sought to show us they had done their promise of protection to their ancestors and mine and to the Great Goddess. We have shared meals, smoke, and stories of Earl Henry. We know all is undisturbed and safe and return to Scotland.

Things seem to have been back on track with the Covenant now that the obligation was given to people who were committed to their vows.

Book 9

Journal of John Wemyss

1514 - 1571

Translated from Latin

March 6, 1543

Completed visit to Western Lands. None has changed.

We have completed our visit to the western lands. Nothing has changed.

Book 10

Journal of David Wemyss

(1535 -1595)

Translated from Latin

May 5, 1565

Events in Scotland have precluded my visiting the Western Lands. I hope that Holy Father and my father will forgive me.

Events in Scotland prevent me from visiting the western lands. May Holy Father and my father forgive me.

This is only the second of fifteen generations of Sinclairs and Wemyss not to make the voyage to the Western Lands to check on the treasures. Thirteen out of fifteen generations completing their obligation at these points in history is an amazing accomplishment.

BOOK II

JOURNAL OF JAMES WEMYSS

1560 - 1640

TRANSLATED FROM LATIN

October 18, 1585

Lord Ruthven's affair has now been concluded and with my father I have visited and returned from a visit to the Western Lands. In an effort to escape the aftermath of Lord Ruthven's treachery we traveled with 11 brethren to ascertain the safety of the treasure which Earl Henry, 1st Earl of Orkney removed from Scotland in 1398. We have concluded our part of the Covenant, and we begin to make plans to transfer the rest of the treasure to the Western Lands before the King confiscates the treasure in the name of England.

Lord Ruthven's trial has finished, and my father and I have gone and returned from a visit to the western lands. It is an effort to get away from Lord Ruthven's treason and so we travel with 11 brothers to decide the safety of the treasure that Earl Henry, first Earl of Orkney took from Scotland in 1398. We finished our duty to the Covenant and start to make plans to remove the rest of the treasure to the western Lands before the English King takes the treasure as his own.

The key players in the Ruthvin Affair included William Ruthvin, (**left**) the First Earl of Gowen, who kidnapped King James VI in 1582, (**middle**). James VI was the son of Mary Queen of Scots (**right**). (Internet/Internet/Internet)

The "Lord Ruthven Affair" was an effort to overthrow the Catholic influence of King James VI (James Charles Stuart, 1566 - 1625), led by William Ruthvin, the 1st Earl of Gowen, who kidnapped the fifteen-year-old king in August of 1582. The kidnapping became known as the "Raid of Ruthvin", but it was short-lived as the king escaped ten months later.[44] Ruthvin was eventually captured, tried, and convicted of treason and sorcery—for good measure to further demonize him—and then beheaded in May of 1584. The story of King James VI— his mother was Mary Queen of Scots—and the political intrigue and scandalous behavior of the key players is fascinating and worth delving into. Prominent people like James Wemyss would have been aware of the events surrounding the entire Ruthvin Affair. It fits that the political fallout at the highest levels of leadership involving the then king of England and Scotland affected the secret efforts of those involved in the Covenant. Once the political situation settled down, the mission of moving the second treasure was then back on track. An interesting side-note is the Ruthvin Affair served, in part, as Shakespeare's inspiration for the play *MacBeth*.

Here we also see a return to the use of sacred numbers. This time in the number of men who traveled to the Western Lands to check on the treasures. James Wemyss, his father David, and 11 brethren make a total of 13, the sacred number of the Goddess.

44. https://en.wikipedia.org/wiki/William_Ruthven,_1st_Earl_of_Gowrie

May 4, 1617

This day we met at Gray's Inn in London with Sir Francis Bacon to discuss the movement of the remaining treasure to the western banks. We meet again in three months' time.

Today we met at Gray's Inn in London with Sir Francis Bacon to talk about moving the rest of the treasure to the western lands. We will meet again in 3 months' time.

The name Francis Bacon (1561-1626) jumped off the page when I first read it, but upon reflection I shouldn't have been surprised.[45] Bacon was a British author, philosopher, and statesman who wrote a famous treatise of a scientific utopian society that was published a year after his death, titled *The New Atlantis*.[46] It is interesting he wrote the fictional work only three years before his name first appears in James Wemyss journal in 1617. Many scholars attribute Bacon's work as frivolous musings of a man who wished humanity could live in a prosperous society where individual rights and equality were paramount to everyone. Little did they know he was a key player in his time with the mission of the Covenant. Instead of being a fictional vision, *The New Atlantis* was the template for what the "Free Templar State" would look like when it came time to recover the treasures and put the plan into action. Little did he know, the plan would begin to come to fruition 145 years after his death, and the second treasure was still decades from making its way to the Western Lands.

September 22, 1621

We met once again with Sir Francis Bacon. We have decided upon a plan to move the rest of the treasure and to mark its presence. We hope to move soon.

Once again, we met with Sir Francis Bacon. We have a plan to move the treasure and to mark its place.

December 30, 1625

45. https://www.britannica.com/biography/Francis-Bacon-Viscount-Saint-Alban

46. https://www.gutenberg.org/files/2434/2434-h/2434-h.htm

Francis Bacon (1561-1626) wrote a novel that told of a utopian society he dreamed of for humanity called, The New Atlantis. The book was published a year after the death of the man and no one knew how intimately involved he was in founding the real New Atlantis that would come to fruition 145 years after his passing. (Internet)

My brother John has been made Baronet of Nova Scotia. Our plans move forward.

John my brother has been made Baronet of Nova Scotia. Our plan moves forward.

April 16, 1626

We meet once again with Sir Francis Bacon, William Cranborne, and Peter Lely at Gray's Inn in London. Our plans are complete.

We met once again with Sir Francis Bacon, William Cranborne, and Peter Lely at Gray's Inn in London. Our plans are complete.

James Weems met with important people who were obviously in on the Covenant and plans to transfer more treasure to North America. Beyond Bacon, Sir Peter Lely (1618 -1680) was a Dutch painter and draughtsman who spent most of his career in England. Francis Bacon often held meetings at Gray's Inn, one of the four Inns of Court (professional associations for barristers and judges) in London. To practice law as a barrister (lawyer) in England and Wales, an individual must belong to one of these inns.

April 22, 1626

King Charles has been crowned at Westminster Abbey and Scotland is once again at peace. We are now able to put our plans in motion.

King Charles has been crowned at Westminster Abbey and it is peace in Scotland. We can put our plans in action now.

May 1, 1627

I have met with the brethren, and we have agreed on the method of transferring the treasure from the Abbey. We shall use the Wemyss fleet and take 3 ships but first we must visit Laon. Our Brethren there await us.

The brethren have met and agree on how to move the treasure from the Abbey. We will use the Wemyss fleet and take 3 boats after we visit Laon. Our brothers there wait for us.

This entry just begs for speculation, and I am happy to oblige. Keep in mind, this is a new batch of treasure we are given little information about. Further, we are not given information about what abbey James is referring to. Based upon the pervasive legends of treasure hidden beneath Kilwinning, our speculation will make that one assumption. James likely wrote this entry from Wemyss property on the northern coast of the Firth of Forth. If so, then the 3 ships mentioned must have traveled down the east coast of England to the northwestern coast of France to travel overland to Laon just west of the city of Reims. From there they must have returned to their ships and then followed a similar route the Templars followed from LaRochelle to the Firth of Clyde and docked the ships near Kilwinning. Once loaded with treasure, those ships must have sailed around the northern part of Scotland back to the Firth of Forth and hid the treasures in the Wemyss Caves. When looking at a map of Scotland, it would have made much more sense to travel overland to Wemyss Caves, but something must have made that logical route untenable and forced them to sail around the dangerous waters of Northern Scotland. The following entries confirm that the risky mission to move the treasures was successful.

September 22, 1627

"The Behumet and remaining gold from Laon has been placed in the Cave of Thieves where we can protect and care for it. There it will remain until the proper time when we can begin our voyage to the Western Lands. We await word from our brethren who have gone to the Western Lands to prepare a place and are anxious for their return. Scotland once again is prey to English raids, and we fear inspection.

The remaining gold from Laon and Behemoth treasure have been stored in the Cave of Thieves where we can protect and take care of it. It will remain there until the time we start our voyage to the western lands. We wait for word from our brothers who have gone to the western lands to prepare a place. We are impatient for their return. The English once again raid Scotland and we worry about discovery.

This is the first mention of a mysterious item called the "Behumet." What exactly that is remains unclear. However, with knowledge of the Templar activities after the capture of Jerusalem in 1118, and specifically their actions inside the Talpiot tomb, we have a clue to what the Bahumet might be.

The Talpiot tomb was discovered in southern Jerusalem in 1980 during blasting a hillside in preparation for the foundation of an apartment building. Ten ossuaries were found inside the tunnels of the burial chamber. Seven were inscribed with names, six in Aramaic and one in Greek. All seven names correspond to members of the first century royal family, including "Jesus, son of Joseph" and "Mariamene the Mara", aka Jesus and Mary Magdalene. This highly controversial discovery shook the world with implications that still reverberate nearly half a century later.

In *Akhenaten to the Founding Fathers*, published in 2013, I explained how the three skulls found on the floor of the burial chamber of the tomb were placed in the south, west, and eastern quadrants consistent with where the three highest officers sit in a Masonic lodge and a Templar Commandery. I claimed then, and still believe, this was a telltale sign of the Knights Templar having entered the tomb after capturing Jerusalem circa 1118, when they also entered a different first century underground ritual chamber that contained four ossuaries covered in lambskin. Other items included scrolls, five metal devices, gold, and also the bones "of a man whose head had been severed with a large heavy axe" and inscribed with the name "Yon." This person was John the Baptist, and the Templar Knights–including the first Grand Master, Hugh de Payans–"*...bagged the bones.*"[47]

I mention this because, like the ritual chamber the Templars found beneath the south wall of the Temple in Jerusalem where they removed the bones of John the Baptist, the ossuaries found inside the Talpiot tomb only contained fragments. These bones had also been collected by the Templars, as they were their biological ancestors. The bones also served as leverage against the Roman Catholic Church, but that is another story for a different day.

So is the Bahumet the bones–or more specifically, the skull–of one of the Royal Family? Could the Bahumet be the skull of Jesus, or Mary Magdalene? There are plenty of reasons to believe this is true. This and subsequent entries leave no doubt of the importance of the Bahumet, and the smart money would be on one of these relics. My money is on either Jesus, or most likely, Mary Magdalene. Just saying...

July 22, 1628

Word has finally arrived from our brethren who have traveled to the Western Lands. They have found a spot of perfection for the Behumet and the treasure but say that Nova Scotia [Acadia] *is now overrun with French and the English. They were forced to go far inland and have left behind eight markers which when followed exactly lead to a wild and unruly land where the natives have shown them great caves in which to hold the treasure. I fear that I am now too old and infirm to assist with moving the treasure and have left the task to my grandson David.*

I have told him the stories of our ancestors both Sinclair and Wemyss

47. Wolter, *Akhenaten to the Founding Fathers*, Page 181, 2019.

and their long involvement with the Templars and the voyages that our long-ago ancestors made to Groenland and the Western Lands. He is still young but understands the importance of reverence and secrecy concerning the treasure. He has been taught well by the brethren and has committed himself to visiting the Western Lands to further our goal of moving the rest of the treasure away from the hands of the English. As soon as his marriage contract is concluded, and he is duly married and leaves an heir he will continue the Covenant.

Our brethren who went to the western lands have finally sent word. They have found the perfect place for the Behumet treasure but say the French have taken over Nova Scotia and the English. They needed to go inland far and have left 8 markers behind that when followed lead to a wild and ----- land where the Indians have showed them grand caves to hold the treasure. I think I am too old and sick to help move the treasure, so I leave the job my grandchild David.

I have told him the stories of our grandfathers both Sinclair and Wemyss and their work with the Templars and the voyages that our distant relatives made to Greenland and the western lands. He is still young but understands the reverence and sanctity of the treasure. The brothers have taught him well and [he] has made a commitment to visit the western lands with the goal of moving the remaining treasure away from English hands. As soon as his marriage contract is done and his is married and has a son he will go on with the Covenant.

Sacred numbers appear again in the form of eight markers leading to what the brethren believed was the "spot of perfection for the Bahumet." Subsequent entries reveal the eight markers leading to the "...wild and unruly land..." where the treasures were hidden.

May 1, 1635

I leave this morrow to visit the Western Lands with my grandson David of Wemyss. I pray that Holy Father and the Holy Goddess will strengthen me and allow me to pass this task to my grandson. We must find the first of the markers left behind by Sir Duncan and secure the help of the Ahherah. They worship the Great Goddess and have been allies of the Covenant for over two hundred years.

Tomorrow, I leave to visit the western Lands with my grandson David of Wemyss. I ask the Holy Father and Holy Goddess to keep me strong so I can pass the job to my grandson. First, we must find the markers left behind by Sir Duncan and ask for help of the Aherrah. They worship the Great Goddess and have been friends of the Covenant for more than 200 years.

Here we are reminded of the "Ahherah/Aherrah"—what the indigenous people in North America were called then—and of their assistance in guarding the treasures for their brothers at this point for 200 years.

BOOK 12

JOURNAL OF JAMES WEMYSS

1590 - 1649

TRANSLATED FROM LATIN

April 18, 1640

My father James of Wemyss has died this day and has left me the obligation of fulfilling the Covenant of the brethren. I once visited the Western Lands thirty years ago but know that my time has passed to complete the Covenant. I must pass the task and the journals of our forefathers to my son David who is aware of the sanctity of our mission. He must ally with the Earl of Murkle to complete this task. Only together can the Sinclair and the Wemyss family please Heavenly Father and Heavenly Mother.

My father James of Wemyss has died today [and] left the job of fulfilling the brothers Covenant. I once visited 30 years ago to the Western Lands, but I know my time has passed to complete the Covenant. I am forced to pass the books of our ancestors and the task to my son David. He must alliance with the Earl of Murkle to complete the task. Together the Sinclair family and the Wemyss family can please Holy Father and Holy Mother."

Book 13

Journal of David Wemyss

1610 - 1679

Translated from Latin

April 20, 1640

My father has passed to me the journals of our forefathers and the obligation to complete the Covenant of the brethren who guard the Templar Treasure and the Behumet. I pray that I am worthy and begin to read the journals.

The books of our ancestors have been passed to me by my father and the obligation to finish the Covenant of the brethren who guard the Templar treasure in the Western Lands. I hope that I am worthy and have begun to read the journals.

August 3, 1640

I have met this day with the Earl of Murkle and we have discussed the journals which were passed to me. He is unhappy that the Wemyss family has continued the legacy and wishes to have the legacy and responsibility returned to the Sinclairs. I have refused, stating that my grandmother Katherine Sinclair knew of the sanctity of the trust given to us and had passed the legacy to us by necessity. He refuses to help me in my journey. I fear that the animosity will make this mission impossible and must let it lie fallow for a time.

I met with the Earl of Murkle today and we have talked about the journals. He is very unhappy that the legacy was passed to the Wemyss family and wants it returned to the Sinclairs. I refused, saying my grandmother Katherine Sinclair knew of the sanctity of the obligation given to us and by necessity passed to our family. He has refused to help with our journey. I feel his anger makes this mission not possible and I must let it alone for some time.

At this point in the Darren Weems copy there are what appear to be two pages with a list of names in alphabetical order that is titled, "Stayed behind 1395, Knight with Sir Dennison."

Arbia (West)
Ardenbourg
Bethune (West)
Biersi
Brabant
Braybrooke
Brennan (West)
Bueria
Burges
Cadeleta (West)
Caestree
Canipenets
Candlebeer (West)
Capons
Clouttying
De Champagne
de Tiny
de Blaise (West)
de Blaise (West)
Denis
Dennison

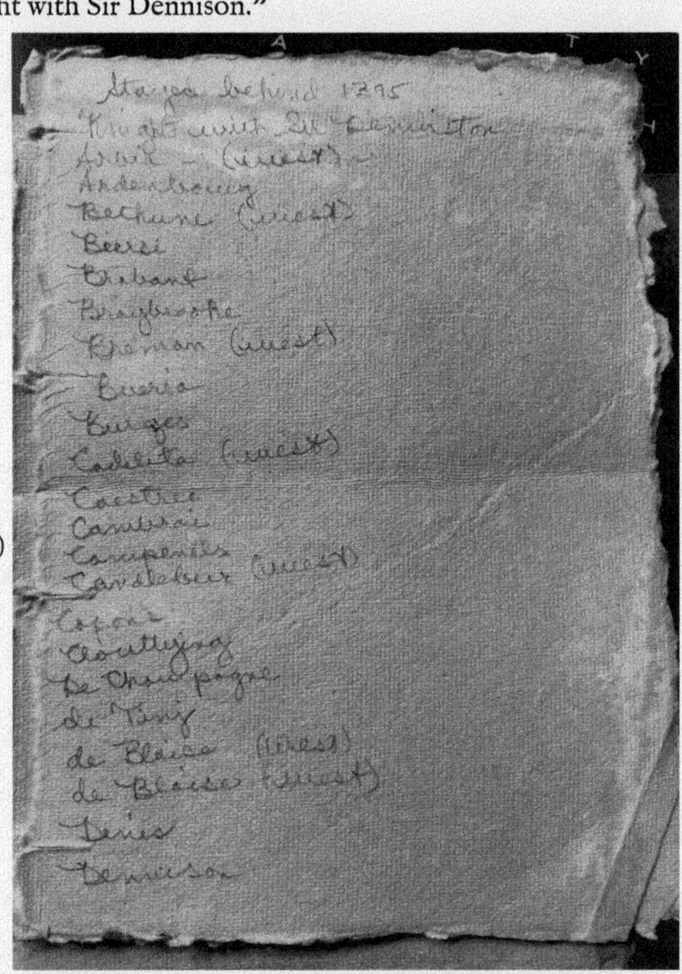

There were two pages loose in the Darren Wemyss copy after the entry of August 3, 1640 that had a list of sixty-four names of the men who stayed behind in 1395. The heading reads, "Knights with Sir Dennison." Presumably the names with "west" to the right were those men who traveled west to explore the New World. (Wolter, 2016)

de Ponthieu
de Roet
Destpal
Doval
Flamiungi
Fuerno
Genieffe (West)
Gerieffre (West)
Ghent
Izenberg
Laningi
Malie
Marion
Merritt (West)
Navarre
Nevers
Nivelles
Olglivie (West)
Perbone
Podicbrand

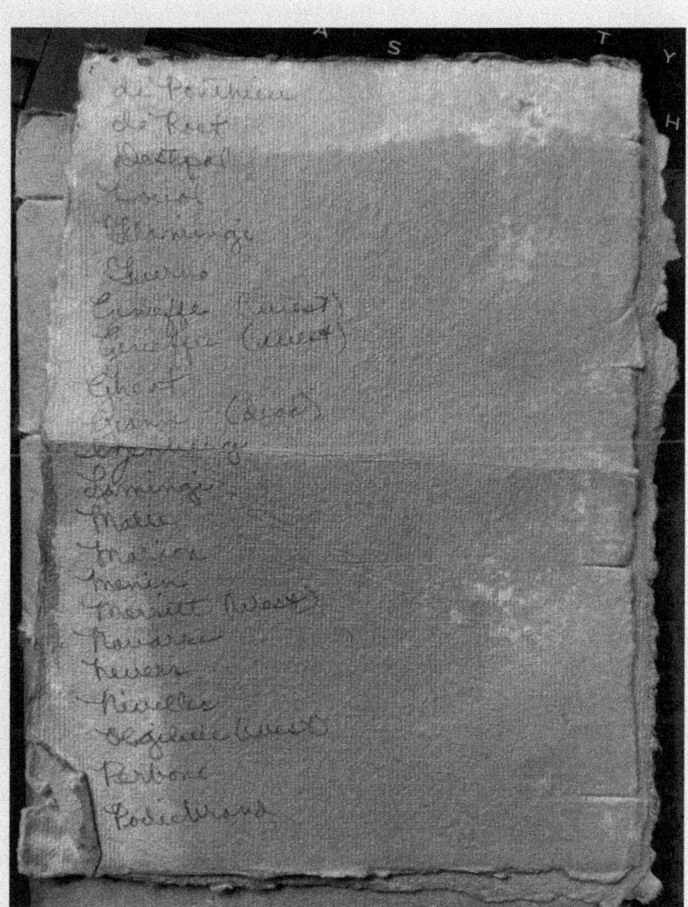

The back of the first page contained twenty-two names with four of the men listed as having traveled west. Curiously, the name Gunn has the word "dead" next to it. One of the Templar knights listed on the *Perequin* ship's list was James Gunn. It's interesting he is listed as dead, as there is a pervasive legend in Westford, Massachusetts that a carving of a sword on a glacial outcrop in the town was made to honor the fallen knight James Gunn. (Wolter, 2016)

Reppe
Sacke
Shirley
Slype
St. Verde
Templemars (West)
Templemars M.
Valara
Varsenacre
Veroequi (West)
Von Sacke
Von Hoyen
Von Part
Von Schaepfer
Von Schudi (West)
Von Seedorf
Von Windegg
Wingfield
Ypres
Zocke

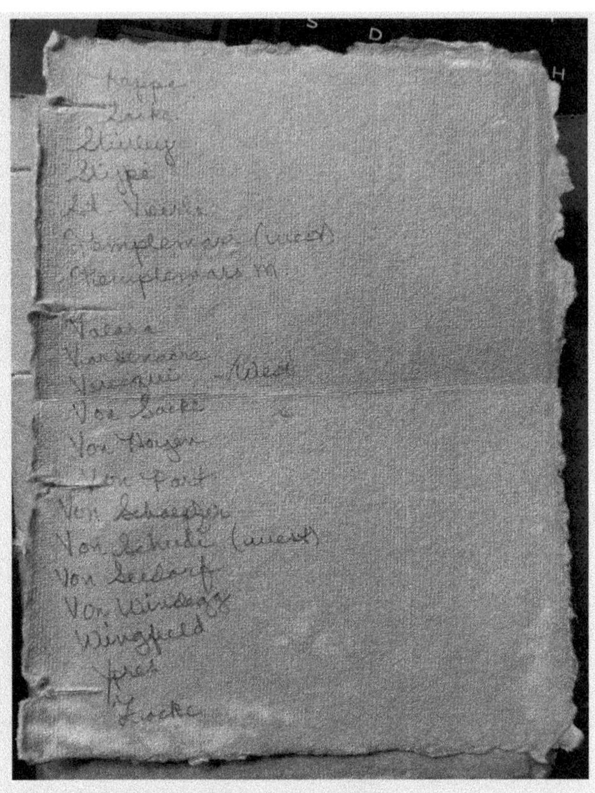

The second page contains twenty names with "west" following three of them, making a total of fourteen men who apparently traveled west. (Wolter, 2016)

Sister Harkin's note to James at the end of the journals she translated:

Dearest James,

I am being sent to Philadelphia and must say goodbye to you, my friend. You have brought me back memories of home and I will miss your lively conversation. I wish I had time to tell you of the stories of Templar treasure beneath the altar at St. Antonies. Your story is amazing and God has told me it is true. I only translated that which was not in English. You should be able to read the more recent ones. I have left the originals in the church library for you. May God bless you and your family.

Agnes

This is where the Sister Harkin translations end and begs the question why she did not translate the lengthy journal entries of James Wemyss which, according to Diana Muir's copy of the journals, were written in Old English. It's hard to say what happened but it is possible that the book was missing, or she ran out of time since this book's entries are lengthy and would have taken significant time to translate and she knew she was leaving. Regardless, we have Diana's copy to work with and, despite the two Latin versions being markedly different, the information conveyed is essentially the same.

I also find it interesting that in her final entry in her personal journal on May 30, 1885 she was skeptical of the stories told in the Sinclair/Wemyss journal. However, in her note to Reverand Weems she wrote she believed the stories were true. At this point we will never know, but her apparent uncertainty is something myself and many others who have read the journals have felt.

Book 14

Journal of James Wemyss
1633 - 1714

Translated from Old English

December 24, 1663

My father has gifted me with the responsibility of fulfilling the family promise and the Covenant of the twelve families and the brethren. I am aghast at the responsibility and must ponder this further. I have read the journals of my forefathers and knew nothing of the Covenant until now. Scotland has been at the mercy of treachery and greed and the longer the treasure remains in Scotland the greater the fear that it will be lost. I must discuss this with my father and the brethren to determine the best course of action to take.

February 10, 1665

A female child named Anne has been born and will someday take her place as queen. I have made a promise to my father to complete the Covenant and must now follow through with the plans that were made years before. I must gather together crew and Brethren to make this possible this coming spring. The longer we wait the greater the danger.

April 25, 1665

The weather is fine, and the ships have been provisioned. Crews with sailing and mining experience have been assembled and we leave tomorrow for the western coast of Scotland to remove the artifacts and gold still resident at the Abbey. We have already secured the Behumet and gold from the Cave of Thieves on board the lead ship the Balfour to be protected by the 12 Brethren aboard. Once we leave the shores of Scotland, we will visit Greenland for fresh water and hope to reach Nova Scotia by the 1st of June.

This entry gives a strong clue as to which abbey the treasure was stored at by saying, "... for the western coast of Scotland ...". Kilwinning is on the west coast of Scotland and has pervasive legends of treasure being stored there.

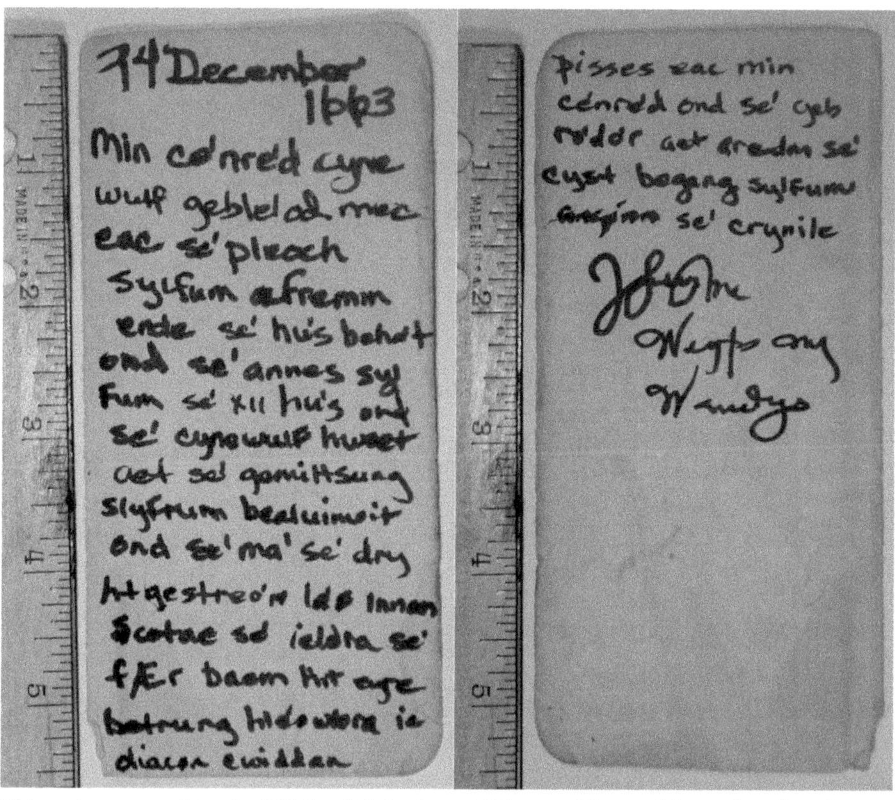

This entry was written in Old English by James Wemyss. He would travel to the Western Lands two years later, bringing more treasure from Scotland and hiding it along the St. Lawrence River, in the Great Lakes region, and beyond. (Wolter. 2018)

May 28, 1665

We have arrived at the Isle of the White Stag and have been greeted by friendly natives who say they have been waiting for us for many years. They say that Nova Scotia is now crowded with Europeans, and they have feared for our return and our safety. We shared a meal with them and smoke the pipe to send our prayers to heaven. I have explained that we have not time to visit the islands where the treasure has been stored previously as we have a great mission to perform. They assure me that the sites are well protected and have not been disturbed.

We further explain that we have new cargo that we must protect and find a safe place for. We must first find latitude 49.88 to the north on the island which was granted to Sir John of Wemyss, Baron of Nova Scotia. We make plans to leave in the morning.

The leader of the Ahherah have asked us to take a spirit woman named Kimi Sokanon with us to aid if we should encounter other natives. She says she is a descendant of a Knights Templar named Cun'Ham. She also speaks Latin and knows the native people and their customs well. She wears a white robe made of the sacred white deer skin and is a comely woman. We agreed to return her to the Isle of the White Stag prior to our return and I give her my cabin on the Balfour as her own. We leave in the morrow with their blessing and prayers.

The island to the north referenced here is Anticosti Island, which is located at the mouth of the Great River, now called the St. Lawrence River.

The mention of Kimi Sokanon being a descendant of a Templar Knight named Cun' Ham–most likely the name Cunningham–is significant but unsurprising and brings to mind another more famous descendant of a Templar Knight much better known to historians. A certain Templar tradition says the young woman Lewis and Clark met in the winter of 1803 was also the descendant of an indigenous woman and Templar Knight from prior to 1700. Her name was Sacajawea, and she helped the famous explorers survive their first winter and successfully travel to the west coast of North America and return.

May 31, 1665

We have arrived at the island which was granted to Sir James and have found a small settlement of Europeans on the eastern shore. We will begin our search on the western shore as instructed by my grandfather.

June 1, 1665

We have found the first marker on a large boulder about 30 feet above the high tide line. It has been marked with the star of the Great Goddess and the alignment to the horizon given by the shadow at noon clearly gives us our next direction. We have calculated the destination to be at 48.39 latitude to the southwest through a large river that is engraved on the rock. We have dug a hole approximately 2 yards deep and have left a small portion of our treasure as instructed. We move on to the next marker.

The 8-pointed star of the Great Goddess is also called the Star of Venus with its eight points radiating from a central focus where a rounded triangular hole was cut into the rock using a straight chisel and hammer. Once cut, a rod is placed into the hole creating a plinth that casts a shadow that points in the direction to travel at a designated time of the day. Since the James Wemyss party was traveling west, the time of day to cast a shadow in that direction would have to be in the morning.

We have already seen the Templars carving a map of the Merrimac River and Lake Winnipesaukee at Tyngsboro, Massachusetts, and here is evidence consistent with the practice.

Inset: The eight-pointed Star of Venus was a Templar symbol often carved into rock to mark important sites. Often a stone hole was cut into the center so a rod or stick could be inserted to cast a shadow as a directional indicator at a designated time(s) of the day. (Internet)

Carved into the bedrock inside the fortification at Hammershus Castle on the Island of Bornholm, is a compass with the four cardinal points and a stone hole at the center. Similar to the Star of Venus carvings Earl Henry Sinclair's men carved in North America, this one was likely used to tell time. (Wolter, 2008)

June 2, 1665

Before traveling down the Great River towards our next destination we must first contact Phillipe Mius d'Entremont and Michel Dupuis of Port Royal. We will ask that they accompany us on our journey as they represent the brethren here in Nova Scotia. Their assistance will be greatly appreciated.

June 3, 1665

The Brethren of Port Royal have joined us and report that they also have been watching the islands in Nova Scotia where previous cargo has been buried. All is safe and secure, and we begin our journey down the river.

June 4, 1665

We have arrived at a small island in the midst of a great river at 48.39 degrees latitude. The marker has been found in the center of the island, but we leave no treasure as we fear the island will be engulfed at high tide. The weather has been treacherous, and we decide to spend the next day waiting for the storm to abate. Even though the marker is clearly marked the stormy weather does not allow us to see the shadow cast by the marking stick for an astronomic alignment. We must wait for a brighter day in order to determine the latitude of our next destination which lies further down the great river.

June 5, 1665

The sun has shown her favor upon us, and we have determined our next destination to be 47.41 latitude. We leave directly.

June 6, 1665

We have arrived at the next destination of 47.41 degrees latitude and discovered another small island which is uninhabited. We have located the marker on the northern shore of the island which shows our next destination to be at 44.44 inland to the northwest. The engraving on the boulder gives us the route to take and we leave a small portion of the treasure here at a depth of 2 yards. Before we leave, we bless this spot and request Heavenly Father and the Great Goddess to watch over it until our return. Twenty men will travel inland to find the next marker while the rest wait along the shore with the ships. Kimi will accompany us inland.

June 9, 1665

We have found the next marker, more by accident than by design and see clearly that our destination will be extremely difficult to reach. The shadow of the marking stick shown by the star of the Great Goddess sends us in the southward direction. An engraving on the boulder shows a high mountain top near a river that travels south at 44.27 degrees latitude. We must plan carefully and have decided to take only two of the ships inland and to leave their cargo there as appropriate. As my grandfather requested, we have left a small portion of our treasure here for the use of our brethren who will follow. We form a triangle and bless this place asking for fortitude and health to reach our next destination. We leave in the morning for the river and hope that our brethren are well during our absence. Kimi will accompany us to the next marker as she says her ancestor Cun'Ham once visited the sacred mountain where a small village of ancestors was located.

June 12, 1665

With the help of the morning star and bright sunlight we have located the correct latitude and anticipate a difficult climb up the mountain to the east. We must stay as close to the correct latitude of 44.27 as possible in order to reach our goal.

The morning star mentioned here is the planet Venus.

June 13, 1665

We have found the marker about three-quarters of the way up the mountain not far from the mountain top. There is a large cave nearby where the light of the morning sun illuminates the western facing entrance. We decided to leave 1/3 of the remaining treasure there in the cave. To do so we must return down the mountain and portage the treasure to this spot. Therefore, we decided only to bring gold and silver to the top. We leave behind a cross made of stones and have covered the cave's entrance with a large boulder.

There is evidence of a small village that once existed on the top of the sacred mountain. It appears to have been abandoned many years ago although there are several smaller caves that hold bones and artifacts belonging to the one-time inhabitants. One cave holds the bones of a tall warrior with a sword nearby. The hilt of the decaying sword identifies him as coming from Normandy centuries ago. Kimi tells us that the ancestors moved westward after the arrival of European settlers to the east. They believed that the mountain was close to God and the Goddess and had lived here for many years before departing. It was from them that they learned the language of Latin and the rituals they now practice honoring the Great Goddess.

It is unclear which mountain is being referred to here. The only thought that comes to mind is Owl's Head Mountain near Stanstead, Quebec, Canada. There is a Golden Rule #5 Masonic Lodge that meets there, and I've heard there is a cave there where solstice rituals take place. It's possible there is knowledge passed down through Masonic circles of treasure being left there, but it's all speculation at this point. I must put Owl's Head on my bucket list.

Leaving a cross of stones as a marker is consistent with tradition. I am curious if the cross is still there, and if it was a Christian cross or a Templar cross, with all arms of the same length.

In today's world the Sword of Normandy refers to Sword Beach in Normandy in Nazi-occupied France, where assaults against the Germans took place in 1944 during World War II. It is kind of ironic for a sword made in Normandy to have been found inside a cave on the mountain where indigenous people lived. It could very well have belonged to a Templar knight who came over with Earl Henry two-plus centuries earlier, or perhaps later. It is hard to say with such sketchy information.

June 17, 1665

We have arrived back at the great river and rejoin our comrades and the other five ships. Now that three of the ships have no cargo, we ask them to return to the island given to Sir John of Wemyss, Baron of Nova Scotia to await us there. It may be as long as 3 months, but they have ample supplies to await our return and have been instructed to fill their cargo hold with the great cod fish of the northern seas.

June 18, 1665

According to the marker left on the sacred mountain our next destination is 45.686 degrees latitude. My grandfather has told me it is located at the edge of one of the great inner seas. The weather is once again fair, and we take great joy in viewing the new land to the north and to the south. Although we have seen natives on the shore, they have not approached us and seem preoccupied with their fishing in the inner sea.

As we approached the end of the second inner sea, we discovered we can go no further. Kimi tells us we must go back and take a small river to the north that will allow us to pass the great rocks and waterfall. This will lengthen our trip, but it is the only way we can proceed.

The "...edge of one of the great inner seas..." must be the site of Eagle Island in Sodus Bay where John Weems Jr. would travel to in 1770, and where I paddled across the bay to the same island in 2018. I scoured the undeveloped center portion of the island for three hours and found nothing.

The "small river" that allowed travelers to bypass Lake Erie and Niagara Falls was the Ottawa River, long known by the indigenous people to bring travelers going west to the top of Lake Huron and what is now Sault Ste. Marie. From there, travelers have the option of both Lakes Michigan and Superior and the gateway to the center of the continent with routes to the Great West.

June 23, 1665

We have arrived at the third inner sea and continue our journey to 45.686 degrees latitude. The weather is once again stormy, and we travel slowly towards our destination praying to God for a safe journey. Lightning has struck the mast of one of our ships but still we persist.

The third inner sea would be Lake Huron.

June 25, 1665

We have arrived at a small island populated with small furry creatures who build their houses with sticks. We can see the southern shore from the island and have located the marker in the center of the island. Once again, we leave a small portion of treasure at a depth of 2 yards and then proceed to our next destination of 46.198 to the north and west. The marker makes it apparent that we must take the center of several rivers in order to journey into the hinterland and we copy the map as best as we are able and will continue our journey after a day's rest waiting for better weather.

The small furry creatures who built houses with sticks were beavers, which were hunted to extinction in the UK in the 16th Century.[48] This is why James Wemyss was unaware of the creature during his time. They were reintroduced to Scotland starting in 2009 and are now a protected species.

June 30, 1665

We thirteen have reached our destination of 46.198 latitude after sailing west for 2 days and then traveling on foot for almost an entire day. The ships have anchored in the river and the remaining Brethren protect the treasure while we explore. Kimi accompanied us and tells us of how her ancestors also visited this land generations ago and found it pleasing. She knows their language and tells us that her white robe will tell them that she is a spirit woman and a friend. With her help we have visited a small village of the people and have been given the use of several horses and 4 carts to use in transporting our cargo. We give thanks to Heavenly Father and the Great Goddess for their assistance and add three native guards to our company as we return to the ships.

Once again, we see the use of the sacred number of thirteen in the group traveling west. Having their spiritual Goddess—and their literal Goddess in the indigenous Spirit woman Kimi—gave the party all the peace of mind and protection they could possibly ask for.

48. https://www.wildlifetrusts.org/saving-species/beavers

July 4, 1665

After two days travel, we have returned to the riverbanks and have placed one half of the treasure in the carts to return to the marker which we found at 46.198 degrees latitude. Thirty of the crew and thirteen Knights will return with the carts. The rest will stay with the ships until our return. The marker resides in a bluff and shows us a cave to the northeast whose entrance faces the west. Inside the cave we will dig into the soft soil and deposit half of the remaining treasure. The remainder we will take to our last destination which the marker shows at 45.52 degrees latitude to the north and west.

July 7, 1665

After much consternation we have dragged the carts across the flat land and circled the small lakes to the place we have selected. Here we leave half of our remaining cargo and ask for the blessing of Heavenly Father and the Great Goddess to protect and ensure its safety. Our three native warriors, one who is the son of the chief, have promised to protect this land until we return and that no one will know of its presence. Once again, we return to the ships knowing we must take the rest of the cargo inland by cart. Kimi and one of the native warriors called Wa'ho'la will accompany us.

July 10, 1665

We now head north and then west to a latitude of 45.52. The land becomes drier as we travel but it is easier for the horses to pull the wagons while the rest of us walk beside them. Native people watch us from the hills but do not disturb us. Kimi's presence reassures them we mean no harm. We carry the artifacts, gold and Behumet that remain and are assured that the ships will remain safe with their crew and remaining Knights until our return. The weather is extremely hot, and an occasional rain is a welcome respite as we continue our journey."

This final location is far to the west, but it is uncertain exactly where it is.

July 20, 1665

After crossing many hills and valleys we have found a marker showing us this is our final destination. The star of the Great Goddess engraved into the stone cast a shadow pointing to caves in the hills to the southwest. This place is considered sacred by the natives and Wa-ho-la and Kimi perform a ritual of thanks and protection before proceeding. A lone rider came to our camp near the marker and has welcomed us. He is able to talk with Wa-ho-la who has explained the mission of the Great Goddess and the promise his people and Kimi's people had made to their ancestors. The rider is pleased with our cause and promises to lead us to the caves in the morning after we have rested. Two other warriors join us with fresh meat at the day ends and we tell stories and eat well with thousands of stars overhead.

July 25, 1665

We have successfully hidden the remainder of our cargo in the hills of the native people. Wa-ho-la has explained that although the warriors come from different tribes, they all have similar stories of men from the east who came at the request of the Great Goddess many years ago. They smoked with their elders and agreed to respect each other's ways in order to please the Great Goddess. The tribes will protect the treasure and wait for the Knights to return to claim in it the future. Tomorrow, we leave to return to the river and then to Sir James's Island.

September 15, 1665

We have returned to the island granted to Sir James and rejoined our comrades who are eager to return to Scotland. Along the way we saw many natives fishing in the great river in hidden canoes with great spears. Many of the men who joined us in this long walk are exhausted but have grown hardened by the journey and renewed by the return voyage. The weather has been fair and warm, and we have all learned patience and faith while on our journey. We pray that the things we leave behind will be well cared for and leave tomorrow for the Isle of the White Stag to return Kimi to her people.

October 28, 1665

We have returned to Wester Wemyss and our mission is complete. It is now up to our brethren across the seas to complete the Covenant when the time is correct to bring forth the New Jerusalem. We pray for their safety and wisdom and pass on the obligation to them in their infancy. May they be led in wisdom and favor by the brethren who have proceeded them to the Americas in their new home. We will ever be here in their time of need.

Book 15

Journal of David Wemyss

1678 - 1730

Translated from Old English

May 7, 1692

Today I leave with my father for Nova Scotia to the west. Father is now the Grandmaster of the brethren and has instructed me in the Covenant of our family and the family Sinclair. With us travel 12 members of the MacDonald clan who survived the massacre at Glencoe. They will settle in Nova Scotia where they will be safe from the Scottish government.

June 2, 1692

Today we arrive at Port La Tour and meet with Brother Phillipe Muis and Antoine LeBlanc. They will accompany us to visit the islands in Nova Scotia where the treasure of Earl Henry Sinclair is buried.

June 12, 1692

Today we visited New Ross, long abandoned by the Templars who came here 300 years ago. Their treasure is still safe as is the treasure on Dover Island which we visited yesterday. The government here in Nova Scotia is in a constant state of change and the Brethren know that soon the treasure must be moved to a safer place. Perhaps by the time I am initiated into the Brethren I will be able to accomplish that goal as my father suggests.

July 15, 1692

We have completed our visit in Nova Scotia and leave today for Cape Breton where we sail back to Scotland on board the Virginia, bound for Edinburg. Before we leave, we visit with the family of Pierre Martin who are longtime friends with our family and the Sinclairs. Brother Pierre has told my father of the political unrest here and my father is saddened. He reminds me that it will soon be my responsibility to care for the locations of the treasure along with Brother Pierre's son also named Pierre. We must be prepared to use force if necessary.

July 17, 1692

Today we leave for home.

8

The Journals of John and John Wemyss Jr:

Books 16 through 20

Book 16

Journal of John Wemyss

1709 - 1771

Written in English

October 24, 1730

Before my father died last evening, he called me to his side and confided the secret of the Covenant between the Wemyss family and the Sinclairs of whom we are descended. Although I am his youngest son, he feels it is best to pass the responsibility to me as I am most likely to visit Nova Scotia as a member of the Kings army. My older brothers are loyal to the King more so than the brethren and as the youngest I am able to travel more easily. I will remember his plea and have taken the journals into my possession. Although he has told me the story, he begs me to read the journals and take them with me always to keep them safe and secret. I regret I cannot read the old English, but my Latin is good, and I shall follow the instructions as best I can. My unit leaves next week for Jamaica, and I must make it my goal to achieve his last requests.

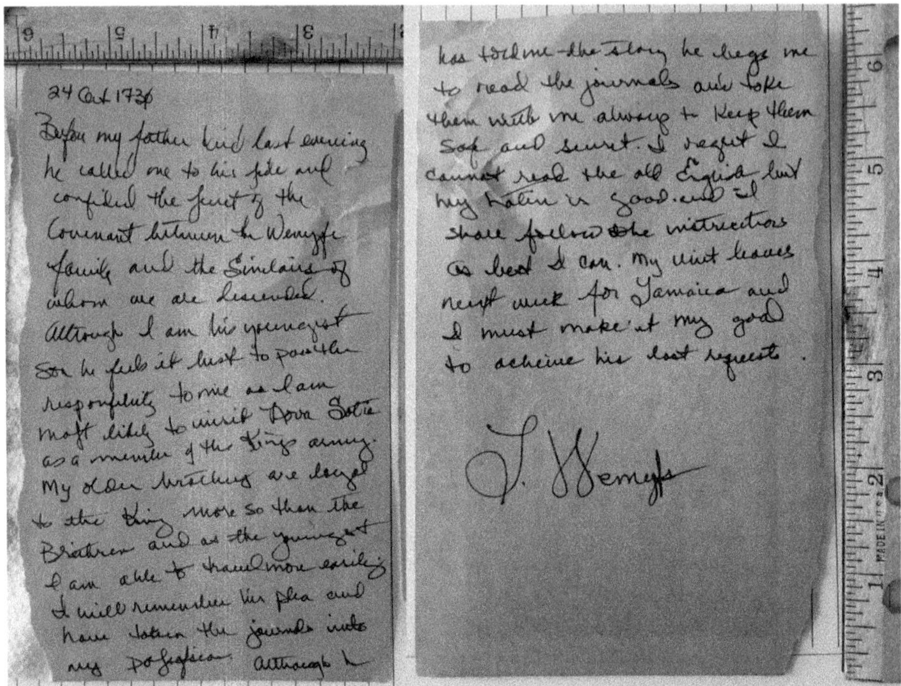

24 Oct 1730

Before my father died last evening he called me to his side and confided the secret of the Covenant between the Wemyss family and the Sinclairs of whom we are descended. Although I am his youngest son he feels it best to pass the responsibility to me as I am most likely to visit Nova Scotia as a member of the Kings army. My older brothers are loyal to the King more so than the Brethren and as the youngest I am able to travel more easily. I will remember his plea and have taken the journals into my possession. Although he has told me the story he begs me to read the journals and take them with me always to keep them safe and secret. I regret I cannot read the old English but my Latin is good and I shall follow the instructions as best I can. My unit leaves next week for Jamaica and I must make it my goal to achieve his last requests.

J. Wemyss

This page chronicles the passing of the journals from David Wemyss to his son John Weems. It is one of only three original pages that survive from the collection Diana Muir once had, but allegedly threw away in 2016. (Wolter, 2018)

September 19, 1731

After being released from our duties in Jamaica we have arrived in Nova Scotia and have been assigned to a small island in the bay to watch the settlement of Halifax and the comings and goings of ships in the harbor. We have built a small stockade on the north side of the island and can view Halifax as well as the shipping lanes to the east. We have been told that pirates also use this island so we must keep a sharp eye. This island is also the same as Dog Island where the brethren have left two caches of treasure. I must endeavor to find them and make certain they are safe. My father had given me instruction as to how the brethren and Sir Francis Bacon has marked their existence. My time on this island gives me ample time to explore and make certain the treasure brought here long ago is still safe.

This entry seems to imply that Sir Francis Bacon may have visited the New World, although there is no historical documentation that he ever did. On the other hand, a skeptic could argue against it. Without additional, more definitive information we will never know for certain.

March 3, 1738

Our unit has been disbanded and sent to New York City in the colonies. We each have been given the opportunity to take up land here in the American colonies. Because of my promise to my father, I look forward to the opportunity to make a new life for myself here in Philadelphia. As a freemason I have Brethren here who are known to me from Scotland who are settling here as well. Many of the men from my unit have taken advantage of the opportunity and each of us has been given 160 acres to make our own.

July 17, 1740

Today I make Isabella Scott, daughter of Doctor John Scott, my wife and companion. Together we settle in Cecil County where we will build a farm and begin a family. I am most happy and think my father would be proud. We have created an assembly of Brethren nearby in Philadelphia and each month I attend to learn more about my responsibilities in the colonies and towards my brethren. We seek to establish an enlightened country and work towards those goals.

John Sr. gives insight into the goals of the brethren from Scotland, and is consistent with the ideology and dreams of the Founding Fathers, of which he was certainly one.

November 8, 1741

Today my first child, a son named John, is born. He is a strong lad and his mother does well. He will be named John Scott Weems in honor of his American birth and heritage and his maternal grandfather.

Here John Sr. welcomes his son who will be the most prolific and detailed chronicler of these journals. As you will read in the coming entries, his actions are nothing short of heroic and I'd be lying if I said I wasn't pleased I share his middle name.

November 11, 1743

Today a daughter Margaret is born. A lass with black hair she looks most like her mother.

February 2, 1745

Another son, Thomas Scott Weems is born this day. Isabella is a strong woman and does well.

April 19, 1746

Another son, Bartholomew is born this day. Johnny has made him his own responsibility and hovers over him.

December 28, 1749

Another daughter Isabella Elizabeth Weems was born this evening. She is a tiny child and has a weak cry, but we pray that she will survive. Her mother is weak from the birth, but the older children help her with the child as they bring her what she needs.

March 28, 1752

A son, David is born this day and named after my father who has been the most influential person in my life. I hope that David will honor his grandfather and become a great man.

April 4, 1766

I met this day with the brethren and have invited six of them to accompany me to Nova Scotia to ascertain that the sites where Templar treasure is buried are still safe and undisturbed. They each come from the Covenant families and although some have been made aware by their fathers of the Covenant and guardianship of the treasure, others are blissfully unaware. Sworn to secrecy, they have accepted the responsibility and will make their families ready for their absence. Each of them understands the gravity of our situation as English subjects but our loyalty to the Lord and to the brethren and a free nation is greater.

This entry sheds important light on two things. First, the mention of "Covenant families" makes clear there indeed were, and still are, bloodline families that remain committed to certain ideological tenants that go back centuries if not millennia. Second, these familial and spiritual bonds and commitments go beyond nationalistic loyalty to one's country. They extend an utmost commitment to higher causes so eloquently said here.

May 25, 1766

The fields have been planted and responsibility given to my brother-in-law David Scott to supervise the farm during my absence. His brother John accompanies us on our journey. We leave tomorrow morning to go north by horseback to Nova Scotia. Along the way we will gauge the political atmosphere in the northern colonies and meet with the brethren along the way.

June 25, 1766

We meet this day with Brother John Secombe in Chester on the edge of Mahone Bay. He and Brother Alpheus Morse have taken us to the nearby islands, and we have seen that all is well. We leave next for the Big Stone Fort, so called by my father, to do the same.

June 28, 1766

"We have met this day with Brother Joseph Peters[49] in Halifax and tomorrow he and Brother Phillipe d'Entremont will take us to Taylor Island where we inspect the treasure site. He is a forceful man and well respected in the community. He will be a good ally for the brethren in Philadelphia if political happenings continue in the same vein. I believe we are headed towards Revolution, and it pleases me that our brethren in Nova Scotia support us in our search for freedom of action and thought.

49. See page 349 for more on Brother Joseph Peters.

June 30, 1766

We end our visit to Nova Scotia by visiting Louisburg where we meet with Brother Pierre Martin Jr. He is the son of the man I met when I was much younger, but he remembers our meeting well. His father instructed him in the responsibilities of the guardianship, and he has endeavored to meet his responsibilities. He has taken us and the other 6 Brethren to Janvrin Island, once known as the Isle of the White Stag, where we meet with members of the native tribe. They are descended from the man who first met our ancestor on the shores of Nova Scotia in 1395. They have honored their commitment to our ancestors and have honored our visit with a feast. We are unable to visit Ebenezer Morton in western New York Province, and so we end our journey at the place where it all began. I return home with a lighter heart knowing that the treasure is there if it should be needed.

It was this entry that confirmed my belief the Isle of the White Stag was in realty Janvrin Island. Also, the man the members of the native tribe descended from has to be Earl Henry's lifelong friend Askoosh.

June 15, 1768

I meet this day with the brethren at the Green Dragon Inn in Boston. In attendance are Ebenezer Morton of western New York Province, Arthur St Clair,[50] George Mason the 4th of Virginia,[51] John Hanson of Maryland,[52] Nathaniel Gorham of Massachusetts,[53] John Dickinson,[54] and William Irvine of Orkney who now lives in Boston. Together we discuss the recent political happenings and the approaching revolution. We must prepare to retrieve the treasure in order to support the Revolution and the establishment of the New Jerusalem. Each is in agreement. We must enlist the help of our eldest sons to do this and will prepare a place for the treasure where it is easily retrieved for the brethren's use. I will

50. https://www.battlefields.org/learn/biographies/arthur-st-clair

51. https://www.britannica.com/biography/George-Mason

52. https://www.thoughtco.com/john-hanson-biography-4178170

53. https://www.archives.gov/founding-docs/founding-fathers-massachusetts

54. https://www.biography.com/political-figures/john-dickinson

meet with the Grand Master this coming week and receive his approval of our plan. If he approves, we will move forward.

Students of the Revolutionary War will recognize the Green Dragon Tavern as a well-known meeting place of Patriots in Boston prior to the onset of the war. I have visited this cramped tavern– which still exists–and imagined many of the people mentioned in John Sr's entry. Most notable is the "Forgotten Founder," George Mason, and General Arthur Sinclair. Perhaps the most famous founder of America, George Washington, is one of the only ones not mentioned in the journals. However, due to his close association to Arthur Sinclair–who advised him on military strategy that helped turn his dismal early record of defeats against the British into important victories that ultimately led to victory–you can be sure Washington was well aware of the mission of the Covenant and the establishment of the "New Jerusalem."

In July of 2020, I found the gravestone of Founding Father, Ebenezer Morton, in the Cemetery of Green in Plymouth, Massachusetts. (Wolter, 2020)

Left: Arthur St. Clair (1736-1818) was born in Thurso, Scotland and was a military general who provided input in several successful battles during the Revolutionary War, earning the respect of George Washington. In 1787, St. Clair served as the president of the Continental Congress. (Wolter, 2020/Internet)

Right: George Mason (1725-1792) drafted the Virginia Declaration of Rights in 1776, and his work influenced Thomas Jefferson's draft of the Declaration of Independence, which then influenced the subsequent state declarations and the nation's Constitution. He refused to sign the Constitution until it contained a Bill of Rights. (Internet)

The Grand Master of Freemasonry in the American colonies at the time of this entry in 1768 was Dr. John Warren. An interesting side note is my good friend and current Grand Master of the Martinist order I was initiated into, Timothy Hogan, is related to John Warren. Tim's ancestor, Dr. Joseph Warren–the Patriot who was initiated by Paul Revere into Freemasonry and was killed at the Battle of Bunker Hill in 1775–is Tim's direct ancestor on his mother's side. When I contacted him to confirm my internet search revealed John and Joseph were brothers, Tim was unaware of it. Needless to say, he was very pleased to hear his distant uncle was directly involved in the mission of the Covenant, and his distant grandfather likely was as well.

Left: John Hansen (1721-1783), painted here like George Mason with his hand parked inside his vest—a telltale sign he was a Freemason—was the first President of the Continental Congress from 1781-1782. (Internet)

Center: John Dickenson (1732 -1808) was an attorney, a politician, and became known as the "Penman of the Revolution."

Right: Nathanial Gorham (1738-1796) served as President of the Continental Congress from June 1786 until January 1787. He was a gifted politician and staunch supporter of the Constitution. (Internet)

Book 17

Journal of John Weems

1741 - 1812

Written in Modern English

May 14, 1769

A courier arrived today from Philadelphia and my father has requested that I return home to deal with an important family matter. My father has never asked anything of me before, so I feel obligated to attend. He has insisted that I stop in Staunton and solicit Brother John Scott to accompany me as Mother has been ill and she wishes to see him. My brother-in-law Richard Gott and sister Margaret have agreed to look after Kitty and my small family in my absence. I hope to be gone only a few weeks and will leave in the morrow to do his bidding.

So begins the first entry of the most prolific writer of the journals, who poured his heart and soul into his patriotic actions and feelings that, prior to the publication of this book, were completely unknown. He and the forty-six men and six African American slaves are previously unknown heroes of the American Revolution who put their lives on the line, just like all those famous Patriots did whose names we all know. Enjoy this deeply personal and amazing experience of a Patriot whose name you've never heard of before but now will never forget.

May 16, 1769

Brother Bible will accompany me as far as Staunton and Kitty has given me a letter to be delivered to her parents there. After many kisses and tearful goodbyes, we are hoping to spend the night in Danville with friends of Brother Bible. It will take 4 days to reach Staunton and another 8 or 9 days to reach Abington. I pray that my family remains well in my absence and look forward to seeing Brother Scott in Staunton.

May 19, 1769

The journey to Staunton was unremarkable and we have arrived at the home of Brother John Scott. He too has been summoned by my father and has reluctantly agreed to travel with us. Although the weather has remained fair it appears a storm is on the way. I have delivered Kitty's letter to her mother and told her of the little babies and how they have grown. My uncle and I shall leave in the morn to continue our journey.

May 20, 1769

A fierce storm has slowed our progress, and we have camped on Lewis Creek for the night. We will continue in the morning.

May 23, 1769

We have finally arrived at the manor after following the river through the Shenandoah Valley and the seashore south of Philadelphia. It is much changed during my absence, yet the manor and farm never change. Mother seems weary and Father is as always. He insists we have a good night's rest before he embarks on this matter. I sense there is urgency in his voice, but we spent the evening talking of family and events since I last saw him 7 years ago. I sketched pictures of the babies for my mother, and she seems very pleased. She thinks that Elizabeth looks like her and that baby William seems healthy and happy.

Entries like this breathe life into the era when drawing pictures of loved ones, instead of taking them with cameras or cell phones, was the norm. John Jr. will do much of this in the coming entries to a level historians rarely, if ever, see.

May 24, 1769

It has taken hours to put my hand to pen and write my thoughts. I now understand why Father has taught us to write our thoughts each evening. Not only do we chronicle the events in our lives, but he has been preparing us for the adventure ahead. When I asked why he did not invite my brother Thomas he replied that although he loved his sons equally Thomas is a slave owner and might be swayed by the prospects of riches. Whereas I am satisfied with my life and do not seek to put myself above other men. I am not certain that I agree with his assessment but will try to do my best to fulfill his wishes.

Father has always taught us that we are the descendants of great kings and queens in Scotland. Father is the grandson of the Earl of Wemyss, the Grandmaster of the Freemasons in Edinburgh. As such he bears the responsibility of a great family. When Thomas and I were of age we were initiated into the Freemasons in Philadelphia and so began our training in trades that would benefit both our country and our lives. I have been trained as a surveyor and engineer while Thomas claims his occupation as a blacksmith and metal worker. We are both educated men although our interests differ.

Father's story of our families' involvement in Freemason activities is confusing and lengthy. He has promised that as I read the journals of my ancestors who have gone before me that I will begin to understand the enormity of my journey. He has put into my safekeeping a small chest of journals that reach back hundreds of years requesting that I begin with the oldest. It is only then that I will understand what the Freemasons and the Templars before them have kept hidden and the efforts taken to preserve it. The Brethren have always kept such secrets, and I have heard rumors for years but have given them no heed until now.

Father is concerned with the current political happenings and has received word that settlers have begun to settle the area of Nova Scotia where we must travel. He has arranged for us to leave on board ship in the morrow for Cape Breton where we are to seek out an alliance with others who would support our cause. My Uncle John Scott will accompany me as he did my father many years ago and acquaint me with the hiding place of what Father refers to only as the Covenant. He has also demanded that I record my journey so that someday I may pass the responsibility along to my own son.

The journey begins.

What struck me in this entry is John's father essentially telling his son how medieval Templarism evolved into modern Freemasonry. It has long been speculated, but in the current era most Masonic scholars say there is no evidence to support the premise. These journals provide conclusive evidence in extensive detail.

May 25, 1769

We have taken passage on board the ship Raleigh. We are laden with iron pots, cups, ladles, and cloth for the natives who trade at Cape Breton. The cabin is small, and Uncle John makes terrible noises while sleeping but I use the time to begin my reading as he sleeps at night. The five-day voyage will give me adequate time to prepare for what is ahead. The weather remains fair, and I hope will remain so. Father has promised to send a message to my family explaining my long absence. I pray that they are well, and that God protects them.

May 28, 1769

We lodge at Fort Western this eve before crossing the bay to Cape Breton. I am not a good sailor and beg the opportunity to stand on firm ground if only for a little while. The ship's crew trade here at Fort Western and I learn that it was founded by Boston merchants. I continue my reading but admit that my mind is confused. I cannot read the oldest documents being written in the old script but have been able to read my father's journal and the three generations before him. It has become clear that his settlement in Pennsylvania was as much to protect the Covenant as it was to begin a new life. They become easier to read as I continue, and I hope to be able to learn more before we land in Cape Breton.

My ancestor the Earl of Wemyss was most explicit in his writings. He admonished each generation of the family to continue the role of guardian for the Covenant. He explains that it is a covenant between the family of Wemyss and Sinclair to protect the holy Templar treasure that was secreted from France to the caves of the Firth of Forth beneath the Wemyss Castle. This was done to safeguard it when the Templars were persecuted and expelled from their homes. While I have learned of the Templar trials during my youth, I had no recollection the family of Wemyss was so closely entangled with that of Sinclair. I was mistaken.

My great grandfather James Wemyss has included a short history of the family, and I know now that the two families are connected through marriage and through obligation to the Brotherhood.

I still do not know the goal of our expedition and am trusting in Brother Scott that his memory does not fail him."

The "old script" he mentions struggling with was Latin, and it appears he was able to read the journals written in Old English. One can understand his confusion without having read the first thirteen journals, but he will soon be enlightened by the older brothers he is traveling with.

June 1, 1769

Constant rain. Will arrive tomorrow at Cape Breton. Brother Scott declines to discuss the diaries with me. He says I must make up my own mind.

June 2, 1769

It has taken longer than expected to reach Cape Breton and the Raleigh has put us off at Isle Royal to return in 4 days. My knowledge of geography is appalling, and I strive to make it better. Brother John has located Pierre Martin who is married to a Escasoni native woman he calls Anne. Their home is a small frame house with a thatched roof but very comfortable even with 8 children. Isle Royal is a small settlement of settlers both Acadian French and native. Tomorrow Mssr Martin is to take us to a nearby island where Uncle John says our ancestors first landed in the New World.

June 3, 1769

Brother John and Brother Pierre said they first visited the island with my father thirty years ago. When Brother Pierre is gone the responsibility of monitoring the island will pass to his son Pierre who is now 8 years old. My French is very weak, but Uncle John and Brother Pierre easily converse with each other in French. Brother Pierre has very little English but some German. I also speak German as my wife is of German heritage.

We arrived at a place called Quarter Moon Cove on the southeast side of the island which they called White Stag Island. Brother John began to tell me in earnest of a young man who would visit these waters as a child fishing with his father. The young man grew up to be Henri St. Clair, Lord of Roslyn Castle, a grandmaster of the Freemasons and an explorer. He tells me how he brought 3 ships and 85 men with him in the spring of 1395 to this island. Here they began their search for a place to hide the Templar treasure that was hidden in the bowels of Wemyss Castle on Firth of Forth. Brother John also told me that today was a special day as the planet Venus would pass through the sky this night giving us the blessing of the Holy Mother. Together we formed a triangle with Brother Pierre and said a prayer to the father to bless this place and our journey. Before we left this place, we carved the year's date on a large boulder 50 paces from the shore to document our journey. Other dates are also given, and Brother John explains that each generation must visit the rock 2 times in their life-time. The first is to be given the task and the second is to pass the task to the next generation. He explained that my father is too ill and asked him to accompany me. The next time I come the task will be given to Brother Pierre's eldest son and to my own son who will journey with me.

The entrance to Well Cave on the northern coast of Firth of Forth in Scotland. The large bell-shaped cave lies directly below the ruins of what was once Wemyss Castle. (Wolter, 2019)

Our next stop will be in Halifax Nova Scotia where we meet with Brother John Fraser. First, we return to Isle Royal and await the Raleigh.

While it is hardly a surprise to learn that Earl Henry Sinclair was a Grand Master of Freemasons in Scotland, there are no formal records that exist today that document this. This entry within these journals serves as that documentation. Here we also see the first specific mention of where treasure was hidden in Scotland. John's mention of the treasure being "*... hidden in the bowels of Wemyss Castle on Firth of Forth.*" must be in reference to Well Cave, which lies directly below the ruins of what used to be Wemyss

Castle. It is a large underground cavern, among many along the shoreline carved out by wave action over thousands of years. I have visited it many times. Our guides told us of a now-backfilled tunnel that used to lead up into the castle. After exploring the cave there is a recess that appears filled in that was likely where that tunnel used to be.

The mention of the planet Venus is significant, as John Jr. and his brethren understood She is the physical manifestation of the Goddess in the heavens who they call upon to bless and protect both themselves and the treasures. In this case, however, there was more to the planet Venus than just being symbolic of Deity. On June 3, 1769 there was a transit of Venus—where the planet moved across the sun relative to earth—that was anticipated by scientists and, as evidenced by this entry, was known also to

While filming an episode of *America Unearthed* in January of 2019, we crawled through a small entrance to film inside Well Cave that lies directly below the ruins of what used to be Wemyss Castle. The journal entry John Weems Jr. made on June 3, 1769, relayed that Templar treasure was hidden inside this cave in the fourteenth century. (Wolter, 2019)

Freemasons, in this case brother John.[55] Further, by forming a triangle—the symobol of Deity—they create an important symbol of Freemasonry, both then and today.

Brother Tom Colvin and I searched for three days on Janvrin Island trying to locate the boulder with dates carved into it but to no avail. Either we simply missed it, which I highly doubt, or erosion of the soft glacial till comprising the island has claimed the stone which now sits beneath the waves.

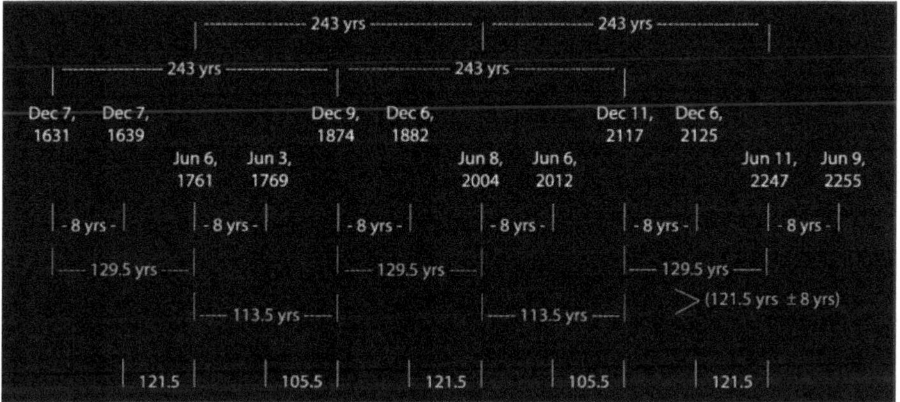

This chart shows the dates of the transit of the planet Venus dating back to 1631. On June 3, 1769 there was a transit of Venus which was documented in Tahiti by scientists on the James Cook expedition. It was also documented by John Weems Jr. in this journal entry. (Internet)

55. https://australian.museum/blog-archive/museullaneous/transit-of-venus/#:~:text=The%20main%20aim%20of%20Captain,which%20assisted%20in%20nautical%20navigation.

Within Freemasonry, the triangle is a symbol of Creator, or Deity and is often depicted with the Eye of Horus—an Egyptian symbol of protection, healing, and wellbeing—within. The most common example is found at the top of the unfinished pyramid on the American dollar bill. This example is found in the center of the rose window of the Cathedral of Saint Helena in Helena, Montana. (Wolter, 2011)

June 5, 1769

While waiting for the Raleigh to return I have read through my Father's journal and have managed to read the first part of Henricus de Santo Claro's journal. Henry, as I shall call him in the future, has visited the island which the Migwaw called the Isle of the White Stag at least four times. His father and grandfather had also visited the isle many times, as did their fathers before them. He tells of how his grandfather brought 100 Knights to the New World who were weary from battle and had no home to return to. Henry also stated how a terrible plague had decimated his homeland, and they had hoped to escape the ravages of both war and health. He also tells that in 1357 when he was eleven his father left behind 2 fishing boats and 20 men who were to find a passage to the inland seas to search for the men who had been left behind years before. They were accompanied by Henry's native friend Askosh whom he had met on his first fishing trip. It makes me wonder what happened to these men as he never mentions their return to Orknades. It is apparent that Askosh had returned to his village. Years later Henry met him again during his old age.

I now understand why we must visit all the places that were visited in 1398. It is to make certain that the treasure left behind is untouched and unknown. Uncle John says it is our duty to protect the ancient sites and to remember our promise to the Aherrah and the Holy Mother.

June 6, 1769

The Raleigh has returned, and I must prepare myself for another sea voyage. Brother Pierre's wife has given me a tea that she says will calm my stomach. Hopefully the weather will remain calm. Before we left, she shared with us some of the myths of her people about white men from the east visiting their villages for many centuries and the things that they had taught each other. The children also danced their native dances for us making me smile at their movements. It makes me miss my children and my wife. I hope to be home soon.

June 8, 1769

We have arrived at Halifax and shall meet with Brother John Fraser for evening meal. The Raleigh will continue to Fort Western, and Brother John tells me that we shall complete the rest of our journey on horseback. I am quite happy with that revelation.

June 8, 1769

Brother John Fraser has told us of the political unrest in Halifax and but assures us that the nearby island where Henry Sinclair visited is still safe and secure. It is not the type of place that settlers would settle and remains unvisited by most people. We three will visit the island tomorrow and say our prayers to fulfill my father's wishes.

This must be McNab (Dog) Island, where the *Katherine* went ashore during a storm.

June 9, 1769

We have visited a small island off the east coast of Halifax which seems to be made entirely of rock except for one small area. There is a bay on the south side where we landed, and Brother John Fraser took us to a spot on the top of cliff where we formed a triangle and said a prayer of protection for the entire island. I asked Brother John where the treasure was hidden but he says only that it is buried 22 feet below the surface and that my father can provide more details. Before leaving we carved the date into the rock to mark our visit.

The number 22 recurs multiple times in John's Jr's entries as the depth treasure was buried at various sites. This number has an important esoteric meaning as it is the number of bones in the human skull, eight in the cranium and fourteen in the face. Other numbers, such as thirty-three, represent the number of vertebrae in the human spinal column. The fact there are thirty-three degrees in Scottish Rite Freemasonry is not an accident. Gnostic groups like the Knights Templar and Freemasons use aspects of the human body, such as the skeleton, in their teachings to pass on secret information to those initiated with certain knowledge. One excellent example is the Kensington Rune Stone that incorporates these numbers (eight, ten, fourteen, and twenty-two) intentionally to convey secret information to other members. Once armed with this knowledge, the Kensington inscription suddenly takes on new meaning upon realizing there is other information being conveyed to those with the "eyes to see."

> *8 Gotalanders* [people from the Island of Gotland, Sweden] *and 22 northmen* [Norwegians] *on this acquisition business/ taking up land* [land claim] *from*
>
> *Vinland* [northeast region of North America] *far to the west. We had a camp near*
>
> *2 sklar* [Sinclair/shelters?] *one day's journey from this stone* [location]. *We were fishing one day, after we came home found 10 men red from blood and death.*

AVM. Save from evil.

There are 10 men by the inland sea to look after our ships, 14 days journey from

this hill [location]. *Year 1362*

Beyond 8 + 14 + 22, it is interesting that the first four numbers in sequence (8 + 22 + 2 + 1) equal the number thirty-three. It's also interesting that there are fourteen individual numbers in the inscription (8 + 2-2 + 2 + 1-0 + 1-0 + 1-4 + 1-3-6-2 = 14). None of this is coincidence.[56]

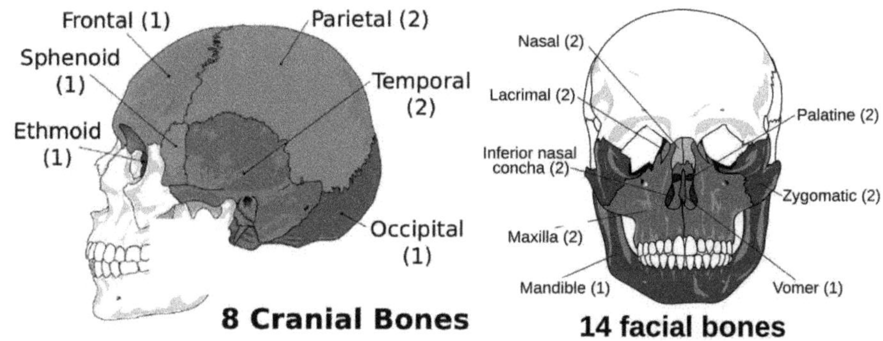

There are eight bones in the human cranium and fourteen facial bones for a total of twenty-two in the human skull. Gnostic traditions incorporate aspects of the human body, such as the number of bones in the body, within their rituals and teachings. (Internet)

June 10, 1769

Today we began our journey inland by horseback with Brother Samuel Morse from Chester, a good friend of Brother Fraser. My horse is a gentle and good-natured mare of cream color and a welcome change from the rocking motion of the waves on board a ship. It takes us about 6 hours to reach a point south down the coast and then many more hours inland along a small river. Here there are ruins of a stone fortification

56. There is a lot more esoteric information embedded within the Kensington Rune Stone inscription and I invite the reader to learn about what the brilliant carver did in my 2019 book, *Cryptic Code of the Templars in America: Origins of the Hooked X*, in Chapter 6, "Cryptic Code on the Kensington Rune Stone."

that Brother Morse tells me was called "Big Stone Fort." It was built by 14 Templars who had been left behind at their own request by Henry St Clare in 1395. Brother Morse explained that it has been abandoned for some time and that he does not know what happened to the brethren left behind. He supposes that they may have traveled southward to combine with other Templars who had stayed behind. Together we formed a triangle and said a prayer of protection and then made a fire to stay the night.

Here again we see the symbolic number of fourteen in the number of Templars who stayed and built the fort at New Ross.

During my first visit to the well at New Ross, I was aware of the stories

Apparent ruins on the McKay property at The Cross. External walls of the alleged "castle" extend onto neighbouring properties of the hill top village.

Photo by Michael Bradley.

This photo taken by Michael Bradley in the 1970s shows what is believed to be the foundation of the Knights Templar fort built by men left behind by Earl Henry Sinclair in 1395 and 1398.

about a fort having been built there by the Templars, and I was curious to see if there was any evidence I could find. Only yards from the well and just into the dense brush I found piles of various sized boulders that looked to have been moved from the lot where the well was. This was certainly not a natural pile of glacial boulders, and many of them clearly showed evidence of having been worked by man. No locals I talked with knew how or when the boulders were moved there, but there was information about an old stone foundation near the well. The foundation was believed to be what remained of the Old Stone Fort built by the Knights Templar. Geological evidence to support this was found in the rounded glacial cobbles used to line the shaft, which is not a technique for modern well construction.

Just into the woods at the edge of the property in New Ross where we filmed an episode of America Unearthed, there was a large field of glacial boulders. They were moved from what was believed to be the foundation stones for a medieval Knights Templar fort mentioned in Sinclair/Wemyss journals. Many of the stones had been intentionally worked by man providing evidence they came from a previously unknown structure. (Wolter, 2012)

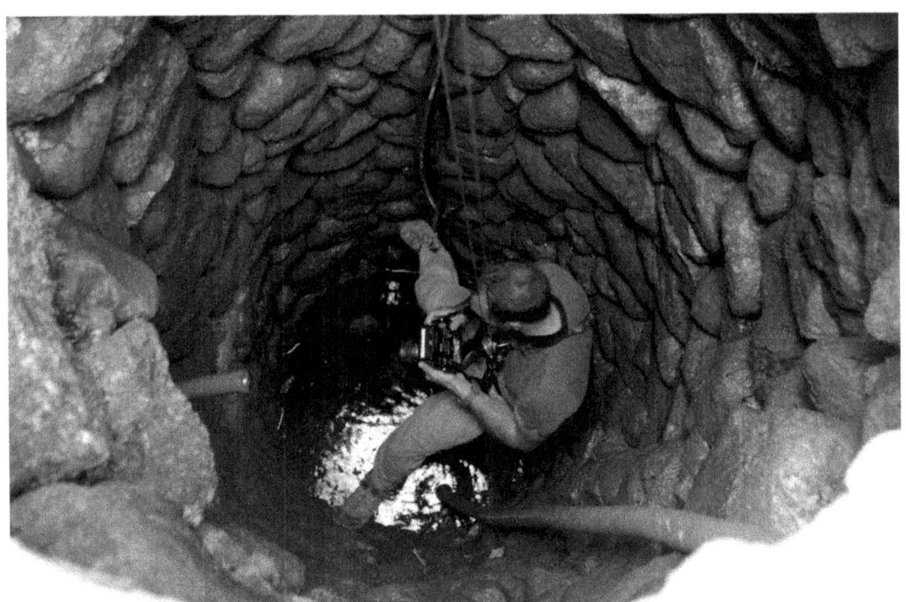

Cinematographer Colin Trienen shoots inside the "Holy Well" at New Ross during filming for an episode of *America Unearthed* in October of 2012. Note the rounded glacial cobbles used to line the shaft, which is not a modern well-building technique. (Wolter, 2012)

June 12, 1769

We return to the coast today and ride towards a river to the South called Gold River to meet with a woman named Mary Neale. During our ride Brother Morse showed us a Norse stone that showed the legend of Sigurd of Sweden.

I nearly fell out of my chair upon reading this entry because not only was I aware of the Norumbega Vineland Rune Stone carving in Mahone Bay, but was already aware of the Ramsund carving in Sweden that dates to 1030 AD. The Ramsund Carving likely was the inspiration for the Mahone Bay carving but is an abbreviated version. On January 26, 2025 I visited the Norumbega Vinland Rune Stone on a cold, clear day. I examined the carvings that were deeply cut into the coarse-grained, granitic, glacial boulder that sat upon the shore. Exactly how old the carvings are is difficult to say, but the mention of the rune stone by John Weems Jr. suggests they are at least 256 years old.

The fact that the so-called Norumbega Vinland Rune Stone is mentioned by John Weems Jr. in his journals—and that he saw the inscription—is simply incredible. The current opinion is that it is a modern creation simulating a similar inscription in the glacially smooth bedrock of Sweden called the Ramsund Carving. This entry changes everything about the age and origin of this amazing inscription. (Wolter, 2025)

The Ramsund inscription was carved into the bedrock in Eskilstuna Municipality, Södermanland, Sweden in 1030 AD. In English it reads, "Hónefr raised [the stone] in memory of Geirmarr, his father. He met his end in Þjústr. Skammhals cut these runes." (By Pbuergler - Own work, CC BY-SA 4.0)

June 13, 1769

We arrived at the house of Mary Neale last eve and have spent the night lodged in the barn. This morning, we gave thanks for the day and then borrowed her boat and together with Brother Samuel Morse we visited a small island just off the coast of Nova Scotia in the Bay of Saint Marquerite. The island is covered with tall oak trees creating a canopy over the center of the island. It is here that Brother John told me the story of the Saint Katherine, *a ship captained by Henry St. Clair in 1398. He tells me that the fleet of 7 ships met with an enormous storm and 2 ships were lost. One sank in the bay of Saint Marguerite, and the* Saint Katherine, *a galley laden with treasure, was lifted from the water and deposited onto this island by a large wave. After 3 weeks they could not free her and were forced to bury their treasure on the island and then burn the ship. The men were then divided between the remaining ships while 3 Knights stayed on the island to guard the treasure until others could return.*

Brother Morse showed me the spot where the treasure had been buried and showed me how the site had been marked with boulders. He then told me how my great, great, grandfather had met with Francis Bacon in London years later and together they had planned how to keep the secret of the treasure and how to mark its location. When next they returned to mark the location only two knights remained and the third had been buried. The two knights then returned to Scotland where they later died.

Brother Morse also explained how the British soldiers had built a small palisade on the north side of the island and showed me where it had stood. He said that my father had been one of the young officers who had been here watching the harbor and bay at the same time that he watched over the treasure. That is how he had met my father. He also spoke of pirates who had often visited the island and were rumored to have hidden treasure there as well. Brother Morse also told us that 3 farmers from the mainland used the island to pasture sheep but that currently none of them lived on the island.

I asked about the other ships, and he told me that the ships had gathered together after the storm and each ship had buried their treasure at the chosen island from the previous voyage. He then showed me by drawing a map in the sand that they had buried treasure at three additional islands in the bay. Overwhelmed with the enormity of their task, I was amazed that no one had found the treasure in the past. Brother John explained that the natives had covenanted with the Holy Mother and with Henry that they would assist in protecting the treasure. If ever settlers came to the area, they were soon run off by offending spirits in the night. Brother John smiled at the idea and Brother Morse stated that he had often seen strange sights in the bay from his home in Chester.

Together with Brother Morse we formed a triangle and said a prayer of protection asking the Holy Father and Holy Mother to protect these places until such time as they were needed. I still did not understand the reason my father has instructed that I be brought here, but trusted Brother John to tell me when the time was right.

Satisfied that the treasure was safe, we returned to the house of Mary Neale for our nighttime meal, giving thanks for our safe journey. Brother John says that in the morning we will begin our journey southward towards home stopping three more places before we return to Philadelphia. First, we would travel south on the coast on horseback until we reach Poboncon where we will take our passage on board a ship to Fort Western.

June 15, 1769

The journey to Poboncon has been very pleasant. The weather is calm and near the sea the breeze is cool and relaxing. Brother Samuel Morse has been to Poboncon many times and is familiar with the trading vessels who come there to trade with the natives. He assures us we will be able to find a vessel to transport both us and our horses which Brother Fraser has given us. Brother John has paid him in silver for the price of the horses and tells me that we will be traveling down the coast towards Rhode Island and Maryland. It will take longer but he states that we must stop at three places which would be difficult on-board ship.

During our ride, Brother John continues to tell me the story of Henry St. Clair and reminds me how he sent half of his fleet back to Scotland and then separated the rest of the crew into two parts. One ship went north towards Louisbourg with five monks to establish a monastery and winery, while the ship continued on to the St Lawrence River to the inland lakes. Brother Morse added that Louisbourg fell in 1758 to the British but there are native families who still talk of the monks who taught their ancestors generations ago.

Brother John also explained that the ship that went north eventually came to Lac de Frontenac where they buried their treasure on a small island before settling in for the winter. Eight men returned overland to the Templar settlement near Massachusetts and joined the men who had settled there. Unfortunately, we will not be able to visit the area as my father could never determine the island they had stayed on.

Now that we have arrived at Poboncon we have news of a ship leaving in the morrow called the Echo. We have secured our passage and will leave for Fort Western in the morning.

I am homesick and I miss my wife. It makes me wonder if I am being a foolish man for believing such a tale of Templar Treasure. I asked Brother John why he believes, and he says that although he has never seen the treasure, he has faith in our brethren and has never seen anything to contradict the story. He has met many men in the brotherhood and all of them have had faith, and he says so must I. I have been taught to believe in the brethren and trust in their teachings. Now I must begin to apply those lessons.

John Jr. has doubts about the story that even today sounds almost too fantastic to be true. I remember being just as moved when John first saw the structure that changed his mind into believing in the mission of Covenant and the treasure he will get to know well very soon.

June 18, 1769

We have been traveling by horseback for 3 days now and plan to stop in Concord New Hampshire to visit with friends of my father. The weather has turned wet again and I welcome a dry bed for the eve. We stayed the first night in Yarmouth, Maine and have made good progress on the road to Boston. I have been able to complete Henry's journals and am now reading those that follow. I wonder what I will tell my own son when he is old enough to understand. So much has changed since Henry St. Clair came to the Americas. I wonder that his dream of a free state can ever be realized.

It is heartening to know that John Jr. did live long enough to see the completion of the Covenant, and the realization of the Free Templar State which started four centuries earlier. He played such a vital role in seeing it to fruition.

June 20, 1769

We have arrived at the village of Westford which is celebrating its founding 120 years ago in 1659. We stayed at Fletcher's Inn on the village square and watched the celebration and listened to the music and children playing. I will continue reading this night to learn more. Brother John tells me that the Wemyss Shipping Lines were responsible for bringing the treasure from western Scotland about 100 years ago. I want to understand what was happening in Scotland that made them seek such a refuge.

June 21, 1769

We met with Brother Thomas Brooks this morning who took us a few miles into the woods and told us the story of how some of Henry St. Clair's men had camped here during the winter in 1395 at Prospect Hill. They chose this spot because it was the highest vantage point over the harbor just a mile or two away. He also gave us a tour of the village and showed us the Westford Academy where young men are educated for the future. After lunch we decided to ride further to Boston and stopped at Harnett's Tavern on the way for refreshment.

This entry appears to add credence to the legend of the carving of the sword at Westford being a memorial to the fallen Sir James Gunn in 1395. What happened and why he died remains a mystery.

June 22, 1769

We have spent the night in Boston at Taylor's Inn across from the Green Dragon Tavern where they talk of politics late into the night. It is difficult to sleep with so much noise, but it makes me feel as if the city is alive. Uncle John asks that we spend time touring the city as it might be a long time before we visit again. He wishes to spend time at King's Chapel to reaffirm his faith. It is a most beautiful church, and we pay our respects to those we knew in the churchyard nearby. We ate lunch on the commons and talked with other travelers about the current political leanings. I am certain we are headed for revolution. We leave in the morn for Newport, Rhode Island where we will meet with Brother Peleg Manchester.

June 25, 1769

We have stayed the night at a small inn on the road to Newport. This morning, we meet with Brother Peleg Manchester who will show us an old monument that Brother John says was built by the Templars who settled nearby.

June 25, 1769

Brother Peleg has shown us what is called the Newport Tower. It has been here longer than the village has been founded. Some say it is a grain mill while others say it was built by the Templars to mark the seasons and to claim the surrounding area for settlement. It is the most unusual place I have ever seen, and I am fascinated by the methods in which it was constructed. As an engineer I can see how it must have been difficult to construct the tower using pressure points. It has 2 stories and has recesses in the stone for a fire and small windows that look out to all the directions of the compass. The sun enters through a different window each season and whomever built the tower had a great knowledge of astronomy. The watcher Baraqijal would have been proud.

The quarry stone used is also unusual and must have taken a great amount of effort to bring to this site. I have sketched a picture of the tower for my wife as I'm certain she would love to see it. After staying the night, we will be returning to Philadelphia. I am anxious to talk to my father about what I have seen. I wonder if his recollections are the same as mine.

It is now 256 years since this entry was written, and the Newport Tower still looks like it did when John Jr. marveled at it back then. The brethren understood then what has been confirmed scientifically today: that the structure was built by the Templars to incorporate extremely precise astronomical alignments. Of course, my favorite is the winter solstice illumination of the egg-shaped keystone at 9:00 a.m. I discovered in 2007, in the west-northwest archway on the inside of the tower. This keystone sits back-to-back with a notched angled keystone on the exterior of the archway. This tells us the builders understood the lessons of the Royal Arch degree, which was known and presented to initiates in the late fourteenth century. I also discovered the two keystones were not centered in the archway, as would normally be done. This is because they document a long-range alignment that starts in the center of the tower, extends through the two keystones and then extends into space in a west-northwest direction to exactly where the Kensington Rune Stone land claim is found, in the geographic center of the North America continent.

The rune stone was a land claim carved, buried, and marked by triangulating stone holes cut into several glacial boulders surrounding it. This would allow a returning party to find it. The Tower itself was also a land claim, just as John Jr. was instructed by his elder brethren that day in 1769.

When Diana shared the journals with me in 2016, I asked her if the sketch John Jr. made was in the material she had. Unfortunately it was not, likely meaning John Jr. gave the sketch to Kitty upon his return. What an amazing piece of history it would be if it was ever found.

The Newport Tower is a two-story stone and mortar structure that stands on eight, round heavy columns the Templars constructed circa 1400. (Wolter, 2018)

On the morning of the winter solstice at 9:00 a.m. the west window in the Newport Tower creates a lightbox that illuminates the egg-shaped keystone in the west-northwest archway. This ingenious alignment marks the shortest day of the year and allegorical rebirth of the sun. (Wolter, 2007)

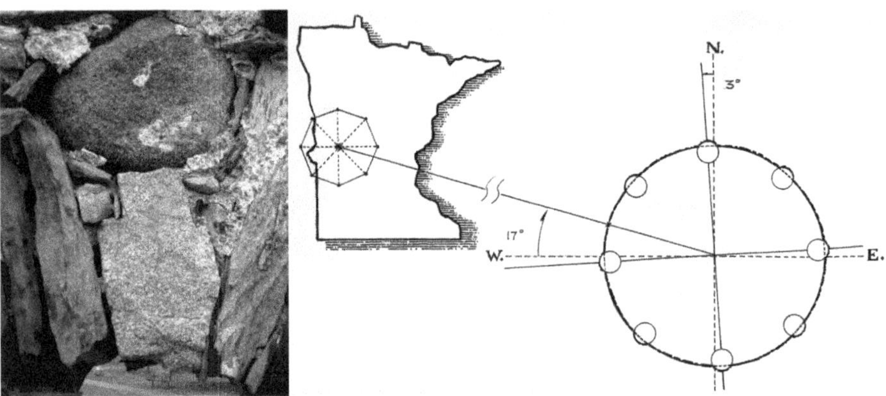

On the outside of the Newport Tower in the west-northwest archway is a notched and angled keystone that was placed back-to-back with the egg-shaped keystone on the inside of the structure. In 2007, it occurred to me that a line from the center of the tower extended through the two keystones west into space extends to the location where the Kensington Rune Stone was discovered in the fall of 1898. (Wolter, 2007/2009)

The split (bottom) and face sides of the Kensington Rune Stone, which is dated to 1362, sits in its cradle at the Runestone Museum in Alexandria, Minnesota. The first three lines of the inscription spells out the who, why, and where, of the purpose of the artifact created as a land claim by the descendants of the disbanded medieval Knights Templar order: "8 Gotalanders and 22 Norwegians on this acquisition mission/taking up land from Vinland far to the west." (Wolter, 2010)

June 28, 1769

We have arrived back in Abington and have been greeted by my mother who is happy to see us. She informs us that Father is in Philadelphia for a meeting of the brethren but will be home in the morning. We look forward to a warm evening meal and a soft bed.

June 29, 1769

Father has arrived home and is pleased to see us. He asked for a report of our findings and Brother John reported that all sites were undisturbed and protected. He told Father of the men we had met with and the places we had visited. Father also asked for a report of political affairs in Boston and in Nova Scotia. Brother John stated that events were unpredictable, and it seems as if both countries are on the verge of war. Father agrees and stated that he had been meeting with the Brethren in Philadelphia about the unrest concerning England and France. He now has more to ask of me, being pleased that I gladly accepted instruction from Brother Scott on our trip to Cape Breton and Nova Scotia with few complaints.

I repeated my doubts about the journals to my Father and he responded, "My grandfather's grandfather and his grandfather before him saw the treasure with his own eyes and helped to move it to the colonies. They wanted to ensure that it was safe and protected until a free nation could be built where God's children could flourish in the bosom of Abraham." He instructed me to be faithful and obey the admonishments of he and the brethren. He promised that God would direct me in my actions if only I have faith.

Father has told me of his meeting with the brethren: John Hanson of Maryland, George Mason of Mason's Island, Arthur Sinclair, Ebenezer Morton, William Irvine, Nathaniel Gorham of Massachusetts, and Joseph Dickinson this past year. They plan to move the treasure and artifacts to Mason's Island where they are preparing a vault to hold them. It will [be] *my job to organize a caravan of 6 wagons and suitable Brethren to assist in moving the treasure to Mason's Island where the brethren will be able to defend it. They are afraid they will lose access to the sites where it is hidden if the British should win the ensuing war. He stated that all of these men and their families were part of the Covenant and would do their best to aid me in my task.*

I am distressed that I will be unable to accomplish this, but Father says I am well prepared and should enlist my brother Thomas for suitable wagons and labor. He gives me 7 maps that he has copied onto unused paper and tells me that each group of 4 or 5 men should reclaim the treasure at each location. Each map is marked with the latitude and marked as to where the treasure resides. I have already visited the islands and will be able to direct them on whom to speak with and where to begin. We are to load the wagons with trade goods for the natives and people of Halifax to justify our journey. He has also included instructions on how to find the last island in western New York, having enlisted the help of Ebenezer Morton. He has asked that I make this journey myself as I must travel through the land of the Onondowaga.

To complete this task, I must take into my confidence those brethren that I trust the most. Father says he trusts my judgment that I will be able to recruit these men in a timely fashion. He has directed me to the Grand Master of the North Carolina Lodge. He suggests that we leave in the spring to recover the treasure and bring it by wagon caravan to Maryland. Brother Hanson and Brother Irvine will assist in ferrying it to Mason's Island in the nearby river.

The candle is dimming and about to go out. I must retire although I know I cannot sleep. Tomorrow I will begin my journey home with Brother Scott. I pray that the Holy Father and Holy Mother protect and direct me in this task. I also pray that my wife Kitty will understand another absence.

Suddenly the gravity of the task John Jr. has been entrusted with hits him. Anyone would be unsure about taking on such a risky and dangerous mission, but as we will see he was more than up to the challenge. This man was a true American hero along with the other men you will soon meet. This is truly one of the greatest stories ever told and represents the truth about how the United States of America was founded.

August 4, 1769

I have arrived home to the loving arms of my wife and children. I have much to consider as I prepare for the task ahead of me. I must travel in 10 days hence to New Town for a meeting of the Lodge. I pray that my brethren will be open to the challenge that faces them.

Book 18

Journal of John Weems

1741-1812

Continued

August 10, 1769

I have spoken with Brother Richard Caswell, and he will arrange a closed meeting for me with the Brethren at the next meeting. I have expressed that all matters must remain secret as much is at stake. He has promised that no record will remain of the meeting and has promised to remind the brethren of their obligations.

This entry reminded me that nearly all of our founding fathers—the ones whose names we know, as well as the ones we don't—like John Weems Jr., were Freemasons. They were also Knights Templar, they just didn't tell anyone. It bothers me that in the modern era almost nobody understands how this country and its constitution were built upon the tenants of Freemasonry. We have forgotten our own past, which brings to mind the phrase we are in danger of reliving: "*Those who do not learn from the past, are destined to repeat it.*"

August 28, 1769

I have recruited 22 men to accompany me to Nova Scotia in the spring of 1770 and have written to my brother Thomas in Abbeville in the 96th District of South Carolina for a promise of 3 wagons and perhaps 6 men to drive and help us with manual labor. I have the promise of 4 wagons from Hillsborough and those recruited here. All are strong men, and we should have ample strength to retrieve what lies buried. I have told them we plan to leave mid-April and may be gone as long as 3 months. They are to prepare their families for their absence and assure them of their return.

It will be several weeks before I receive a reply from my brother, but I have much to occupy my time here. The fields are in need of attention and soon we will have crops to harvest. I must also build another corn house and smoke house before then.

Here we see number 22 again. Freemasons and Templar Knights always think about using symbolic numbers whenever possible.

September 6, 1769

Today Lizzie is four years old. She is a lively child with a large imagination. Kitty baked her a special cake today to celebrate.

September 15, 1769

We have completed the harvest in the south fields and have stored it all in the new corn house. Tomorrow, we start slaughtering 6 pigs and 2 cattle for the winter larder.

October 2, 1769

We are prepared for the winter months and during this week the Church Brethren assist with collecting dry wood to put in the barn for winter fires. I also must remember to caulk the roof in the place that it leaks and replace the old shingles. Kitty is busy making a new winter dress for Lizzie and long pants for baby Willie. John is only 18 months old but he is beginning to talk although he runs everywhere. His tiny hands explore everything.

October 11, 1769

The barn is stocked with wood for the winter and hay has been stored for the horses. We plan for a church feast to celebrate the harvest this Sunday after services.

October 23, 1769

Brother Bible's wife Anna has taken ill after the birth of her third child. Kitty and Margaret will care for her for the next few days. The children are fussy but sugar candy keeps them happy. They dislike my cooking and grimace while eating. They make me laugh and I miss my wife less.

November 1, 1769

Anna Bible died this morning from fever. She will be buried tomorrow in the churchyard. Brother Bible is weary but thankful she did not suffer longer. He holds tight to his children and asks only that the Lord receive her with grace.

It is entries like this that remind one how we take childbirth almost for granted in our time, when it was a very dangerous undertaking back then. That said, my own daughter—a type 1 diabetic—nearly died from preeclampsia giving birth to her daughter Kinzlee a couple of years ago. Thankfully we had a good outcome in our case.

November 12, 1769

Willie has fallen off his rack and has broken his left leg. Kitty has wrapped it with linen, and I will ride for the doctor for medicine. He cried constantly although he tries to be brave.

November 13, 1769

Willie is much happier now that his leg is set and rewrapped by Doctor Biddle. Lizzie hovers over him like an angel and brings him anything he wishes.

November 16, 1769

Today is my 5th anniversary of my marriage to Kitty. We celebrate with a special dinner with Brother Richard Gott and his wife Margaret who is my sister.

December 5, 1769

We received our first snow today. Winter has arrived.

December 24, 1769

Kitty has stayed up late finishing the Christmas presents for the children. I have made Lizzie a cornhusk doll, carved a whistle for Johnny and a boat for Willie. Last week I bought a shawl for Kitty while visiting Greeneville. I hope she will be pleased.

December 30, 1769

We have received another heavy snow. The horses refuse to leave the barn and I tripped over the pig while trying to feed them. Lizzie laughed at the dirt and mud when I returned to the cabin. Kitty was not as happy.

January 5, 1770

Johnny turns 2 years old today. He is a big boy and looks like his Grandfather Dengler. His grandparents would be proud as he is already learning his numbers. Kitty keeps them busy during the day as it is too cold to be outside in the winter garden.

January 15, 1770

The church Brethren gathered together today to celebrate the birth of twins to Brother and Sister Thompson. Both boys are healthy and were baptized this day and given the names of Andrew and Ambrose Thompson. The Baptism was followed by a lunch at the Church.

February 4, 1770

We have visitors from Pennsylvania who arrived late last night. Gordon Little and his brother Theophilus are traveling south and could go no further on the road. They bedded in the cabin near to the fire. They leave this morn after a hearty breakfast. They bring news of political affairs back east and talk of revolt in the colonies.

February 22, 1770

I attended a meeting of the brethren last night and listened as they spoke of political unrest in Massachusetts, Virginia and Pennsylvania. I worry that my father and his friends are involved somehow as they are very opinionated. Brother Smith lectured on the need for temperance and tolerance, but I fear few were listening.

March 15, 1770

Another large snowstorm has kept us indoors for 3 days. I have created a path to the barn but the animals are restless and are anxious to be let loose. We keep warm in the cabin and play games with the children.

March 22, 1770

Kitty gave birth this day to another son whom we named George Wright Weems. He is a strong lad with blonde hair. He will be baptized this Sunday at a meeting. Kitty is doing well, and Lizzie is doing her best to help her with the baby.

April 1, 1770

I have recruited the following men and have received a response from my brother with a promise of 4 wagons, 4 men and 8 slaves to assist us in our travels. He is unable to accompany us as the farm requires his attention and his wife is expecting a child during that time. He is sending our brother Bartholomew in his stead, who will be of great assistance. I make this list as a record of our journey so that they may be blessed by the Holy Father and Holy Mother in their journeys.

1. *John Weems*
2. *Abraham Bailey*
3. *John Caswell*
4. *Joseph Ballard*
5. *Samuel Craig*
6. *John Fannin*
7. *Moses Boynton*

8. *George Cummins*
9. *James Frazier*
10. *James Lynch*
11. *Joseph Montfort*
12. *Benjamin Hilliard*
13. *Oliver Howse*
14. *John Powell*
15. *Peter Copeland*
16. *Daniel Lovel*
17. *Samuel McCracken*
18. *Joseph McCullough*
19. *Elijah Roberson*
20. *Theophilus Thompson*
21. *John Noe*
22. *Richard Gott*

The men from 96th District should arrive in the next few days. I am looking forward to seeing my brother Bartholomew. It has been almost 5 years since we have talked. Bart is a huge bull of a man but is kind and gentle. My brother Thomas assures me that he has full authority over the slaves he is sending. He also says he would like to see the slaves freed once their job is completed as they have served his wife's family well for many years and have earned their manumission. Once again, I have enlisted Brother Bible to look after my family. Kitty will also have the assistance of my sister Margaret Gott in our absence. I assure her that we will return within 3 months' time and beg her to forgive my absence.

Upon reading this entry the first time I was stumped by the word "manumission." I had never heard it before, but it was clearly defined in this entry.

April 6, 1770

My blood brother Bartholomew has arrived with a retinue of 20 men and 4 wagons of tobacco for trade with the natives in Nova Scotia. He brings with him 6 slaves for whom he has papers of manumission so that they may be released to freedom after we have completed our journey.

The men he brings are all Freemasons of an advanced degree. This evening will be spent in explaining our duty to the men who have gathered. We shall leave in 2 days' time after the horses are sufficiently rested and the wagons prepared.

The following is a list of the men who have arrived with Brother Bartholomew.

1. *John Ash*
2. *John Bailey*
3. *William Byers*
4. *William Berry*
5. *Matthew Bradley*
6. *John Caldwell*
7. *George Caughman*
8. *Rev Thomas Clark*
9. *Peter Dancer*
10. *John Edwards*
11. *William Ellis*
12. *John England*
13. *Patrick Calhoun*
14. *Robert Haddon Jr*
15. *Moses McCarter*
16. *Moses McCarter*
17. *Robert Swain*
18. *William Vickery*
19. *James Webb*
20. *James Richey*
21. *Samuel Ball (Freed slave)*
22. *Ambrose Weems (freed slave)*
23. *Hannibal Weems (freed slave)*
24. *Solomon Weems (freed slave)*
25. *Honest Redfearn (freed slave)*
26. *Barkabol Redfearn (freed slave)*

April 7, 1770

My children are captivated with their Uncle Bartholomew, and he has spent the morning giving rides on his shoulders to Lizzy and Willie. Bart has never married but it appears he adores the children. This day will be spent readying the farm for my absence and finishing the corn house. We leave in the morning after daily prayers and asking for the Lord's protection in our journey.

April 8, 1770

Word has arrived in Hillsboro of a battle in the streets of Boston on the fifth of March in which at least five were killed.[57] *Citizens are angry at the numerous taxes and demand representation in the provincial congress. It bodes bad news for our journey, and I worry that we might be stopped on the road to Nova Scotia. We must not be misconstrued as a small army and must take greater care to appear as merchants. We postpone our journey and will meet this eve to discuss our final plans before leaving on the morrow."*

The Battle of Boston occurred on March 5th, 1770, and became known as the Boston Massacre. Five civilians were killed by British troops in a skirmish started when a frightened British soldier discharged his gun, inciting his comrades to open fire on the unruly crowd.

The Boston Massacre occurred on March 5, 1770 when British troops opened fire on an angry mob in downtown Boston. (Internet)

57. https://www.britannica.com/event/Boston-Massacre

April 8, 1770

We have taken great care to pack the wagons with common articles for trade. Brother William Johnston has secured three wagons of farm and trade goods and seed with an eye for a fair profit in Halifax. Brother Fanning has also secured the necessary papers we need and silver to pay the duties if any be demanded. The Regulators have been appeased by Brother Gott and they turn a blind eye to our activities as they presume us to be honest farmers and merchants.

We have covered the dried tobacco and cotton bales from last fall's harvest in South Carolina with sturdy wool blankets that can be used on our return to obscure our goods. Each man has prepared his own pack with enough rations to last two months and shot and powder for his musket. We have amongst us only 10 bayonets and have hidden them beneath the wagons in case of need against the natives. We hope to reach Halifax within two months and will procure digging tools once there. We plan to ferry the wagons across at Fort Western to shorten the journey.

Each group of 5 men will meet with Brethren we have met before and will be guided to the correct island via boats that we will secure in Halifax. Whatever we can deliver back to the brethren in Boston will be ferried by boat back to the wagons which will stand on the Halifax quay. We must as always be extremely careful as the British occupy Halifax. I have made arrangements to buy furs and goods to return to Hillsboro as proof of a good trade. We will then travel down the coast to Poboncon where 3 ships will be waiting for us as arranged by my father. He feels it best to return by sea rather than by land as British troops patrol the roads regularly. Only the trade goods will return by wagon with half of our men led by my brother Bartholomew. The rest will return by sea. I know I will be ill the entire way.

Before we leave in the morn, I have made arrangements to hide the journals in a brick vault built for burials at the Church with the permission of the rector who is also a brethren. He has promised that they will be safe until my return and promises to look after our families as well. After my return from the church, I will spend my last eve with my wife and children. I have promised to build a proper two-story brick house for

Kitty upon my return as she tells me our small family continues to grow. I leave with her Solomon, a freed slave sent by my brother Thomas to help her with the farm in my absence. He is an amiable lad and has promised to do as she asks until my return. He is well skilled in farming and the forge and is gentle around the children.

The Regulators were a group of citizens in North and South Carolina who took up arms against corrupt colonial officials between the years of 1765 to 1771.[58] Because John Jr. lived in North Carolina it makes sense he likely would have encountered the Regulators, preferring to stay on their good side by being fair and upright in his negotiations with them.

Book 19

Journal of John Weems
1741-1812

Written in modern English

April 9, 1770

We have left this chilly morn up the Trading Path and hope that the weather will warm as we head east to Staunton. We will take the same route as Brother Scott, and I took for familiarities sake. Upon my return I will ride through western New York to fulfill my promise to my father. First, we must secure what we can in Nova Scotia.

April 27, 1770

We travel approximately 20 to 25 miles per day and should reach Baltimore shortly. The journey has been unremarkable so far and the weather remains fair, yet chilly with an occasional rain. Those we pass on the road are friendly and ask for news of the Carolina territory. Many are going that way in search of new beginnings and good farmland. We wish them well and continue on.

58. https://www.battlefields.org/learn/articles/regulator-war

Cover page of the lambskin map and linen journal book #19, written by John Weems Jr. in 1770. I snapped this photo while examining it on September 19, 2016. (Wolter, 2016)

April 29, 1770

We have overnighted at Baltimore and restock our rations so that we can continue to Philadelphia. The horses are well rested, and we should arrive in Abington in 5 days. More British troops are seen on the road, but they pass us by as soon as we explain we are merchants on the way to market. Our papers from Brother Fanning serve us well and so far, there have been no incidents.

May 5, 1770

We have arrived at the manor and Father and Mother are excited to see us, especially Bartholomew who has been absent for 6 years. We camp outside by the barns and the men are excited for a day or two of rest. The horses have been released into the fields after a visit to the farrier and the wagons are sheltered in the barns against any rain or bad weather. Samuel Ball, one of Thomas's freed slaves whom he has trained as a blacksmith, has taken over Father's forge and with the help of the other men is strengthening the wagon wheels and wagon tongues against the rough roads ahead. Thomas has treated his slaves well and I find them well trained and able to read and write. Samuel tells me that Master Thomas and his mistress Elizabeth has provided a school and church for them and that he will miss them both.

Many write letters home and Father has promised to dispatch them as soon as possible. Before we continue Father wishes to address the brethren at the Friends Academy where I attended school, and has sent a courier to Philadelphia to request the presence of the Lodge Grand Master. It is there that we will make final plans and instruct the brethren in the reasons behind our journey. We will meet in the morrow after a good night's sleep and evening meal. After supper Father began interviewing the men I had recruited. I hope he finds them satisfactory.

The name Samuel Ball instantly brought to mind the same name associated with the Oak Island mystery. We covered this topic in the book I published with Donald Ruh in 2024, *Oak Island, Knights Templar, and the Holy Grail: Secrets of the Underground Project Revealed.* We concluded they were not the same person, as this Samuel Ball was several years older than the Samuel Ball who became very wealthy in the area of Mahone Bay in the 1800s. That man was born in 1765 and would have been four years old when this mission commenced.[59]

The original May 5, 1770 entry by John Weems Jr. on page one of the twenty-four-page journal Book 19. (Wolter, 2016)

59. Wolter/Ruh, Page 7-13, 2024.

May 6, 1770

My Father, having been raised to the status of Master Mason in the 46th British Regiment, presided over the meeting which was attended by William Ball of Philadelphia and Benjamin Franklin the former Provincial Grand Master of Pennsylvania. The brethren gathered in the schoolhouse and for 3 hours were impressed upon by the presiding brethren the importance of their mission. We were each divided into groups of 5 and told to embrace each other in the coming journey and to learn to trust and depend upon each other as it would become vitally important in our task.

The presiding Brethren also imparted their knowledge of current political events and told us that it was immensely important that the Templar Treasure find its way back to the Grand Lodge to assist in the oncoming war. We would soon lose control of the territory in Nova Scotia and the brethren feared it would be lost if not retrieved straight away. They also reiterated that secrecy was of the utmost importance and that we would be always surrounded by British troops and subjects who might report our every move.

In January of 2021 I visited the Quaker Friends School in Abington, Pennsylvania. The school still stands and has been added onto six times. Duing our visit the groundskeeper showed us the original space where that private meeting took place on May 6, 1770. (Wolter, 2021)

hope I confirmed them satisfactory.
May 6, 1770

My father, having been raised to the
status of Master Mason in the 46th British
Regiment, presided over the meeting which
was attended by William Ball of Philadelphia
and Benjamin Franklin the former Provincial
Grand Master of Pennsylvania. The Brethren
gathered in the school room and for 3
hours were impressed upon by the
Presiding Brethren the importance of their
mission. We were each divided into
groups of 5 and told to embrace each
other in the coming journey and to
learn to trust and depend upon each
other as it would become vitally important
in our task.
The presiding Brethren also imparted
their knowledge of current political
events and told us that it was
important that the Templar Treasure
find its way back to the Grand Lodge
to assist in the upcoming war. We
would soon loose control of the territory
in Nova Scotia and the Brethren feared
it would be lost if not retrieved straight
away. They also reiterated that secrecy
was of the utmost importance and that
we should always be surrounded
by British troops and subjects who might
report our every move.

The original May 6, 1770 entry by John Weems Jr. on page two of Book 19. This entry is arguably the most impactful and inspiring entry in this journal. (Wolter, 2016)

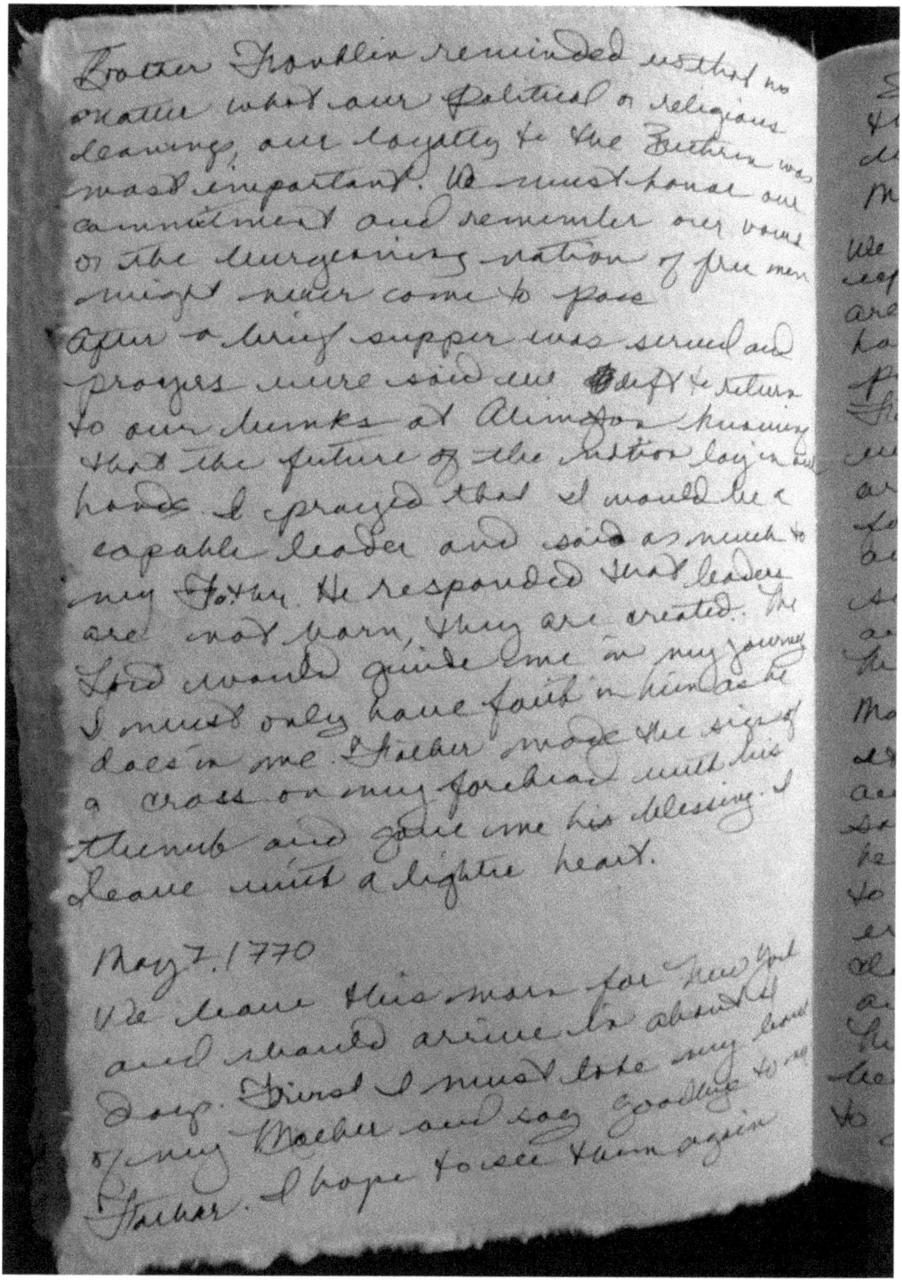

Brother Franklin reminded us that no
matter what our political or religious
leanings, our loyalty to the Brethren was
most important. We must honor our
commitment and remember our vows
or the burgeoning nation of free men
might never come to pass.
After a brief supper was served and
prayers were said we left to return
to our bunks at Alington knowing
that the future of the nation lay in our
hands. I prayed that I would be a
capable leader and said as much to
my Father. He responded that leaders
are not born, they are created. The
Lord would guide me in my journey
I must only have faith in him as he
does in me. Father made the sign of
a cross on my forehead with his
thumb and gave me his blessing. I
leave with a lighter heart.

May 7, 1770
We leave this morn for New York
and should arrive in about 4
days. First I must take my leave
of my Mother and say goodbye to my
Father. I hope to see them again

This is the continuation of the original May 6 and 7, 1770 entries by John Weems Jr. on page three of Book 19. "Brother Franklin" is undoubtedly Benjamin Franklin. (Muir, 2016)

Brother Franklin reminded us that no matter what our political or religious leanings, our loyalty to the brethren was most important. We must honor our commitment and remembers our vows, or the burgeoning nation of free men might never come to pass.

After a brief supper was served and prayers were said we left to return to our bunks at Abington knowing that the future of the nation lay in our hands. I prayed that I would be a capable leader and said as much to my Father. He responded that leaders are not born, they are created. The Lord would guide me in my journey. I must only have faith in him as he does in me. Father made the sign of a cross on my forehead with his thumb and gave me his blessing. I leave with a lighter heart.

For me, this was the most important and moving entry of the entire corpus of the journals. Especially after having been in the space at the Quaker Friends' School in Abington, Pennsylvania where this meeting took place. When I closed my eyes and stood silent in that room, I could almost hear Benjamin Franklin's voice imparting his wisdom on the young brethren who were about to put their lives on the line for the sake of the new Republic that was about to be formed. These men didn't know their efforts would result in an eventual historic victory over the British and the founding of the most powerful nation on earth. I get chills every time I read John Jr's words. They will always resonate in my heart and soul.

May 7, 1770

We leave this morn for New York and should arrive in about 4 days. First, I must take my leave of my mother and say farewell to my father. I hope to see them again soon but am fearful the road that lies before us will be fraught with difficulty.

May 12, 1770

We arrived in York City yesterday and set up camp on the edge of the city. There are British troops everywhere, but we have been stopped only once before passing through the city. As my father suggested, when asked

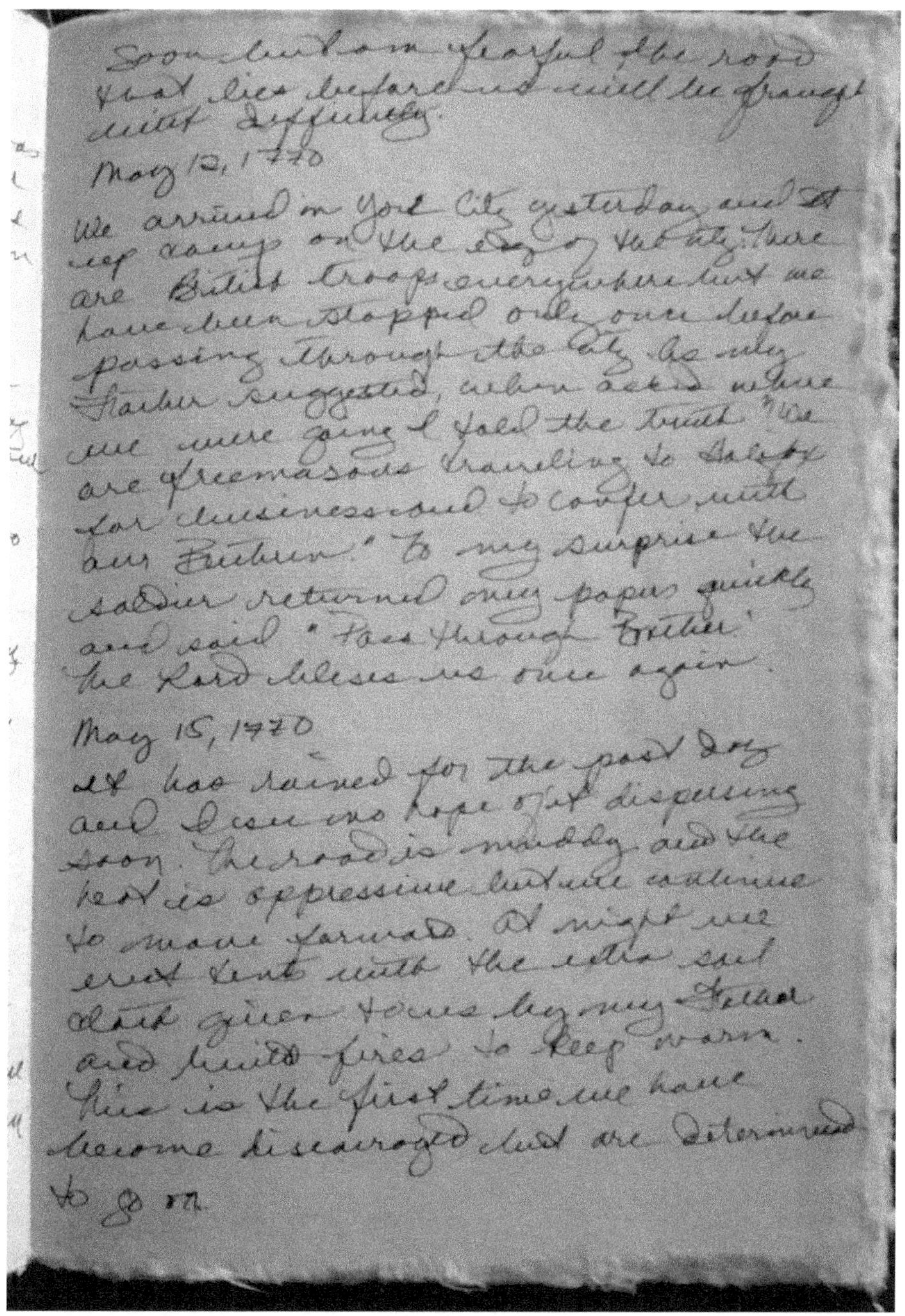

soon but am fearful the road that lies before us will be fraught with difficulty.

May 12, 1770

We arrived in York City yesterday and set up camp on the edge of the city. There are British troops everywhere but we have been stopped only once before passing through the city. As my Father suggested, when asked where we were going I told the truth "We are freemasons traveling to Halifax for business and to confer with our Brethren." To my surprise the soldier returned my papers quickly and said "Pass through Brother." The Lord blesses us once again.

May 15, 1770

It has rained for the past day and I see no hope of it dispersing soon. The road is muddy and the heat is oppressive but we continue to move forward. At night we erect tents with the extra sail cloth given to us by my Father and build fires to keep warm. This is the first time we have become discouraged but are determined to go on.

These are the May 12 and May 15, 1770 entries by John Weems Jr. on page four of Book 19. (Muir, 2016) *where we were going I told the truth, "We are freemasons traveling to Halifax for business and to confer with our brethren." To my surprise the soldier returned my papers quickly and said, "Pass through Brother." The Lord blesses us once again.*

This simple entry contains a powerful message about the profound impact of Freemasonry during this time. Once recognized as a brother, there was then, and still is now, a common bond through a shared experience and an oath to conduct oneself "on the level" with other brethren regardless of their faith or their national allegiance.

May 15, 1770

It has rained for the past day, and I see no hope of it dispersing soon. The road is muddy, and the heat is oppressive, but we continue to move forward. At night we erect tents with the extra sail cloth given to us by my father and build fires to stay warm. This is the first time we have become discouraged but are determined to go on.

May 18, 1770

Bad luck has visited us this day. Brother Joseph Ballard's horse stepped in a gopher hole and Brother Ballard was thrown to the ground, breaking his left arm. He says he can continue but when we arrive in Boston will leave it to the doctor to determine.

May 22, 1770

We have arrived in Boston and have sought out a doctor to care for Brother Ballard's arm. He says that once it is set properly, he should be able to continue as long as he limits his activity. I suggest that he drive one of the wagons to prevent further injury and he is satisfied with my reply.

The town seems uneasy and British troops are ever present near the centre of town and the quay. We will circumvent the town and continue north after a night's rest in the stables and replenishing our rations.

May 18 1770
Bad luck has visited us this day Brother
Joseph Ballard horse stepped in a gopher hole
and Brother Ballard was thrown to the ground
breaking his left arm. He says he can continue but
when we arrive in Boston will leave them to
the Doctor to determine.

May 22, 1770
We have arrived in Boston and have sought
out a Doctor to care for Brother Ballards arm. He
says once it is set properly he should be able to
continue as long as he limits his activity. I
suggest that he drive one of the wagons to
prevent further injury and he is satisfied
with my reply. The town seems uneasy and
British troops are now present near the centre
of town and the quay. We will circumvent
the town and continue north after a nights
rest in the stables and replenishing our rations

May 23, 1770
Overnight we heard shouting and yelling
as a barn was burned to the ground not
far from where we are billeted. We are
anxious to be on our way and will leave
right after breaking our fast.

May 24, 1770
We were stopped by British soldiers upon
leaving the town but once again Brother
Flemmings papers were accepted and we paid
a small bribe of 1 pound sterling for each
wagon to be on our way. I look forward
to reaching the quiet road before us and
hope to arrive at Fort Western without

The original May 18 to May 24, 1770 entries by John Weems Jr. These entries chronicle the beginning of the journey from Abington, Pennsylvania to Nova Scotia to recover the Earl Henry treasures hidden in 1398. (Wolter, 2016)

May 23, 1770

Overnight we heard shouting and yelling as a barn was burned to the ground not far from where we billeted. We are anxious to be on our way and will leave right after breaking our fast.

"Billet" is another word I had not heard prior to reading the journals. It is a place where soldiers stay for a short while.

May 24, 1770

We were stopped by British soldiers upon leaving the town but once again Brother Fanning's papers were accepted, and we paid a small bribe of 1 pound sterling for each wagon to be on our way. I looked forward to reaching the quiet roads before us and hope to arrive at Fort Western without further incident.

June 2, 1770

We have arrived at Fort Western without incident and have camped beside the harbor to await a ferry to Nova Scotia. It will take several trips, but each group of men is gladdened that we are near our goal. It may take 2 days to complete the passage to Nova Scotia, but the men are enjoying the sun and warm weather. Several have taken to fishing off the quay and we shall have fish for dinner with any luck.

June 5, 1770

All have arrived safely at Poboncon and have been met by a group of natives led by a silver haired man who calls himself Kaleboo. He speaks good English and says that he learned at a missionary school when he was a child. He claims that the Holy Mother – or spirit woman – of their village admonished him to bring 5 others and meet the ferry that brought the Warriors of God. He says they are also Gods Warriors and would accompany us on our journey if we would so allow. They have been waiting for 10 days and are happy to see we have arrived safely.

I pondered this for a moment, and realizing it would be good to have a native translator, accepted his assistance. I could only suppose that one

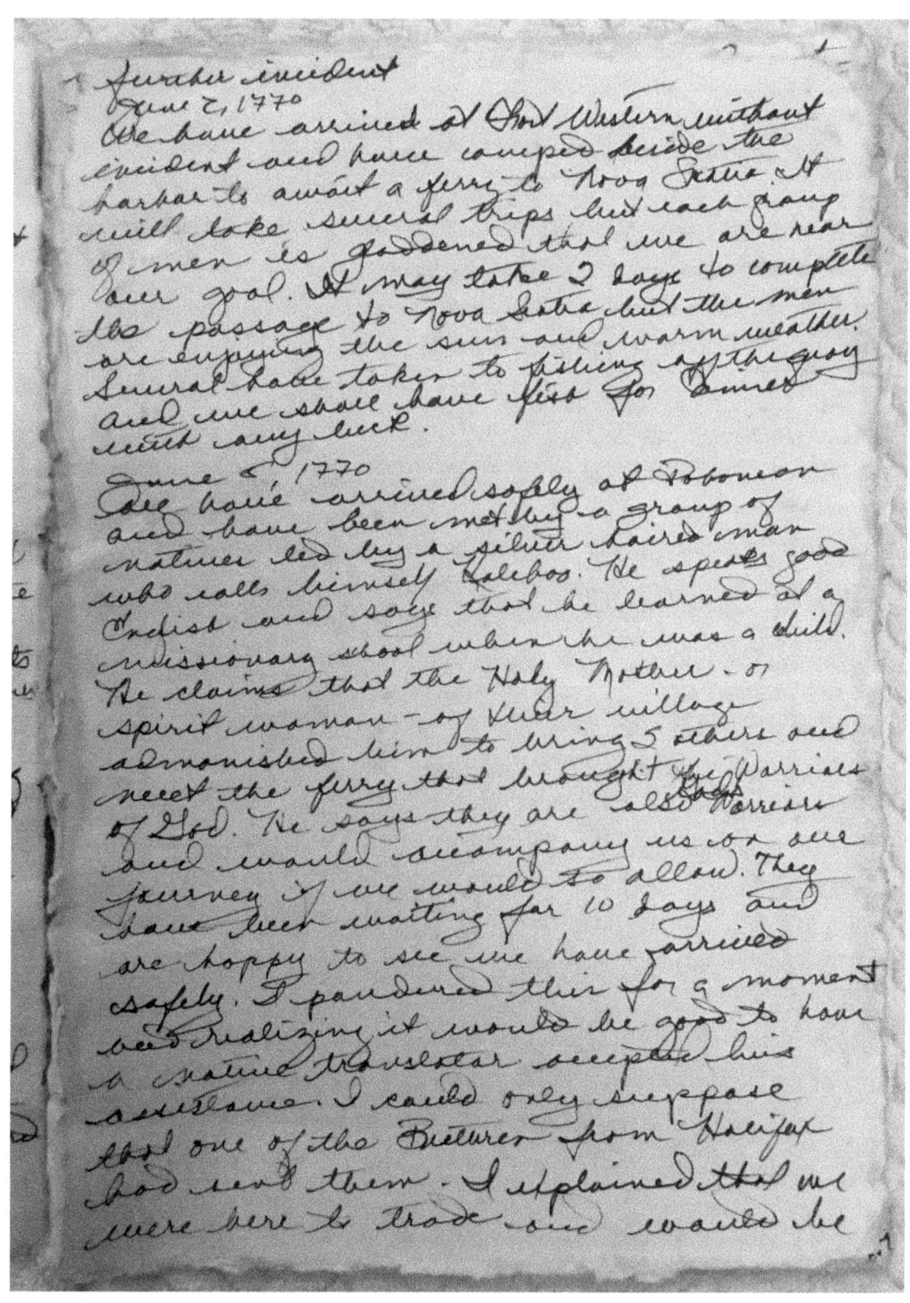

further incident
June 2, 1770
We have arrived at Port Western without
incident and have camped beside the
harbor to await a ferry to Nova Scotia. It
will take several trips but each group
of men is gladdened that we are near
our goal. It may take 2 days to complete
the passage to Nova Scotia but the men
are enjoying the sun and warm weather.
Several have taken to fishing off the quay
and we shall have fish for dinner
with any luck.

June 5, 1770
We have arrived safely at Pobomcoup
and have been met by a group of
natives led by a silver haired man
who calls himself Kaleboo. He speaks good
English and says that he learned at a
missionary school when he was a child.
He claims that the Holy Mother - or
spirit woman - of their village
admonished him to bring 5 others and
meet the ferry that brought the Warriors
of God. He says they are also Warriors
and would accompany us on our
journey if we would so allow. They
have been waiting for 10 days and
are happy to see we have arrived
safely. I pondered this for a moment
and realizing it would be good to have
a native translator accepted his
assistance. I could only suppose
that one of the Brethren from Halifax
had sent them. I explained that we
were here to trade and would be

Journal entries John Weems Jr. made on June 2 and June 5, 1770. (Wolter, 2016) *of the brethren from Halifax had sent them. I explained that we were here to trade and would be making several stops on the way to Halifax where we would meet with our brethren. He nodded his head in understanding and he and his men began to help disembark the wagons from the ferry.*

John was wise accepting the assistance of Kaleboo and his men. It appears the commitment of support and assistance of the indigenous people to the Covenant was unbroken even after four centuries. This undying commitment by the indigenous people must be respected and honored, especially after the way they were treated by the colonists during settlement in the eighteenth and nineteenth centuries. It was nothing short of genocide, and when we celebrate our 250th anniversary of the birth of America we should honor their contribution as much as the brave patriots like John Weems Jr., the Freemasons named here, and African American slaves who traveled with him to complete the Covenant and establish the New Jerusalem.

Within 2 hours we have emptied two wagons of trade goods that was meant for the natives here. They are eager to have metal pots, blankets and sturdy cloth and greet us with warm smiles. In return they provide us with digging implements, picks, shovels and food supplies for our trip. After a good nights rest we will once again commence on our journey up the coast to Chester. Our first stop will be at Gold River where one empty wagon and one of the teams will remain at Mary ONeale's home. We have divided the brethren into teams that include a wagon driver, a native and several brethren. We will go our separate ways after we reach Chester, hoping to meet up again after 2 weeks.

Father has given us the best locations for the islands as possible that were obtained during their trip in 1766. He has also written letters to each of the brethren that I carry enlisting their assistance as each of them knows exactly the places we are searching for. We will need to procure a number of boats in each place to ferry men and equipment back and forth to the wagons. Each team will require a surveyor's compass and adequate food supplies and blankets to cover their cargo once retrieved.

making several stops on the way to
Halifax where we would meet with
our Brethren. He nodded his head in
understanding and he and his men
began to help disembark the wagons
from the ferry. Within 3 hours we have
emptied two wagons of trade goods that
was meant for the natives here. They are
eager to have metal pots, blankets, and
sturdy cloth and greet us with warm
smiles. In return they provide us with
digging implements, picks, and shovels
and food supplies for our trip. After a
good night rest we will once again
commence on our journey up the coast
to Chester. Our first stop will be at Gold
River where one empty wagon and one of
the teams will remain at Mary Oheals
home. We have divided the Brethren into
teams that include a wagon driver, a
native and several Brethren. We will
go our separate ways after we reach
Chester, hoping to meet up again after 2
weeks.
Father has given us the best locations for
the islands as possible that were obtained
during their trip in 1766. He has also
written letters to each of the Brethren
that I carry enlisting their assistance
as each of them knows exactly the
places we are searching for. We will
need to procure a number of boats

The continuation of the John Weems Jr. entry on June 5, 1770. (Wolter, 2016)

The staging place at the mouth of the Gold River is very near present day Oak Island. It has become extremely famous for the treasure that was hidden there in 1395 and, according to the Cremona Document, was recovered in 1769.

After we have secured what we have come for, Brother Peters and Brother Fraser will assist us in buying goods for our return to Maryland. The ships that Father has arranged for us at Halifax will meet us there on June 24th [St. John the Baptist Day, a very important day in Templarism and Freemasonry to this day]. *After we have loaded our cargo, we will stop at Chester and Gold River to retrieve our brethren where there is less scrutiny from the British troops.*

Team 1 Island at 44.4812 Ship Perequin
Will meet with Brother Joseph Peters of Halifax

1. *John Weems*
2. *Joseph Ballard*
3. *Samuel Craig*
4. *John Fanning*
5. *Moses Boynton*
6. *James Webb*
7. *Honest Redfearn (Black) (Driver)*
8. *Kaleboo (native)*

Team 2 Island at 44.4523 (Ship Apricitas)
Will meet with John Smith of Gold River

1. *George Cummins*
2. *John England*
3. *Patrick Calhoun*
4. *James Frazier*
5. *James Lynch*
6. *Joseph Montfort*
7. *Benjamin Hilliard*
8. *Ambrose Weems (Black)*
9. *Kesegook (native)*

in each place to ferry men and equipment back and forth to the wagons.
Each team will require a surveyor's
compass and adequate food supplies
and blankets to cover their cargo once
retrieved. After we have secured what we
have come for Brother Peters and Brother
Fraser will assist us in buying goods
for our return to Maryland. The Ships
that Father has arranged for us at
Halifax will meet us there on June 28th.
After we have loaded our cargo, we
will stop at Chester and Gold River to
retrieve our Brethren where there is
less scrutiny from the British troops.
Team 1 island at 44.4812 Ship Peregrin
will meet with Brother Joseph Peters of
Halifax
John Weems, Joseph Ballard, Samuel
Craig, John [illegible], Moses Boynton,
James Webb, [illegible] [illegible] (Black driver)
[illegible] (native)
Team 2 Island at 44.4523 Ship Apricitas
will meet with John Smith of Gold River.
George Cummins, John [illegible], Patrick
Calhoun, James Frazier, James [illegible]
Joseph Montfort, Benjamin Hubbard, Ambrose
Weems (black) [illegible] (native)
Team 3 Island at 44.43815 Ship Ortus
Will meet with John Fraser of Halifax
Oliver House, John Powell. Peter Copeland,
Daniel [illegible], Samuel McCracken Joseph McCulloch
Moses McCarthy S. Hannibal Weems (Black) [illegible]
(native)

The continuation of the John Weems Jr. entry on June 5, 1770. It includes the list of names on teams one (*Perequin*), two (*Apricitas*) and three (*Ortis*), named after the ships that carried and deposited their treasures in 1398. (Wolter, 2016)

Team 3 Island at 44.43815 (Ship Ortus)
Will meet with John Fraser of Halifax

1. *Oliver Howse*
2. *John Powell*
3. *Peter Copeland*
4. *Daniel Lovel*
5. *Samuel McCracken*
6. *Joseph McCullough*
7. *Moses McCarter Sr*
8. *Hannibal Weems (Black)*
9. *Mooin (native)*

Team 4 Big Stone Fort (Ship Fortunae)
Will meet with John Secombe of Chester

1. *Theophilus Thompson*
2. *John Noe*
3. *Moses McCarter Jr*
4. *John Ash (driver)*
5. *John Bailey*
6. *William Byers (driver)*
7. *James Richey*
8. *Yap Team (native)*

Team 5 Island at 44.5135 (Ship Katherine)
Will meet with Alpheus Morse of Chester

1. *Richard Gott*
2. *John Caswell*
3. *Abraham Bailey*
4. *Matthew Bradley*
5. *Robert Haddon Jr (wagon driver)*
6. *William Vickery*
7. *Elijah Roberson*
8. *Robert Swain*
9. *Samuel Ball (Black) (driver)*
10. *Weisis (native)*

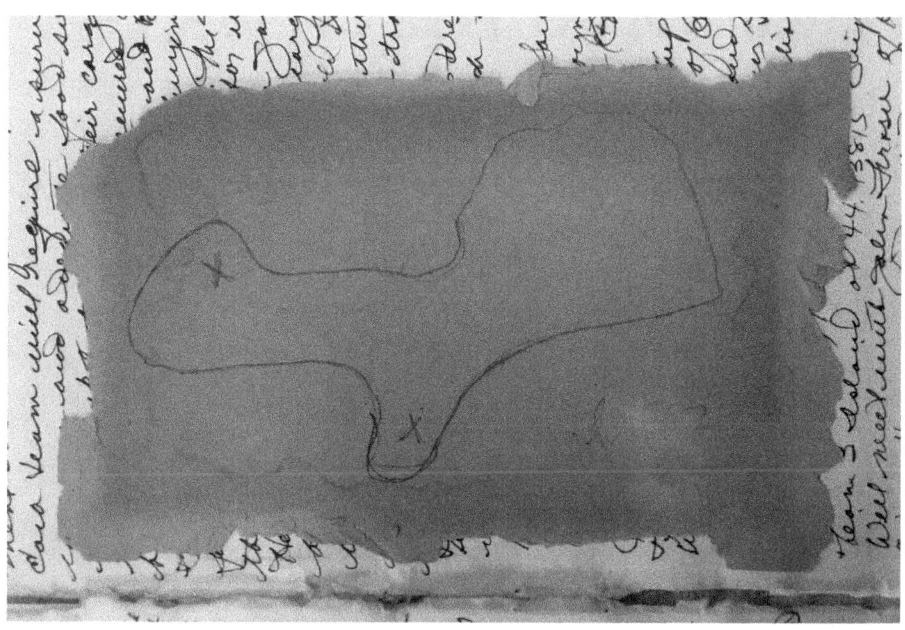

It was between pages seven and eight of John Weems' journal, Book 19, where I found a paper map of what appears to be Dog Island (McNabb Island). It shows where two treasures were deposited, marked by two X's, from the *Katherine* which was washed up on the island during a storm in 1398. (Wolter, 2016)

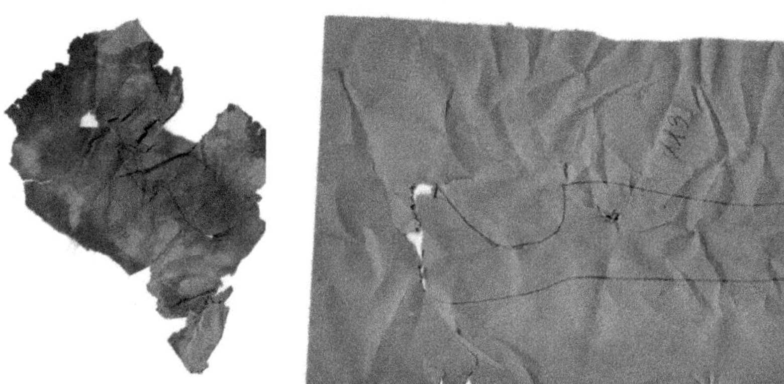

These pictures are of two additional maps, presumably of islands where treasure was buried by Earl Henry Sinclair and his men in 1398. (Muir, 2016)

Team 6 Island at 44.516 (Ship Somnium)
Will meet with Samuel Morse of Halifax

1. *Bartholomew Weems*
2. *John Caldwell*
3. *George Caughman*
4. *Rev Thomas Clark*
5. *Peter Dancer*
6. *John Edwards*
7. *William Berry*
8. *William Ellis*
9. *Barkabol Redfearn (Black) (Driver)"*

June 8, 1770

The natives do not have horses and so they ride with the wagon driver, regaling us with stories and myths of their people. Along the way I have learned several Mi'kmaq words and have heard their stories of how men from the East visited their people more than 10 centuries ago in stone canoes with wings like a bird. In the evening when we camped, they told us of the legend of Zichinni a red-bearded man who taught them to fish with nets and stayed for one year with their ancestors who befriended them. They told also of how these men's descendants had returned only 150 years earlier and brought with them a big rock that their grandfathers had helped to disembark. I am anxious to learn more as we travel and although homesick for my family am beginning to enjoy the journey.

Zichinni is likely the name "Zichmni" for Earl Henry Sinclair as told in the Zeno Narrative. If so, we learn an interesting and previously unknown detail about him, which is that he had a red beard–and likely red hair as well. This should not come as too big of a surprise, as he mentions his daughter Margaret was born with "red hair and blue eyes" like her mother as he wrote in the May 1, 1365, entry.

We have arrived at Gold River at the house of Mary ONeale. She is pleased to see us and accepts the letter from my father and has agreed to help us. She arranges for boats that we can use at Lunenberg to reach two

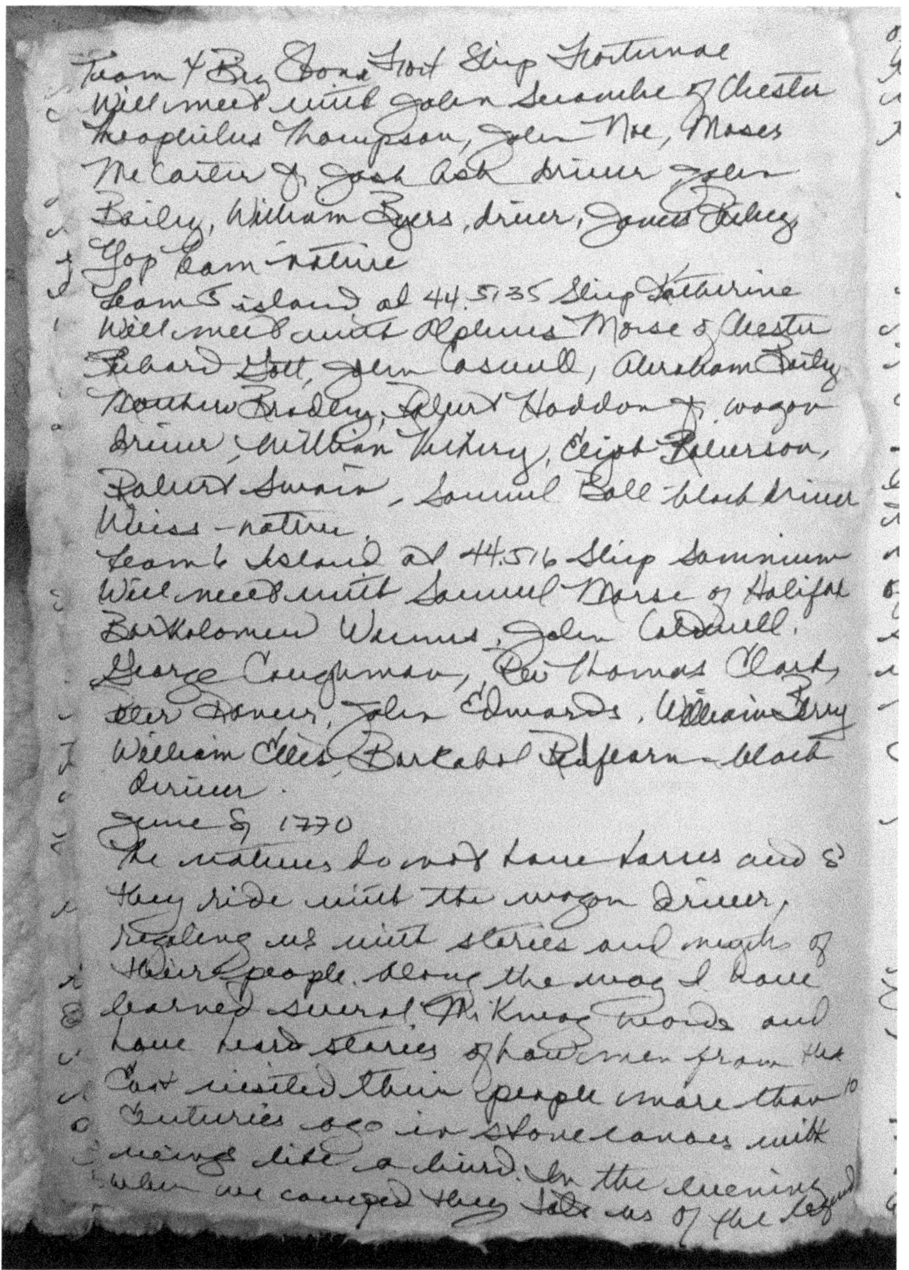
Team 4 Big Stone Foot Ship Fortunae
Will meet with John Secombe of Chester
Theophilus Thompson, John Noe, Moses
McCarter & Josh Ash driver John
Baily, William Byers, driver, James Bailey
Gop team native
Team 5 island at 44.5135 Ship Katherine
Will meet with Alpheus Morse of Chester
Richard Gott, John Caswell, Abraham Baily
Matthew Bradley, Robert Haddon & wagon
driver William Petery, Elijah Robertson,
Robert Swain, Samuel Ball black driver
Weiss native
Team 6 Island at 44.516 Ship Somnium
Will meet with Samuel Morse of Halifax
Bartholomew Weems, John Caldwell,
George Coughman, Rev Thomas Clark,
Peter Dinner, John Edwards, William Perry
William Ellis, Barkabel Redfearn black
driver.
June 8 1770
The natives do not have horses and so
they ride with the wagon driver,
regaling us with stories and myths of
their people. Along the way I have
learned several Mi'Kmaq words and
have heard stories of how men from the
East visited their people more than 10
centuries ago in stone canoes with
wings like a bird. In the evening
when we camped they told us of the legend

This photo shows the continuation of the June 5 entries by John Weems Jr.—listing ships for teams four (*Fortunae*), five (*Katherine*), and six (*Somnium*)—and the beginning of the entry made on June 8, 1770. (Wolter, 2016)

of Tickenni a red bearded man who taught
them to fish with nets and stayed for one
year with their ancestors who befriended
them. They told also of how these men's
descendants had returned 150 years
earlier and brought with them a big
rock that their grandfathers had helped
to disembark. I am anxious to learn
more as we travel and although
homesick for my family am beginning
to enjoy the journey. We have arrived
at Gold River at the house of Mary O'Neale
She is pleased to see us and accepts the
letter from my Father and has agreed
to help us. She arranges for boats that
we can use at Lunenburg to reach two
of the islands we must visit. She
sends a courier to John Smith whom
we will meet on the coast in the
narrows. He will lead a team whose
goal is nearby and will return to Mary
O'Neale's when they have finished their
task & await our return.

June 9, 1770

John Smith arrived early this morn
and set off with the team whose objective is close by. The rest of us leave for
Lunenburg and Chester within the hour.
It frustrates me that I will have no news
of them until we return. I put my
trust in them and in God and pray
that they will be protected. We have seen
no British Fisherman troops as of yet, and hope to appear

The remainder of the June 8 and 9, 1770 entries made by John Weems Jr. (Wolter, 2016) *of the islands we must visit. She sends a courier to John Smith whom we will meet on the coast in the morrow. He will lead a team whose goal is nearby and will return to Mary ONeales when they have finished their task to await our return.*

June 9, 1770

John Smith arrived early this morn and set off with the team whose objective is close by. The rest of us leave for Lunenbourg and Chester within the hour. It frustrates me that I will have no news of them until we return. I put my trust in them and in God and pray that they will be protected. We have seen no British troops as of yet and hope to appear as fishermen.

June 10, 1770

We have arrived in Chester and the team that needs to visit the Old Stone Fort has taken 2 wagons and begun their journey inland after meeting up with Brother John Secombe. Chester is a small town of only about 12 small wood houses and four or five native dwellings. It has a good harbor, and several fishing vessels are at anchor. Another team of the brethren led by Richard Gott will remain here where they will use two boats to complete their task at a nearby island. Brother Alpheus Morse has accepted our request for assistance and will assist them in reaching their goal tomorrow.

This eve Kaleboo told us the story of Dog Island where we must not go. He says our feet will burn and our guts will broil as the island is cursed. The men laugh and say that God will protect them. Kaleboo is not so certain and makes the sign of the cross and spits on the ground to ward off bad sprits. The men laugh even harder. Each night the natives pray to their Holy Mother and ask her to protect us all. I have grown to know that they are good simple people who care greatly for their families and friends. In that we are alike.

In the morning the other three teams will continue on towards Halifax where we will be met by Brother Fraser, Brother Peters and Brother Morse. On our way one team will split off to the other side of the Bay with Brother Peters while the other two teams travel on with

June 10, 1770
We have arrived in Chester and the team that needs to visit the Old Stone Fort has taken 2 wagons and begun their journey inland after meeting up with Brother John Secombe. Chester is a small town of only about 12 small wood houses and four or five native dwellings. It has a good harbor and several fishing vessels are at anchor. Another team of the Brethren led by Richard Gott will remain here where they will use two boats to complete their task at a nearby island. Brother Alpheus Morse has accepted our request for assistance and will assist them in reaching their goal tommorow. This eve Kaleboo told us the story of Oak Island where we must not go. He say our feet will burn and our guts will broil as the island is cursed. The men laugh and say that God will protect them. Kaleboo is not so certain and makes the sign of the cross and spits on the ground to ward off bad spirits. The men laugh even harder. Each night the natives to their Holy Mother and ask her to protect us all. I have grown to know they are good and simple people who care greatly for their families and friends. In that we are alike. In the morning the

The beginning of the entry made on June 10, 1770. (Wolter, 2016)

other three teams will continue on
towards Halifax where we will be met
by Brother Fraser, Brother Peters and
Brother Morse. On our way one team
will split off to the other side of the
bay with Brother Peters while the other
two teams travel on with our trade goods.
When we have completed our tasks
we will meet with the ships arranged
by my Father at the quay on the 24th
of June and will make our way
towards Chester to retrieve the other
three teams. From there we go to Gold
River and prepare for our journey
home. We have alotted two weeks time
to complete each of our tasks and if
it should not take that long, we are to
continue back to Gold River. If any of
the teams runs into trouble they are
to send a courier to either Halifax or Chester.
I worry that the men may become
reticent but am assured they will do
their best. We hope that each team will
travel safely and encourage them to
stay the course acting as fishermen
and merchants. The next two weeks
will seem very long. We will regather
together on June 25th or 26th at Mary
O'Pearls to journey home to our
families.
June 13, 1770
We have arrived at Halifax a goodly
sized town with 3 church's and many

The remainder of the June 10 entry and the beginning of the June 13 entry. (Wolter, 2016) *our trade goods. When we have completed our tasks, we will meet with the ships arranged by my Father at the quay on the 24th of June and will make our way towards Chester to retrieve the other three teams. From there we go to Gold River and prepare for our journey home.*

We have allotted two weeks times to complete each of our tasks and if it should not take that long, we are to continue back to Gold River. If any of the teams runs into trouble, they are to send a courier to either Halifax or Chester. I worry that the men may become reticent but am assured that they will do their best. We hope that each team will travel safely and encourage them to stay the course acting as fisherman and merchants. The next two weeks will seem very long. We will regather together on June 25th or 26th at Mary O'Neales to journey home to our families.

It is clear the mission was well-planned with contingencies in place in case of trouble.

June 13, 1770

We have arrived at Halifax, a goodly sized town with 3 churches and many taverns and places of business. My team has emptied the wagons with the help of Brothers Fraser and Morse who have gotten a good price for the tobacco and cotton. With the silver we have earned we purchase fishing equipment, nets, and digging equipment which we have hidden in the wagon under the sailcloth that we use for a tent each night. Even after purchasing the equipment, we have made a goodly profit for my Brother Thomas on his goods.

The weather remains pleasant, and we look forward to reaching the island we seek tomorrow evening. Brother Alpheus says he knows the exact location of the cache left on the island and has helped us to assemble the needed equipment and two boats which we place in the now empty wagons. The island is uninhabited, and we should be undisturbed."

June 14, 1770

We have traveled overland southward and arrived on the coast near the island we seek. There are a few small farms nearby but no British

taverns and places of business. My
team has emptied the wagons with the
help of Brothers Fraser and Morse who have
gotten a good price for the tobacco and
cotton. With the silver we have earned
we purchase fishing equipment, nets,
and digging equipment which we have
hidden in the wagon under the sail
cloth that we use for a tent each night.
Even after purchasing the equipment we
have made a goodly profit for my
Brother Thomas on his goods. The weather
remains pleasant and we look forward
to reaching the island we seek tomorrow
evening. Brother Cephus says he knows
the exact location of the cache left on the
island and has helped us to assemble the
needed equipment and two boats which
we place in the now empty wagons. The
island is uninhabited and we should
be undisturbed.
June 14, 1770
We have travelled overland southward
and arrived on the coast near the
island we seek. There are a few small
farms nearby but no British troops who
are mostly centered in Halifax to the north.
We have set up a temporary camp behind
the boulders for the wagon driver and
Brother Morse who will wait for us
on the shore with the horses and the
wagons. We can see the island offshore

The remainder of the June 13 entry and beginning of the June 14 entry. (Wolter, 2016) *troops who are mostly centered in Halifax to the north. We have set up a temporary camp behind the boulders for the wagon driver and Brother Morse who will wait for us on the shore with the horses and wagon. We can see the island offshore and if he has any difficulties he is to set a signal fire, and the same with us. In the morning, we will take the two boats we acquired in Halifax to the island and begin our search.*

June 15, 1770

Brother Fraser has accompanied us to the island, and we have anchored our boats on the east side of the island, making certain to secure them against the tide. Brother Fraser has led us approximately 200 paces inland to a grassy area which he says he visits each year. Here we will pitch a tent and begin our dig.

June 21, 1770

It has taken many days to dig down approximately 22 feet to find the treasure left by the Perequin. Each night we pitch a tent over the hole to protect it from the rain which has been intermittent throughout the week. We have made 6 trips back to the camp on shore and have stowed the treasure, mostly silver and gold coin, in the wagons. Brother Craig and Brother Boynton have agreed to stay on shore to guard the cargo along with Kaleboo. Satisfied that we have found everything there is to be found, we fill the hole back up and form a triangle to say prayers of protection for this place. We are thankful that God has watched over us as we have worked, as no one has been injured and we are all in good spirits.

June 24, 1770

This day we returned to Halifax to search for the ships my Father had arranged. The wagons have been stored in a warehouse owned by Brother Fraser and we walked to the pier. As we grew nearer the pier, I recognized the lead ship Lord Elcho, a ship of the Wemyss Shipping Lines from Fifeshire, Scotland. I had only seen the ship twice while in harbor at Philadelphia but knew it on sight. I was equally surprised when the captain of the ship came down the pier to greet me. He is James Wemyss, my cousin from Wester Wemyss in Scotland whom I have not

and if he has any difficulties he is to set a
signal fire, and the same with us. In
the morning we will take the two
boats we acquired in Halifax to the
island and begin our search.
June 15, 1770
Brother Fraser has accompanied us to
the island and we have anchored our
boats on the east side of the island,
making certain to secure them against
the tide. Brother Fraser has led us
approximately 200 paces inland to a grassy
area which he says he visits each
year. Here we will pitch a tent and
begin our dig.
June 21, 1770
It has taken many days to dig down
approximately 22 feet to find the treasure
left by the [illegible]. Each night we pitch
a tent over the hole to protect it from
the rain which has been intermittent
throughout the week. We have made
6 trips back to the camp on shore
and have stowed the treasure mostly
silver and gold into the wagons. Brother
Craig and Brother Boynton have agreed
to stay on shore to guard the cargo
along with Daliboo. Satisfied that we have
found everything there is to be found,
we fill the hole back up and form a
triangle to say prayers of protection
for this place. We are thankful that God
has watched over us as we have
wandered as no one has been injured
and we are all in good spirits.

The entries made on June 15 and 21, 1770. (Wolter, 2016)

seen for many years. He is of an age to my brother Thomas and I and he played together as children when they visited Philadelphia. He is now a Captain in the King's Navy but also a Master Mason. It is good to see him, and we embrace whole heartedly. He is akin to our task and promises that he shall do his best to assist us. Because of his Loyalist views he is certain he will have no problem in leaving port and in fulfilling his duty to our family and to the brethren.

June 25, 1770

This day we have secured our cargo on board the Elcho, the Balfour, and the Harray and are ready to sail for Mahone Bay. I look forward to learning if they were able to find the treasure from the Ortus.

The *Ortus*, you might recall, went down in [illegible] in 1398 in the same storm that grounded Earl Henry's ship, the *Katherine*, onto Dog Island, now called McNab Island. There will be no more mention of *Ortus*, which leads one to believe it might still be at the bottom of the bay.

June 27, 1770

A bright belt of light illuminates the night sky as a comet passes overhead. It grows brighter each night, and the brethren see it as a sign from God that he is pleased with our efforts as he provides light to work by. The blacks see it as a bad omen though and need to be reassured that all is well. Kaleboo says it is the blessing of the Holy Mother and lifts his arms in praise as he dances in the light. He begs the brethren to join him and while some do others are reticent.

We have stopped at the Northeastern peninsula of Mahone Bay and have retrieved Brother Howse team. They were successful in finding the cache with the help of Brother Fraser and Mooin, the native who says he has been there many times to protect the treasure. I now realize that the natives have been protecting the treasure in our absence and are thankful to the Holy Mother for sending them to assist us."

This comet was called Lexell's comet and was discovered by astronomer Charles Messier on June 14, 1770.[60] Messier noted it first became visible

60. https://cometography.com/pcomets/1770l1.html

June 24, 1770
This day we have arrived in Halifax to search for the ships my Father has arranged. The wagons have been stored in a warehouse owned by Frazier and we walked to the pier. As we grew nearer the pier I recognized the lead ship Lord Elcho, a ship of the Wemyss Shipping Lines from Fifeshire, Scotland. I had only seen the ship twice while in harbor at Philadelphia but knew it on sight. I was equally surprised when the captain of the ship came down the pier to greet me. He is James Wemyss my cousin from Wester Wemyss in Scotland whom I have not seen for many years. He is of an age to my brother Thomas and I and we played together as children when they visited Philadelphia. He is now a Captain in the Kings Navy but also a Master Mason. It was good to see him and we embraced whole heartedly. He is akin to our task and promises that he shall do his best to assist us. Because of his Loyalist views he is certain he will have no problem in leaving port and in fulfilling his duty to our family and to the Brethren.
June 25, 1770
This day we have secured our cargo on board the Elcho, the Balfour and the Harvey and are ready to sail for Mahone Bay. I look forward to leaving

The entries made by John Weems Jr. on June 24 and 25, 1770. (Wolter, 2016) to the naked eye on June 20, and the Chinese said by July 12 it was no longer visible. I find this verifiable astronomical event to be very strong evidence in support of these journals.

June 28, 1770

We have returned to Chester and have been reunited with our brethren and the three teams who had been left behind. Each team reports that they were successful in finding the treasure except for the team of Richard Gott who visited Dog Island. They were able to retrieve the cache of silver and gold coin on the northeast beach but were thwarted by the water when digging a tunnel on the south shore. It will take a greater effort to retrieve the second cache, and we resolve to return at a later date. The natives say they will watch over it until our return.

The team of Brethren who visited the Old Stone Fort reported that they were able to find the cache at the bottom of the well in a small anteroom. The well has only the barest of water and they were able to retrieve the treasure, mostly gold artifacts and parchments that were stored dry and secure in the adjoining cave. They report that the Old Stone Fort is barely recognizable as it has fallen in disrepair. People avoid it as they say it is haunted.

The team who visited the third island reported that they too had been able to find the cache from the Somnium after digging only 22 feet at the spot that they were shown. Again, it was mostly gold artifacts, crosses and statues, several golden menorah and gold and silver coin. All treasure has now been stored on board the ships and we make our way to Gold River.

The comet above is still very bright but we see it as a sign of protection and thank God for his constant presence.

Reading that a treasure was recovered from the well at New Ross which I had been lowered into while filming the *America Unearthed* episode was a shock to say the least! Treasure aside, it was reassuring to know that we were on the right track, it was just two and a half centuries too late!

if they were able to find the treasure
from the Ortus.
June 27, 1770
A bright belt of light illuminates the
night sky as a comet passes overhead.
It grows brighter each night and the
Brethren see it as a sign from God that
he is pleased with our efforts as he
provides light to work by. The blacks see
it as a [illegible] bad omen though
and need [illegible] to be reassured
that all is well. [illegible] says it is the
blessing of the Holy Mother and lifts his arms
in praise as he dances in the night.
He urges the Brethren to join him and
while some do others are reticent.
We have stopped at the Northeastern
peninsula of Mahone Bay and have retreived
to Brother [illegible] team. They were successful
in finding the cache with the help of
Brother Fraser and Nooir, the native
who says he has been there many times
to protect the treasure. I now realize that
the natives have been protecting the
treasure in our absence and are thankful to the Holy Mother for sending them
to assist us.
June 28, 1770
We have returned to Chester and have
been reunited with our brethren and
the three teams who had been left behind.
Each team reports that they were successful
in finding the treasure except for the
team of Richard [illegible] who raided Dog
Island. They were able to retrieve the
cache of silver and gold coins on the

The entries made on June 27 and 28, 1770. (Wolter, 2016)

northeast beach but were thwarted by
the water when digging a tunnel on
the south shore. It will take a greater
effort to retrieve the second cache and
we resolve to return at a later date. The
natives say they will watch over it
until our return. The team of Brethren
who visited the Old Stone Fort reported
that they were able to find the cache at
the bottom of the well in a small anteroom
The well had only the barest of water and
they were able to retrieve the treasure
mostly gold artifacts and parchments that
were stored dry and secure in the adjoining
cave. They report that the Old Stone Fort is
barely recognizable as it has fallen in disrepair. People avoid it as they say it is
haunted. The team who visited the third
island reported that they too had been
able to find the cache from the Sonnieur
after digging only 22 feet at the spot that
they were shown. Again it was mostly
gold artifacts, crosses and statues, swords
golden menorah and gold and silver
coins. All treasure has now been stored
on board the ships and we make our
way to Gold River. The comet above is still
very bright but we see it as a sign of
protection and thank God for his constant
presence.
June 29, 1770
We have arrived at Gold River and Brother
Smith and Brother Cummins group has
rejoined our retinue. They report that the
treasure from the Aprintas was more

The entries made by John Weems Jr. on June 28 and 29, 1770. (Wolter, 2016)

difficult to find but after digging 3
different holes were able to locate it.
It consists mostly of parchments in long
cement like tubes sealed against the weather
and gold artifacts chains and gold and
silver coin. All the treasure is now stored
and we prepare to return to Hartford
as the comet watches silently overhead.
We will wait at Mary O'Neals for our
brethren bringing the wagons to join us.
The Brethren welcome the respite and
have spent many hours playing in the
sand and water. They will be brown
as the natives before we return home.

July 3, 1770

The wagons that were left in Halifax
and Chester have now joined us filled
with furs and salted fish. They will
return overland with 30 of the Brethren.
and the other three wagons that will be
filled with lumber when they reach the
province of Maine. They will continue to
Philadelphia where we will meet them.
after having arrived by ship. We will arrive
a week or more in advance but are relieved
that our mission is almost complete.
The comet overhead has begun to dim and
I regrettably take my leave of it as we
head south onboard the Elsho. My
cousin James has asked me to share his
cabins and the ships heavy with cargo
are much calmer than those I remember
on my previous voyage. Even so my
stomach still roils at the motion of
the waves.

Entries made on June 29 and July 3, 1770 (Wolter, 2016)

June 29, 1770

We have arrived at Gold River and Brother Smith and Brother Cummins group has rejoined our retinue. They report that the treasure from the Apricitas was more difficult to find but after digging 3 different holes were finally able to locate it. It consists mostly of parchments in long cement-like tubes sealed against the weather and gold artifacts, chains, and gold and silver coin. All the treasure is now stored, and we prepare to return to Maryland as the comet watches silently overhead. We will wait at Mary O'Neales for our brethren bringing the wagons to join us. The brethren welcome the respite and have spent many hours playing in the sand and water. They will be brown as the natives before we return home.

July 3, 1770

The wagons that were left in Halifax and Chester have now joined us filled with furs and salted fish. They will return overland with 30 of the brethren and the other three wagons that will be filled with lumber when they reach the province of Maine. They will continue to Philadelphia where we will meet them after having arrived by ship. We will arrive a week or more in advance but are relieved that our mission is almost complete. The comet overhead has begun to dim, and I regrettably take my leave of it as we head south on board the Elcho. My Cousin James has asked me to share his cabin and the ships heavy with cargo are much calmer than those I remember on my previous voyage. Even so my stomach still roils at the motion of the waves.

July 6, 1770

The sea has been calm for 3 days and now a thunderstorm threatens. I shall have to find the chunder bucket for this eve. We still have 5 more days before we reach Maryland. I am anxious to have this journey over and return to my family. I miss my wife's good cooking and my children's laughter. I must remember to take them each something from Philadelphia when I return.

July 8, 1770

"The storm has passed, and my cousin James has invited the 4 Brethren who accompany the cargo to dinner in his cabin. It will be a night of frolic, and I look forward to a night of conversation. All goes well so far and although we have passed 2 British patrol ships none have bothered us as we raise the Union Jack.

Aboard the *Elcho*, captained by James Wemyss,—John Weems Jr's cousin from Wester Wemyss in Scotland, when they passed a British ship they flew the Union Jack flag to avoid suspicion. (Internet)

July 11, 1770

Maryland is within our sights, but Cousin James tells me the water is too shallow to accommodate the ships. We shall anchor at the Three Sisters and use whale boats to take our cargo further ashore.

July 12, 1770

The Elcho has four whale boats aboard, but it will take at least three trips to remove all the cargo from each ship. The Balfour and Harray anchor nearby and Brother James Lynch and I must first contact Brother John Hanson at Oxen Hill to arrange for delivery. His nephew farms at Oxen Hill and I understand that Mason's Island, our final goal, is nearby.

July 13, 1770

Brother Lynch and I have met with Brother Hanson who has been anxiously awaiting our arrival along with Brother Charles Peale of Annapolis Maryland.[61] *They took us by boat to Mason's Island where Brother George Mason was awaiting word of our arrival. He has promised to have carts available at his dock to unload the cargo and he has shown us a brick vault. It is approximately 27 feet square and lies within view of his two-story home on the northeast side of the island. The vault*

61. https://www.mountvernon.org/library/digitalhistory/digital-encyclopedia/article/charles-willson-peale

July 6, 1770
The sea has been calm for 3 days and now a thunderstorm threatens. I shall have to find the thunder bucket for this one. We still have 5 more days before we reach Maryland. I am anxious to have this journey done and return to my family. I miss my wife's good cooking and my children's laughter. I must remember to take them each something from Philadelphia when I return.

July 8, 1770
The storm has passed and my Cousin James has invited the 4 Brothers who accompany the cargo to dinner in his cabin. It will be a night of frolic and I look forward to a night of conversation. All goes well so far and although we have passed 2 British patrol ships none have bothered us as we raise the Union Jack.

July 11, 1770
Maryland is within our sights but Cousin James tells me the water is too shallow to accomadate the ships. We shall anchor at the three sisters and use whale boats to take our cargo further ashore.

July 12, 1770
The Elias has four whaleboats aboard but it will take at least three trips to remove all the cargo from each ship. The Balfour and Harray anchor nearby and Brother James Lynch and I must first contact Brother John Hanson at Oxen Hill to arrange for delivery. His nephew farms at Queen Hill and I

The entries made on July 6, 8, 11, and 12, 1770. (Wolter, 2016) *lies at least 10 feet below the surface and the entrance to the east has been dug down to allow entrance. He states that it lies 1000 paces from his home, and he is able to see it at all times of the day. He owns the island in its entirety and has spent the previous two years building this vault for its intended use with the assistance of the brethren. He assures me that it will be a fitting and secure place for the treasure we have brought.*

Charles Wilson Peale was an American artist who painted George Washington and several other Revolutionary War-era heroes. George Mason owned all of what is now called Theodore Roosevelt Island. It sits in the Potomac River right behind and a little north of the Lincoln Memorial in Washington D.C.

We also see more use of sacred numbers. This time the number twenty-seven—for the dimensions of the secret vault on Mason's Island—is approximately ten megalithic yard units, which itself is the number of perfection in Freemasonry, which can only be achieved upon death. The megalithic yard is 2.722 feet in length and is calculated using the planet Venus. Freemasons associate Venus with the Goddess in the heavens, and George Mason used the sacred measurement to construct his vault buried, not coincidentally, ten feet below the surface.

Left: Charles Wilson Peale was a Freemason and famous painter of people like George Washington and other Revolutionary War heroes. (Internet)

Right: This bronze statue of the "Forgotten Founder" George Mason is sitting on a marble bench at his memorial at the National Mall in Washington D.C. The Templar treasure was stored inside an underground vault on Mason's Island,where he lived. It is now called Theodore Roosevelt Island. (Wolter, 2017)

Mason's home originally stood on the southern end of the island and, in 2017, I was able to find a few bricks and mortar that are still on the site. From there I paced off one thousand steps which put me on the northern end of the island at a location that looked as if the vault could have been constructed there. All we need to do now is use ground penetrating radar to see if the vault, or even remnants of it, are still there.

July 14, 1770

It has taken the greater part of the day to transfer all the cargo up the Potomac River to Mason's Island. I was enlisted by Brother Hanson to inventory the cargo as it was placed in the vault and was surprised at the amount of treasure we had recovered. The inventory was given to Brother Mason upon completion, so I do this from memory. In total there are more than 40 chests of coin, 25 gold crucifixes of varying sizes, 12 menorahs of varying sizes, numerous parchments and paintings kept in tubes made of crushed lime and clay. Only a very few of them have been opened to the weather and all seem in good repair. There also are 6 arks made of gold and silver of various sizes, 3 heavily decorated with filigree and winged creatures, 4 stone boxes that contain remnants of bone, a stone box of broken stone tablets, an emerald tablet, several bloodied swords and lances, two of which are broken. One stone box contains flasks of mysterious substances, but I am reluctant to ask what magical solutions they contain. Several casks of jewels and numerous other gold and silver artifacts fill the empty space. It was late evening before we closed the door to the vault which was then sealed with mortar made of crushed lime and shells. The entrance was then covered with soil and made invisible to those who knew not where it lay.

A group of 10 and 14 masons encircled the tomb and we blessed the vault and asked Heavenly Father to bless and protect this place against time and the ravages and greed of war. Cousin James left under the light of lanterns and returned to the ships. My Brethren and I would leave by horseback for Philadelphia in the morn after staying the eve at Oxen Hill. My heart feels lighter now that my task has been completed and I shall sleep a heavy sleep this night.

understand that Mason's Island our final
goal is nearly.
July 13, 1770
Brother Lynch and I have met with Brother
Hanson who has been anxiously awaiting
our arrival along with Brother Charles Peale
of Anapolis Maryland. They took us by boat
to Mason's Island where Brother George
Mason was awaiting word of our arrival.
He has promised to have carts available at his
dock to unload the cargo and has shown
us a brick vault. It is approximately 27
feet square and lies within view of his two-
story home on the northeast side of the
island. The vault lies at least 10 feet below
the surface and the entrance to the vault
has been dug down to allow entrance.
He states that it lies 1000 paces from his
home and he is able to see it at all times
of the day. He owns the island in its entirety
and has spent the previous two years
building this vault for its intended use with
the assistance of the Brethren. He assures me
that it will be a fitting and secure place
for the treasure we have brought.
July 14, 1770
It has taken the greater part of the day
to transfer all the cargo up the Potomac
River to Mason's Island. I was enlisted by
Brother Hanson to inventory the cargo
as it was placed in the vault and was
surprised at the amount of treasure we
had recovered. The inventory was given to

The entries made on July 13 and 14, 1770. (Wolter, 2016)

My breath was taken away the first time I read this entry. Part was disbelief and part was due to how spot-on I would have expected the treasure to be. The voluminous amount of gold and silver was expected, but the rest was an exercise in all the items I had encountered in my years of research into the history of the esoteric aspects of the Templars. The crucifixes and menorahs and the traditions they represented were certainly part of the Templar mission of obtaining leverage against the religious institutions that sought use and control the Templars, especially the Roman Catholic Church.

The gold crucifixes and menorahs are amazing artifacts that were no doubt adorned with jewels and of immense value. However, the six arks are arguably the most perplexing since biblical accounts leave one to believe there was only one Ark of the Covenant within the Holy of Holies in Solomon's Temple. Those familiar with the legend of Enoch know he built a secret vault nine levels below the altar where a copy of all the true treasures were kept. This means there were at least *two* arks. If there were two, then there would likely be many more as certain Templar traditions know. In the Cremona Document there is a page that has instructions on how to build an ark. If so, this means the secret of the Ark of the Covenant isn't where it is, but how to make one.

The most important relics by far in my opinion, were the "*...4 stone boxes with remnants of bone...*" These no doubt were the mortal remains of important people and almost certainly people important to *them*. Recall my comments on the controversial Talpiot tomb from southern Jerusalem (page 183). Inside the burial chamber ten ossuaries, or bone boxes, were found. Seven were inscribed with names, six in Aramaic and one in Greek. The names were as follows:

Yeshua [Jesus], son of Joseph
James, son of Joseph, brother of Yeshua
Maria
Joseph
Mathew
Judah, son of Yeshua
Mariamene the Mara [Greek]

When the ossuaries were found there were only bone fragments inside, welded to the bottom and sides of the boxes. The majority of the bones had already been removed. The question is who removed them? A strong argument could be made that the Templars removed the remains from the tomb during their time in Jerusalem during the Crusades and they are now here in America.

The box with broken stone tablets immediately brings to mind the biblical story of Moses and the Ten Commandments. If the Templars did find the actual stone tablets connected to Moses, it would be an immensely powerful artifact to have in their possession.

The Emerald Tablet is an ancient document that contains cryptic alchemical secrets first created by Hermes. Medieval philosophers credit the tablet with holding the secrets of "The Philosopher's Stone" and how to convert metallic gold into monatomic gold, or "Manna." Powdered gold is said to hold the secret to eternal life when ingested, and produces a convection cell which creates no waste and endless energy. Manna is also said to be what powers the Arks of the Covenant. The flasks of mysterious substances are likely by-products of alchemical processes, perhaps even manna in liquid form.

John Jr's final comments are interesting as he mentions ten and fourteen masons, not twenty-four, "...encircled the tomb...". In addition to ten, fourteen is also a sacred number, associated with the death of Osiris in the Egyptian mysteries when his body is cut up into fourteen pieces and placed along the banks of the Nile River for the crocodiles to eat. There are also fourteen bones in the human face. It is no coincidence these numbers also occur within the Kensington Rune Stone Inscription, "...10 men red from blood and death..." and "There are 10 men by the inland sea [Lake Superior] to look after our ships, 14 days from this hill. 1362.". John called the sealed vault a "tomb" which removes all doubt the stone boxes with "remnants of bone" were human remains.

July 15, 1770

The remaining 11 Brethren and I have traveled the greater part of the day towards Philadelphia which lies 4 to 5 days to the North. Our mood is

Brother Mason upon completion & I do
this from memory. In total there are more
than 40 chests of coin, 25 gold crucifixes of
varying sizes, 12 menorah of varying sizes
numerous parchments and paintings kept
in tubes of crushed lime and clay. Only a
very few of them have been opened to
the weather and all seem in good repair
There also are 6 arks of gold and silver of
various sizes, 3 heavily decorated with
filigree and winged creatures, 4 stone boxes
that contain remnants of bone, a stone box
of broken stone tablets, an emerald tablet,
several bloodied swords and lances;
two of which are broken. One stone box
contains flasks of mysterious substances
but I am reluctant to ask what magical
solutions they contain. Several casks of
jewels and numerous other gold and silver
artifacts fill the empty space. It was late
evening before we closed the door to
the vault which was then sealed with
mortar made of crushed lime and
shells. The entrance was then covered
with soil and made invisible to those
who knew not where it lay. A group
of 10 and 14 masons encircled the tomb
and we blessed the vault and asked
Heavenly Father to bless and protect this
place against time and the ravages
and greed of war. Cousin James left

This entry by John Weems Jr. on July 14, 1770 details the list of incredible treasures he and the forty-six brethren and six slaves had recovered in Nova Scotia. (Wolter, 2016)

under the light of lanterns and returned to the ships. My Brethren and I would
leave by horseback for Philadelphia in the
morn after staying the eve at Oxen Hill
My heart feels lighter now that my task
has been completed and I shall sleep
a heavy sleep this night.
July 15, 1770
The Remaining 11 Brethren and I have
travelled the greater part of the day
towards Philadelphia which lies 4 to 5 day
to the North. Our mood is jovial as we
move forward and we take note of
the well-kept farms and will stay the
night in Baltimore at an inn where
we rest the horses, borrowed from Brother
Hanson's nephew for the trip. British troops
frequent the road but only once were we
stopped. We explained we were returning
home to my Father's house in Philadelphia
and were given leave to go on our way
July 19, 1770
We arrived back in Abingdon and were
joyously welcomed by my Father and
Mother. Before I took my rest Father
insisted on a report and I told
him all I remember of retrieving the
treasure, our journey to Maryland and
the inventory that now resides in the
vault. He was pleased to hear that we
had few problems and reminded me
that my mission is not complete. I
must still travel on horseback to western
New York province to contact Brother
Ebenezer Morton. He has given me the

The entries made on July 15 and 19, 1770. (Wolter, 2016)

jovial as we move forward and we take note of the well-kept farms and will stay the night in Baltimore at an inn where we rest the horses, borrowed from Brother Hanson's nephew for the trip. British troops frequent the road but only once were we stopped. We explained we were returning home to my father's house in Philadelphia and were given leave to go on our way.

July 19, 1770

We arrived back in Abington and were joyously welcomed by my Father and Mother. Before I took my rest Father insisted on a report and I told him all I remember of retrieving the treasure, our journey to Maryland, the inventory that now resides in the vault. He was pleased to hear that we had few problems and reminded me that my mission is not complete. I must still travel on horseback to western New York province to contact Brother Ebenezer Morton. He has given me the location of the island we are to find as being at 43.256 degrees' latitude. He explained that it is an island in a protected bay inhabited by the Onodawgo people. We are to ask for a native woman named Hatenotha when we reach the Seneca. She will accompany us to the edge of the great lake. He suggests that Bartholomew accompany me and the other men should return home to their families. He has given me a bag of silver to give each man 10 silver pounds for their journey. He has promised to direct the wagons to Hillsboro as soon as they arrive, but insists we leave in the morning for New York Province as it is 8 days journey from Philadelphia and we must cross the mountains of the Seneca Indians.

I am disappointed that I am not to go directly home to my family but I understand my father's urgency. He had been unable to locate the cache years earlier and was concerned that it was still safe. He did not ask me to return it to Maryland but simply to ensure its existence. I have promised to fulfil his request if only he shall make certain that Mother sends good sturdy cloth to Kitty for her use and the children. He has promised to do so and I go to bed with a lighter heart.

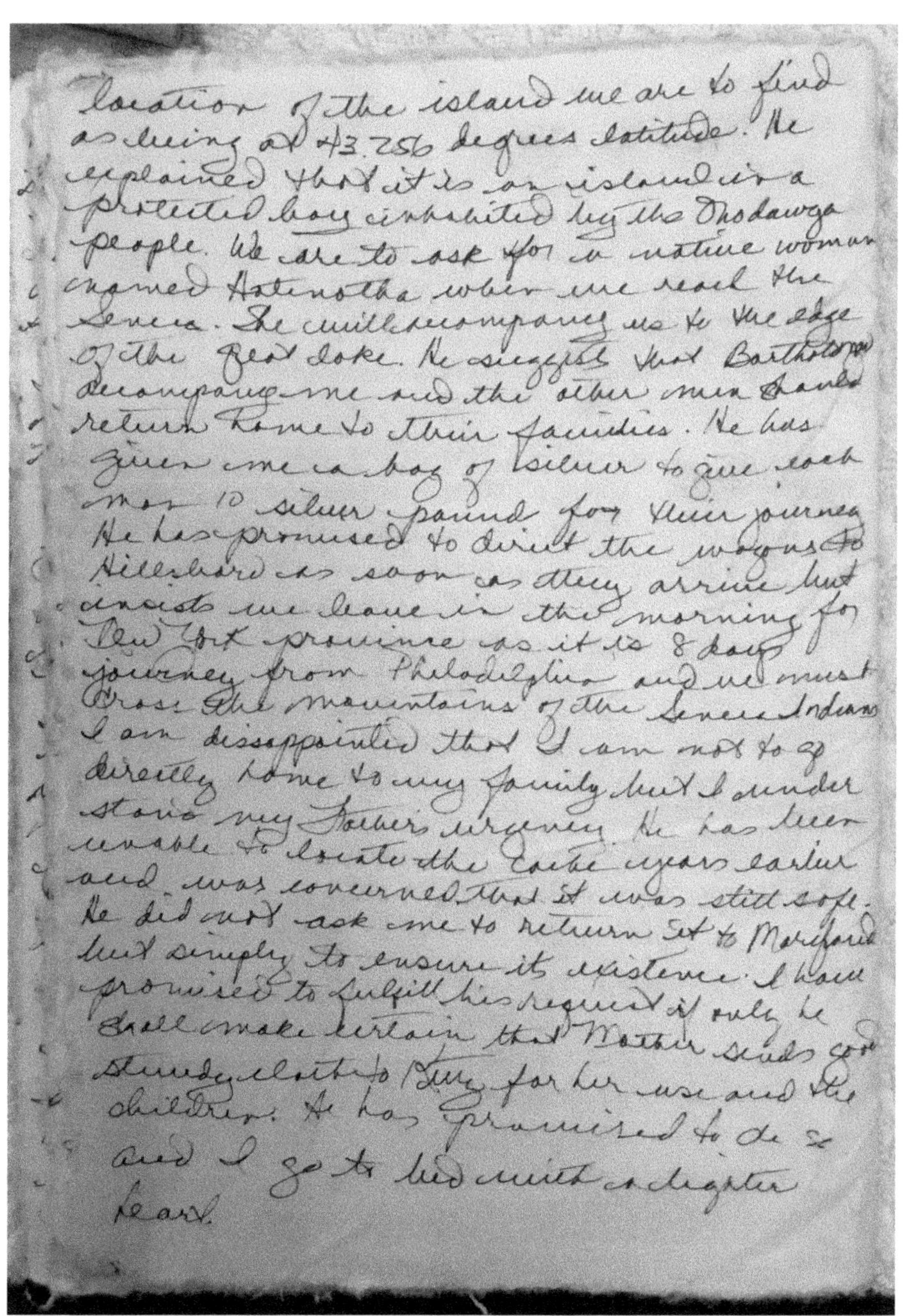

location of the island we are to find
as being at 43.256 degrees latitude. He
explained that it is an island in a
protected bay inhabited by the Onodawga
people. We are to ask for a native woman
named Hatenotha when we reach the
Seneca. She will accompany us to the edge
of the great lake. He suggests that Bartholomew
accompany me and the other men should
return home to their families. He has
given me a bag of silver to give each
man 10 silver pound for their journey
He has promised to direct the wagons to
Hillsboro as soon as they arrive but
insists we leave in the morning for
New York province as it is 8 days
journey from Philadelphia and we must
cross the mountains of the Seneca Indians
I am dissappointed that I am not to go
directly home to my family but I under
stand my Father's urgency. He has been
unable to locate the cache years earlier
and was concerned that it was still safe.
He did not ask me to return it to Marford
but simply to ensure its existence. I have
promised to fulfill his request if only he
shall make certain that Mother sends good
sturdy cloth to Kitty for her use and the
children. He has promised to do so
and I go to bed with a lighter
heart.

The final entry made by John Weems Jr. in Book 19 on July 19, 1770. (Wolter, 2016)

Book 20

Journals of John Weems

1741-1812

July 20, 1770

Brother Bartholomew and I leave this morning for western New York Province. Father has given me lengthy instruction on where to stay on the way and the route to take over the mountains. The weather is fair although hot and Mother has given us rations and food to last us for 10 days. She promises to send presents to the children and Father agrees that after visiting western New York we should proceed home to North Carolina. We can send a letter through Brother Morton as to what we find on the island and he will be satisfied. Father gives me a letter of introduction to Brother Morton and has procured travel papers for us. He gives us both his blessing and wishes us safe travel.

July 22, 1770

We have followed the Schulykill River now for 2 days and will begin overland to the Susquehanna River. The first night we camped by the riverside near Union where Brother Ebenezer Morton joined us. The second night we camped at Windsor, a small village of 5 or 6 houses. Brother Morton has been waiting for us this past month and tells us he has been scouting for land to purchase in anticipation of settlers coming from eastern New York province. He is eager to see Western New York Province and accepts our letter of introduction from Father. He offers his help and knowledge of the Indians and tells us of the meeting he was present at two years ago when they first planned on retrieving the treasure. He is a Patriot and admonishes us that many of the Indians are allied with the British so to keep our views private.

We have enjoyed warm weather during the past few days and have seen many travelers. Each greets us pleasantly and tells us that the road is without peril. Most are men who look to trade with the Indians, and we also saw French missionaries who are headed north.

We have yet to see any Indians, but Father has told us not to raise our muskets to them but to extend our hand in friendship. Tomorrow, we start northwest over the Blue Mountains to find the East branch of the Susquehanna River which will take us most of the way to the island we seek. I am hopeful that we meet some Indians on the way who can help direct us to Hatenotha.

Brother Morton is a quiet man, but he and Bartholomew have found common ground in the evening and tell stories of the 96th District where Brother Morton has never been. He is not a slaver and has many questions about how the blacks are handled and treated. Bart assures him that he and our brother Thomas treat them humanely and fairly. Brother Morton also tells us of his wife and three children, one a babe in arms. He is anxious to find land where he can raise a large family and build a home. In this we share a common goal.

For students of history these musings by John Jr. are an exceptional treat. I have wondered what went through the minds of the people who lived during these times, and especially the mind of a Freemason. I am reminded of the different times it was for Freemasonry, as we have seen throughout these journals. Knowing who your friends were and, more importantly who your enemies were, was key. That is why the secret passwords, hand gestures, and handshakes were so important. Today, they are purely symbolic. Back then it was literally a matter of life and death.

July 24, 1770

We have found the banks of the East branch of the Susquehanna and for the first time have been greeted by Onondaga Indians on horseback from the Old Indian Fort just a few miles to the North. I have asked for directions to Hatenotha, and they simply directed us north up the river. She is known to them and one of them, a tall young man with white feathers in his hair, tells us that she is a spirit-woman and a woman of exceptional beauty and skills. The man named Kanowa speaks both English and French, and is known to Brother Morton. He will accompany us for a day or two until we reach the land of the Onondaga where we will be able to find Hatenotha.

As we ride, we have passed several native villages along the banks of the Susquehanna. The people live in long houses made of wood and bark and surround their gardens and animals with wooden stockades. The children run loose and seem happy with their games and the women are bare chested in the gardens where they grow corn and vegetables. The men we have seen wear feathers in their hair but no war paint and greet us with a simple wave of the hand. Mostly they travel by canoe in the river and walk while on land. We make certain to camp the night in an area removed from their village so as not to alarm them. Kanowa says they are a friendly people but have retreated behind the mountains due to the settlement on the eastern side. They are not a confrontational people but will protect what is theirs.

I can't help but feel bad about how the indigenous people would be treated starting at about this time. For all the virtues of the brethren who put their lives on the line for the Covenant and the free nation they sought to create, it came at a terrible price for the indigenous people. They already had their free nation and welcomed visitors from across the seas. It is heartbreaking to think about the genocide that was to come. It will forever be the biggest stain on one of the most amazing historical stories ever to unfold.

July 26, 1770

We have reached the lands of the Onondaga and Kanowa says we will reach the village of the Onondaga tomorrow and will find Hatenotha there. From there we will travel northeast along the edge of the Cayuga Lake until we reach the great lake. Brother Morton is becoming impatient but Bartholomew and myself are eager to reach the great lake after which we can head home.

July 26, 1770

We have arrived at the village on the banks of the Kasonda and find the young Indian men there surprisingly fierce. We have been told that there are many conflicts to the east in the Mohawk Valley with settlers and are pleased to find that Hatenotha is eager to help us. She greets us with a traditional Indian greeting, strength be within you. She is a woman of my wife Kitty's age but is of yet unmarried. She is quite beautiful and has brilliant black hair that she keeps in a braid decorated with feathers and shells from the lake. She is the daughter of the headwoman and will someday take her mother's and grandmother's place as the spirit-woman of their tribe. It will be her obligation to tell the stories and legends of her people and to teach the people of their ancestors. She greets Kanowa with a smile and I doubt she will be unmarried for long.

Hatenotha told us that her ancestors have a long memory of working with the visitors from the eastern seas and that they have protected their memory through song and story for almost 400 years. She is happy that we have come because her tribe may soon travel south to avoid the invading settlers and conflict. She has agreed to take us to the island near the great lake in the morning. We stay this night at the edge of the Cayuga Lake under the protection of the local chief.

The description of Hatenotha and her obligations as a sprit woman is impressive and worthy of note. Her people respect and honor their elders, traditions, and their history, which included not only Earl Henry Sinclair and his men, but many others who came from different places around the world. Hardly the "savages" they were called to justify killing them and taking their land, they are highly intelligent and gracious, and even today we can still learn a lot from our indigenous friends. All one has to do is treat them with respect, be sincere in our overtures, and most important of all, listen and we will learn.

July 29, 1770

The journey to the edge of the great lake has been a wet but uneventful journey. We have traveled on horseback on the side of the Cayuga Lake and have passed many small native houses. Each night we camp by the edge of the lake and are surprised to see many canoes on the lake fishing with spears. Hatenotha is well known by them, and they wave to her as we pass by on horseback. Kanowa has accompanied us and tells us legends of his people and the animals of the mountains as we ride. We arrived at the edge of the great lake this evening and were greeted by members of the Seneca tribe who are known to Hatenotha and Kanowa. We will borrow three canoes from them in the morning to reach the island in the middle of the bay. She says she has been here every summer with her family and knows the area well. A childhood friend called Owehya'eyu invited us to eat with them this evening and we camp nearby her elder's long house.

July 30, 1770

Brother Morton, Brother Bartholomew and myself have traveled with Hatenotha and Kanowa from the edge of the lake to the island which they call Neoga, which means big island. The island is used as a summer home for the Indians who share the bay with their neighbors. There are many canoes on the shore and several camps. Hatenotha says that we should visit the highest point of the island where legend says the cargo of the great dragon ship is buried. Once we arrived at the highest spot on the island, she told us the story of her ancestors and how they had befriended the men of the great dragon ship who stayed the winter many centuries before.

She told us how they had traveled down the long river from the North with a crew of 26 men in a ship that carried a great treasure. They stayed for the winter and anchored their ship near the sand chimneys at the mouth of the bay. They hunted rabbit and deer during the cold month and traded stories and metal tools with her ancestors. They told great stories of the land they came from over the Eastern seas. She recounted a story of small ugly magical men who inhabited the land where they came from and told us and of the huge sea monsters. They also shared stories of farming and fishing and spoke of their God and how he had sent them to the Western Lands. Over the winter they shared many beliefs and rituals, many of which have survived in her people's lodges and are still used. Most of the men left in the dragon ship when the bay thawed but a group of 8 with long swords stayed behind and later left-over land towards the east to join with their countrymen. Although they were never heard from again her people had kept their promise and visited this spot each summer to say a blessing and protection and chant the rituals they had taught them. The island was considered blessed, and many young people would come here to celebrate their arrival at adulthood and to renew the promise to their ancestors.

The Brethren formed a triangle and blessed the spot and Hatenotha chanted a prayer with her arms raised to the sky in her native language to ask the Holy Mother to protect this place and those who visit. We were relieved to see that the site was undisturbed. Trees had since grown on the spot and a large flat granite rock marked with an eight-pointed star marked the spot where they had buried their treasure. After visiting Neoga Island, we visited the sand chimneys and marveled at the natural wonder of them. I could envision how it would make a perfect vantage point for the sailors during the winter months. It gave a view of many miles up and down the great lake.

It was late afternoon before we returned to the shore, but we were satisfied that whatever lie beneath the capstone on Neoga Island was well preserved and protected. As long as the natives were here it would always be preserved and protected.

The "sand chimneys", as Hatenotha called them in 1770, are at Chimney Bluffs State Park and are comprised of weathered glacial clay deposits that served as geographic markers for people sailing on Lake Ontario. (Wolter, 2019)

July 31, 1770

"This day we leave for home and must retrace our route to Abington and my Father's home. There is no need to send a letter as we are told it is much safer to return the way we had come then to travel south along the great lake. From Abington we will follow the Great Trading Path back to our families and friends. We pray for a swift and safe return.

On May 8, 2019, I paddled across Sodus Bay to Eagle Island to look for the Goddess Stone used to mark one of the treasures hidden by Earl Henry's men in 1398. I didn't find the stone and almost had to swim back when my blow-up canoe sprung a leak, but I had a great time regardless. (Wolter, 2019)

9

Analysis

Here is where the rubber meets the road with these incredible journals. Yes, they tell what is possibly the greatest historical story that has never been told. However, before we can make that claim we must do a critical analysis of the material and present factual evidence that not just supports their authenticity, but hopefully, proves it conclusively.

To put many of the points supporting authenticity of the documents into proper context, we need to bring in another set of controversial documents that deal with the same subject matter: the Cremona Document.

My friend Donald Ruh and I have been working on the myriad encrypted messages, maps, letters, and artifacts of the Cremona Document for nearly twenty years now, and it tells essentially the same story as the journals, yet the journals and the Cremona Document have no known connection to each other.

Don and I will be publishing the definitive volume on the Cremona Document in 2026. I would suggest the reader become familiar with the Cremona Document materials published to date by reading my two previous books, *Oak Island, Knights Templar, and the Holy Grail: Secrets of the Underground Project Revealed*, and *Cryptic Code of the Templar's in America: Origins of the Hooked X*.

To provide corroboration for these journals, I will be sharing pertinent information from the Cremona material, but first a brief synopsis of the Cremona Document.

BILL JACKSON AND DONALD RUH

In the summer of 1968 Donald Ruh and his best friend from childhood, William "Bill" Jackson—who were twenty-six and thirty years old at the time, respectively—took a boat to Bannerman Island in the Hudson River to snorkel and scuba dive. They were looking for munitions in the armory that had been blown off the island during an explosion in 1920. During their searches, Don happened to find two decorative ornaments from flower gardens on the island that were blown to the eastern shore of the river. Don knew Bill's wife Murial was a gardener and gave them to him. A year later, Bill's five-year-old son Mark was playing in his mother's garden and grabbed one of the ornaments. It broke off and fell to the ground. The ornament then broke open and inside they found two artifacts hidden inside. One item was a four-inch-long clay tube sealed with beeswax that contained two parchments. The other artifact was a hockey-puck-sized brass device that contained metal inserts.

One insert had the word "Onteora" etched into the metal. This led Bill to Europe to visit an antique book dealer in France where, among other

Donald Ruh holds the brass device found hidden inside a decorative ornament he discovered at the spot where he's standing along the shore of the Hudson River. The ornament had been blown off the island by an explosion of munitions stored on Bannerman Island seen behind him. (Wolter, 2022)

items, he purchased a pamphlet published in 1718 titled, *The Application of French, Welsh and Scots to the American Indian Language.* The word "Onteora" was in the pamphlet and it led Bill to find the descendants of the authors. In December of 1970, Bill met with Gustave Benvenuto in Rome, who showed Bill the Cremona Document and gave him a page containing information about the scuttling of one of six ships on the southern coast of Newfoundland in 1178. The ships were part of an expedition to North America that began in Wales. Their mission was to travel to the Temple of the Goddess in what is now the Catskill Mountains in upstate New York. The leader of the expedition was a Templar knight named Sir Ralf De Sudeley who was to recover biblical era scrolls from Europe hidden in North America sometime before the year 1000 CE

While rounding the southern coast of Newfoundland, one ship hit rocks and could not be repaired so it was scuttled. The document included detailed information on the location of the ship, and Bill recruited Don to search for the sunken ship. In August of 1971, Bill and Don not only found the ship, but also recovered the mast, some of the decking, and the keel of the ship. This convinced Bill the story was true, so later that year he returned to Rome and purchased the entire Cremona Document from Benvenuto. Bill and Don then spent the next six years hiking the Catskills searching for the Temple of the Goddess. On October 11, 1977, they found the tomb of Altomara, who died in a skirmish between local tribes. Inside the small cave in the mountains, they found her ashes and numerous artifacts left as offerings. During this time, Don was unaware of why Bill was so fixated on traveling to Newfoundland and the Catskills. This would not be fully understood until many years later.

Bill Jackson was a medical doctor and, in 1994 he realized he was dying from arterial sclerosis and Parkinson's disease and decided to sell the document to the Vatican. At first glance this might seem like the worst place to sell this compendium of important Knights Templar documents, maps, letters, and artifacts. However, Bill had a plan in place that resulted in the best possible outcome, even though it took thirty years to play out.

Four years after Bill passed away his son Mark signed an agreement with Don, turning over all his father's research—which included the brass device that started everything in 1968. Four years later, Don discovered two floppy discs hidden behind a framed print Bill had given Don in 1996. One of the discs contained a copy of *A Year We Remember* translated into English, which is the story of Sir Ralf de Sudeley's mission to recover scrolls in North America. The pages Bill sold to the Vatican were written in Theban script, used by the Templars beginning in the early twelfth century. The same floppy disc also included eleven pages of Bill's commentary about the story that shed valuable light on his mindset and the level of research he had conducted over the twenty-three years he had the document (1971–1994).

After finding the floppy discs and getting context as to why Bill took him to Newfoundland and the Catskills, Don contacted me and, together with colleagues David Brody, Steve St. Clair, and Grant Wolter, we hiked up Hunter Mountain to the site of the Temple of the Goddess in July

Don Ruh discovered two floppy disks hidden inside an envelope and taped to the back of a print when he tried to throw it away during spring cleaning in 2008. Bill Jackson gave Don the picture in 1996 and had put on the discs a story titled *A Year We Remember,* and eleven pages of his commentary about the twelfth-century mission to recover biblical era scrolls hidden in North America. (Wolter, 2021)

On July 1, 2009 David Brody and Donald Ruh discovered an inscribed stone buried roughly two and a half feet deep at a location pinpointed using the Compass and Square map found in Altomara's Cave. (Wolter/Wolter, 2009)

of 2009. Using a map found in Altomara's tomb and carvings of Theban symbols on the mountain we found an inscribed stone we called the "In Camera Stone". The stone was a vital piece of evidence that helped us make progress in understanding this vastly complicated story.

In 2013, Don had a roll of 35 mm film from Bill's material developed which had pictures of the pages of the original document he sold. These included four maps of the northeast coast of North America, key pages of esoteric knowledge, and several photos of the long-lost biblical document called *Book of the Wars of the Lord.*

It would be four more years before the next key moment came in the form of a package from Bill Jackson's daughter, Melissa, which included a letter from her father written in 1996. The letter explained how Bill had pulled two original maps from the documents he sold to the Vatican. Also included in the large envelope was what tuned out to be the first page of the Theban script of *A Year We Remember.*

At first, we didn't understand why Bill had pulled this page, but it didn't take long to figure it out. On the back side was a map of where the Templars had entered an underground tunnel system, which led to an underground ritual chamber filled with treasures they had recovered from under the South Wall of the Temple Mount in Jerusalem in 1118. Apparently, Bill did not want the Vatican to have this knowledge, but even more important

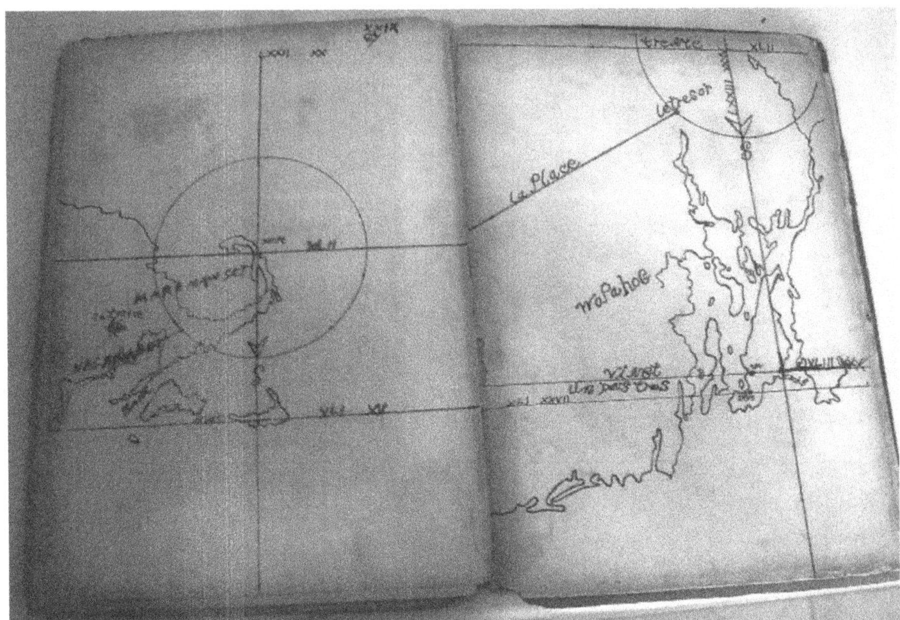

Two of the four hand drawn maps of the Cape Cod and Narragansett Bay areas. This picture was one of several photos Don Ruh received upon having a roll of 35mm film developed he received from Bill Jackson's estate in 2004. The photos were taken by Jackson before he sold the originals to the Vatican in 1994. (Courtesy of Donald Ruh)

is what was on the top of the front page. In Latin were the words *Aelis Capitolina*, the old, first-century name for Jerusalem. This was the cipher phrase necessary to decode the pages Bill had sold to the Church. This led to the realization that Bill had essentially sold the Vatican a worthless document. Sometimes I can hear Bill laughing in his grave, which makes me chuckle too. As wonderful a surprise as this was, it was only the beginning of the magical moments Bill would posthumously provide us.

Over the next six years, Don received six different caches of documents, maps, and artifacts from his deceased colleagues at the private security company he and Bill had worked for until 1994. It became obvious to us that Bill had disseminated the most important parts of the Cremona Document to these colleagues, with strict instructions that upon their deaths the material would go to Don. Bill said as much in a letter he wrote to his colleague John Lennon, which Don received in a package from Lennon's estate in the summer of 2020.

In total, Don received documents from the estates of John Drake (2019), John Lennon (2020), Dan Spartan (2021), and Dave Rian (2022). In the fall of

Don Ruh is the only person that took my research seriously and has helped me with it over the years so I include this portion to him but wish to do so after I have departed this earth. Since he is the youngest of the Spartan personnel I think he will survive long enough for the current political situation in America to have passed on leaving what I hope will be a more open government with less red tape.

In a letter written in 1996 by Bill Jackson to his colleague and friend, John Lennon, he explained why he left his Cremona Document material to his friend Donald Ruh. (Courtesy of Donald Ruh)

2022, after finding a small treasure by information contained in the puzzle box left for Don by Dan Spartan, we pondered whether there was anyone left from the company whom Bill might have left Cremona Document material with.

Don and I were resting next to a creek we had just crossed after our treasure hunt in the Adirondack Mountains when I turned to him and asked, "Is there was anyone left?"

At first, he said "No." He then thought for a moment and said, "Bill had a girlfriend…" A few months later we contacted his girlfriend's cousin, who had been given a cache of documents a couple years before she died in 2021. In January and February of 2023 Don received six encrypted messages which included two pages of sketches of the tunnel system and mechanisms used in constructing the underground workings on Oak Island, and a map.

Left: The box Don Ruh received from his colleague Dan Spartan in 2021. Inside were numerous artifacts and documents Bill Jackson had given to Dan to give to Don upon his death. Most notable was Map Eight which is 3' x 2' in size and has thirteen parts. (Wolter, 2021)

Right: One of over a dozen pages that contain six encrypted messages Don received from a friend named Roberta in 2023. (Courtesy of Donald Ruh)

It took two months to decode the six messages, which revealed a trove of information about the Templars' activities starting in 1304 through the recovery of the multiple treasures hidden in North America in 1769/1770.

The Covenant

It is clear from the beginning of the journals the mission they called "The Covenant" was to establish a sanctuary called the Free Templar State in the land–as stated on the Kensington Rune Stone–"far to the west". It was a sacred mission which began at least three years prior to the suppression of the Templars by the King of France and the Roman Catholic Church, who combined their authorities to arrest, interrogate, torture, and eventually burn as many of the knights as necessary to force them to produce their treasures to help get Philip the Fair out of debt, and to line the already-rich coffers of the Church. On October 13, 1307 the arrest order came down, after which roughly 600 Templars were arrested in France and their headquarters in Paris was raided by agents of the King and the Church. When the vaults were opened, however, they were empty. The order had obviously been tipped off about the arrest and had already removed their treasures. In the following decoded message Don received in 2023 we learn a great deal about what happened leading up to and just after the putdown.

> "*The power of God is within you. This is the final writing of this report. First done in MCCCVIII* [1308] *and revised three times till MCMVIII* [1908]. *The final putting of the relic is told here MDXCVII* [1597]. *In MCCCIV* [1304] *Louis de Grimoard by order of Grand Master Jaques DeMolay ar*[r]*anged for three ships to embark from LaRochelle to locale de Ramsey and Point de Arye and Leith de Saddel dans* [in] *le* [the] [Isle?] *de* [of] *Man with the pilot* [navigator?] *Francisco DeLeon, they embark to Harris West Isle for designer* [architect?] *Paolette Justinian Roach. Set sail Mars* [March] *XXI* [21] *for the brethren in northern the northland. [Scotland?] This is the account of the journey and the CCC* [300] *year project to secure the relic now held by Lionel de Waldern III XLIV* [44] *years old abo*[a]*rd le Gaspard also captained by Philip d' Armon with a crew of LVI*

[56] *and I chest of jewels and jewelry with the relic. Philip d' Armont, relative of Pierre in Lo Tutore* [Italian: The Guardian] *with a crew of LXXIV* [74] *and III chests of gold and silver bars. He also carries Ibrahim Muhammad Al-Zacara, maker of structure. Caption Juan de Alvarez from Garda Portugal in Le Vallant with chart maker Sotomon Yzarbo son of Licinius and a crew of LXVIII* [68] *with V chests of gold and silver coin completes the trio. They ar*[r]*ive at the observatory in Juin* [June] *XXI* [21] *and leave Jillet* [July] *XXI* [21] *for the land of the Wasuta and the Mickimacks."*

There is a lot to unpack in this, and the bulk of it will have to wait for the next book, but let's tie as much of it as we can to the mission of the Covenant. First, the Templar's Grand Master at the time, Jacques DeMolay, appears to have known the end was coming and began preparations to get the treasures and the relics out of Europe and eventually to the Western Lands three years before Friday the 13th, 1307. We know there reportedly were eighteen Templar ships docked in the port of LaRochelle on the west coast of France. From there three ships loaded with treasure and relics made their way due north to the Isle of Man. It appears from the mention of "Saddel" the three ships made their way north again to Scotland. This message seemed to have been delivered from above, for in May of 2022 I had already traveled to the Island of Arran and made important discoveries about exactly where the Templar treasures were hidden—most likely immediately after the putdown in October of 1307—and how they made their way to Wemyss Caves located along the Firth of Forth.

Saddell Abbey

It was a colleague's idea to travel to Saddell Abbey and I was more than happy to visit this site, especially when they said it was Cistercian. In my opinion the medieval Templars and Cistercians are one and the same, and it might be my one and only chance to see it so far out on the Kintyre Peninsula in Western Scotland. It was a beautiful, sunny day when we pulled up the grassy road to the ruins that were once Saddell Abbey. There was something magical about this place that both of us could feel. There was only one stone archway left standing, and the remaining ruins were rather sparce. After exploring what was left of the building, we wandered through the cemetery remarking on the many gravestones adorned with a skull and crossbones.

Left: A drone captured the few remaining ruins and cemetery of Saddell Abbey. (Wolter, 2022)
Right: Several grave slabs exhibited the skull and crossbones. (Wolter, 2022)

Next to the cemetery was a modern shelter. Inside were about twenty grave slabs on display, roughly a dozen of which had effigies of Templar Knights fully adorned in chainmail, armor, shields, and swords. It felt so right being here and we speculated the three ships that left La Rochelle on October 12, 1307 must have been here after their initial stop at the Isle of Man. It would be our discoveries the next day on the Isle of Arran that prompted us to change our working hypothesis about where the three ships, loaded with treasure, stopped first.

Island of Arran

Before leaving the ruined abbey, I flew my drone and took some great aerial video and pictures of the site. From there we hustled our way to catch the ferry to the Isle of Arran. Upon our arrival we drove a half hour to our hotel in the town of Brodick. We would visit a site at King's Cave and arrive late the next morning for the three-and-a-half-mile round-trip hike. After changing into our hiking boots, we walked up to the interpretive sign at

There are about twenty medieval grave slabs that line the interior of the modern shelter at Saddell Abbey on the Kintyre Peninsula in Western Scotland. (Wolter, 2022)

the start and we both noticed something very unexpected. On the sign was a picture of King Robert the Bruce, for whom the caves were named. What made our jaws drop was the write-up that went with the photo, "King's Cave may be traditionally linked to Robert the Bruce's visit to Arran in 1307." We looked at each other and in unison said, "1307?"

Interpretive signage at the beginning of the three-and-a-half-mile hike at Kings Cave included a picture of King Robert the Bruce who visited the caves three months prior to the putdown of the Templars in October of 1307. Could Bruce have been scouting locations to hide the Templar treasures that disappeared just prior to the arrest order? (Wolter, 2022)

Subsequent research would reveal The Bruce had visited Arran, and the island was where the legend of the determined spider that kept spinning its web despite setbacks originated, which inspired King Robert to press on despite his setbacks in battle. This tale with the spider reportedly happened in February of 1307,[62] but another source puts him at King's Cave in August of 1307, only two months prior to the suppression of the Knights Templar. It didn't take long for our minds to race in an obvious direction: was Robert the Bruce scouting a location to hide the treasures that would be whisked out of France before they could be confiscated by King Philip the Fair and the Roman Catholic Church? Even before seeing the cave itself, we both knew we were onto something important. On an incredibly scenic hike to the cave, we speculated the three ships left the Isle of Man and made their way to King's Cave to offload the valuable cargo and then make their way directly across the Firth of Clyde to Saddell Abbey. The Cistercian monks living there would have welcomed their brethren happily and provided food and shelter.

Our theory was rapidly coming together, and when we finally arrived at the main cave what we found there only solidified everything. It was huge on the inside, with an entrance that faced to the south and was not visible from the water. We stood in the footsteps of King Robert the Bruce, imaging him realizing he had found the perfect place to bring the sacred Templar treasure from France.

The entrance to King's Cave is not visible from the Firth of Clyde and would have been the perfect hiding place for Templar treasure in 1307. King Robert the Bruce scouted this cave on the Isle of Arran only a few months before the suppression of the Templars on October 13, 1307. (Wolter/2023)

62. https://www.bbc.co.uk/scotland/education/as/warsofindependence/info.shtml?loc=cave2

The ruins at Kilwinning still stand over underground tunnels and chambers where Templar treasure was likely hidden for a time during the early-to-mid fourteenth century. (Wolter, 2021)

KILWINNING

The exact timing of the movement of the treasures is unknown. However, it seems likely the fugitive Templars would have begun moving the treasures east to Wemyss Caves not long after its arrival at King's Cave. The next logical step would have been at Kilwinning, an abbey built by a little-known group of master craftsmen called the Tironensians.[63] I had been to Kilwinning a few times already and were well-acquainted with the legends of Templar treasure being hidden within chambers and tunnels beneath the Abbey. The Templars would definitely have been trying to keep one step ahead of their enemies—keeping this rich and sacred treasure moving was a must.

We suspect the treasure—and the fugitive Templars—made their way to Wemyss Caves shortly after the Battle of Bannockburn. Earl Henry himself wrote about how their service turned the tide against the British, leading to the greatest victory in the history of Scotland on May 1, 1395:

63. https://www.encyclopedia.com/history/encyclopedias-almanacs-transcripts-and-maps/tironensians

> *We travel with Knights Templars remaining in 120 numbers, descended from Templars at Bannockburn that my grandfather led to search for a free Templar State. We also look for good places to bring the Treasure of the Templars still hidden in Scotland.*

Because of this, two of the most prominent clans in the Scottish Lowlands, the Sinclairs and the Wemyss, would have been obligated to protect the Templars and the treasures. That temporary sanctuary for the next several decades for the fugitive Templars and their descendants was Wemyss Caves.

Wemyss Caves

Well Cave was certainly one of the caves the Templars sought refuge in, and is one I have visited multiple times. It is very large and could easily house multiple families. It sits directly below MacDuff Castle, which belonged to their descendants, the Wemyss, in the fourteenth century. Archaeologists today acknowledge that Christian monks lived in the caves in the fourteenth century. More recently, remains of a forge were excavated and carbon-14 testing of associated organic material also dated to circa 1400 CE.

Earl Henry had several entries discussing activities of the Templars and their descendants in the caves throughout the latter half of the fourteenth century, and how they and their treasures were brought to the Western Lands in 1395 and 1398 as part of the Covenant.

Forrester/Sinclair Connection at Rosslyn

One of the most important and intriguing aspects of the journals is the lists of the Templar Knights and crew that were aboard each ship that sailed to the Western Lands in 1395 and 1398. This presents an incredible opportunity to vet these names which, although a Herculean task, has already yielded interesting and unexpected results. One of the most interesting examples I was able to confirm myself was the name of Adam Forrester who was listed as one of eleven Templar Knights aboard the *Orknades*, during the 1398 expedition.

My investigation into Sir Adam Forrester led to two small churches in Scotland. The first was Corstorphine Church a few miles east of Edinburgh. In January of 2019 I visited this small church and found Sir Adam Forrester's name at the top of a list of his descendants—who were prominent citizens of Edinburgh. Below Sir Adam's name is the name of his eldest son John, who is buried beneath one of three life-size effigies carved in stone inside two recesses of the church. Beside him is the effigy of his wife. Her name was Jean Sinclair, the third of five daughters and three sons Earl Henry Sinclair had with two wives (Margaret and Jean). Jean was named after her mother and was born on April 18, 1383.

> *Today a daughter Jean was born in Corstorphine while her mother was visiting. She is a weak and tiny child, but her mother insists she will survive. I pray for them both. They return home as soon as they are strong enough.*

1. SIR ADAM. Provost of Edinburgh three times, from 1373. Founded a Chapel at Corstorphine, 1376. Deputy Chamberlain of Scotland, 1388. Keeper of the Great Seal of Scotland, 1391. Ancestor of the Forresters of Drylaw, and Le Forestier in France.

2. SIR JOHN (1). Keeper of the Great Seal of Scotland, from 1420. Master of the Household to James I, 1424. Founded this church about 1429. Chamberlain of Scotland from 1429. Buried here. Ancestor of the Forresters of Niddry.

The names of Sir Adam Forrester and his son, Sir John Forrester, are the first two names listed on an interpretive display inside Corstorphine Church in eastern Edinburgh, Scotland. (Wolter, 2019)

Not only is it probable Sir Adam Forrester was well known to Earl Henry Sinclair since they traveled together to the Western Lands in 1398, but the fact Henry's daughter, Jean, was married to Forrester's son makes it a certainty they knew each other well. Beyond this is another curious connection between the two clans that is found in the other small church in Scotland: Rosslyn Chapel.

While filming inside Rosslyn Chapel for an episode of *America Unearthed* in 2019, I discovered something that I had not seen in the church during my previous visits. Carved into a horizontal beam in the southeast corner of the ceiling was what I had thought to be a Mason's mark. However, upon closer examination I concluded it wasn't a Mason's mark due to it being larger, carved deeper, and being the only one of this unique symbol I could find. I have spent a lot of time searching the chapel for Mason's marks in the past and knew of about a dozen or so marks throughout the building. This carving was different, and when I visited Corstorphine Church, I found the answer to the mysterious symbol in Rosslyn Chapel.

Below the carved effigies of Sir John Forrester and Jean Sinclair are five family crests in shield form. The second from left crest contains the hunting horn symbol of the Forrester clan and the engrailed cross of the Sinclairs seen all over Rosslyn chapel. (Wolter, 2019)

Directly below the recess with the effigies of Sir John Forrester and Jean Sinclair were five family crests in the shield style. The second from the left was divided into three parts with the left side having three examples of the same strange symbol I had seen carved into the ceiling beam at Rosslyn Chapel. It was the hunting horn symbol of Clan Forrester, the ancestral keepers of the forests where members of Scottish high society in the region held hunting parties. Here we have an indisputable connection between the two clans, as the carving in Rosslyn would have been added at some point after construction of the chapel began in 1446. This would have been after

The effigies of Sir John Forrester and Jean Sinclair lie within a recess in Corstorphine Church in east Edinburgh, Scotland. (Wolter, 2019)

Carved into a ceiling beam in the southeast corner of Rosslyn Chapel is a large hunting horn symbol of the Forrester Clan. The symbol could be an acknowledgment of the close association of the two clans, consecrated by the marriage of Sir John Forrester and Jean Sinclair shortly before construction of the chapel began, sometime after 1446. (Wolter/2019)

the marriage of John Forrester and Jean Sinclair sometime only a decade or two earlier. While this fascinating connection between the Forrester and Sinclair clans in the late fourteenth/early fifteenth centuries doesn't prove the veracity of the journals by itself, it does provide powerful corroborating evidence in support of their authenticity.

Mason's Island

Another curious aspect of the journals is the mention of the recovered treasures being brought to a small island in the Potomac River in the area of what would soon become known as Washington, D.C. Mason's Island is now called Theodore Roosevelt Island and is now a park that contains an impressive monument to the 26th President of the United States. This, of course, led to me to undertake multiple visits to the island to see if the information in the journals was consistent with what was on the ground.

There are several paths that traverse the roughly north-south aligned island in the middle of the river. The first thing I found was the location of Founding Father George Mason's residence. After a short hike I found an interpretative display clearly showing the location of the house where it stood in 1770. From there I hiked into the woods to see if there were any clues to its exact location and, after a short search, I found a few fired bricks with mortar attached half buried in the ground. They were at the spot that corresponded to the interpretive map, and I felt confident the house was once here.

From this location I started to pace off the 1,000 steps toward the north end of the island. After making a beeline through the woods I found the path leading though the center of the island. I was within a couple hundred feet of the north end of the island when I reached 1,000 paces. Immediately to my right the land dropped off steeply, roughly twenty to thirty feet. I hiked into the brush to the base of a steep rise facing west and was struck by how the steep terrain at the correct distance from the location of the George Mason residence seemed to fit the description of the vault perfectly:

> *He has promised to have carts available at his dock to unload the cargo and has shown us a brick vault. It is approximately 27 feet square and lies within view of his two-story home on*

the northeast side of the island. The vault lies at least 10 feet below the surface and the entrance to the east has been dug down to allow entrance. He states that it lies 1000 paces from his home, and he is able to see it at all times of the day.

After scouting the area along the steep drop, I started looking for bricks and mortar that could be remnants of the secret vault and it didn't take long to find some. Despite the promising discovery, I quickly reeled my excitement in realizing the materials could be from other structures that were known to have been constructed on the island. The other sobering thought was if the vault was still there it would likely still be intact as it was constructed below grade. The bricks I found were likely from some other structure from the past that is no longer standing. However, based on the information from the journals and what I was able to learn on the ground, the secret vault constructed by George Mason could very likely still be there, waiting to be discovered underground. If so, I certainly don't hold out hope there would still be treasure inside it, other than a forgotten coin or a small part of an historic artifact, though even an empty vault would be an incredible treasure and would further validate this amazing story.

Lexell's Comet and Venus Transit

One of the things that struck me after reading the journals was mention of a comet in the sky, multiple times, and the acknowledgment of what was apparently a transit of Venus. Both astronomical occurrences are exceedingly rare and noteworthy. Lexell's comet is named after Swedish astronomer Anders Johan Lexell (1740-1784) and could have been easy to view since it should have been very bright in the sky for several days in 1770. That it is noted by John Weems Jr. isn't that surprising as he was an educated and observant man. For me, this lends enormous credibility to the journals because why would a forger insert something as random, virtually unknown, and potentially trivial to anyone else at that time in history.

The same is true in the mention of Venus during one of its historically known transits across the sun. John Weems Jr. doesn't say the word "transit" but apparently, within Freemasonry at that time, the astronomical movements of Venus were important, as noted by the prominence of the five-pointed star that will be detailed in the Sacred Numbers section. The symbol was so important, and the movements of the planet so well understood by Freemasonry—and the Knights Templar who preceded them—that the Founding Fathers chose the pentagram as the iconic symbol of the Free Templar State. This would eventually lead to having fifty stars emblazoned on the nation's flag.

Beavers

At first, I didn't think much about the comment made about *"...small furry creatures who build their houses with sticks."* by James Wemyss while in North America in 1665. Upon reflection and investigation, it proved to be more significant than I realized. Clearly, Wemyss had never seen or heard of creatures so common on this continent. It turns out there were no beavers in Scotland or the UK during his lifetime because they had been hunted to extinction a century earlier. So, it turns out this seemingly innocuous comment about a curious creature may hold great significance. Silly as it seems, beavers are interesting creatures with their chewing abilities and large, flat tails, and to see one for the first time in a foreign land probably would be noteworthy. It just feels authentic, and minor as it may seem, it could be one of the more convincing pieces of evidence supporting the authenticity of these documents.

Internal Evidence

Perhaps one of the most compelling and convincing aspects of the journals that supports authenticity is what is collectively called internal evidence. In this case, I'm talking about things like sacred numbers, codes, and esoteric symbols within the documents that only those initiated into the secret knowledge would understand. Numerous examples of esoteric symbols are found within the Sinclair/Wemyss journals, as well as within the Cremona Document. What makes this evidence so compelling is how so few have any idea of what these are, let alone how to use them. It is just so unlikely that any kind of forger, modern or past, would have working knowledge of such detailed, highly guarded symbolism to be able to create documents such as these.

SACRED NUMBERS

One aspect of the internal evidence is the use of sacred numbers. Very few individuals have any knowledge of these sacred numbers. Other than independent study of esoteric traditions like Gematria, only those who have been initiated into Freemasonry, Templarism, or other like traditions have any knowledge of these sacred numbers. Those with such knowledge understand the significance of eight, thirteen, and twenty-one, and how they are a telltale calling card to like-minded individuals—a kind of "this is us" signature. These three numbers are part of the Fibonacci Sequence—also called the Golden Ratio—which, in this context, relates to the sacred and secret veneration of the life-giving Goddess.

To fully appreciate this aspect of the journals, we need to take a close look at the most iconic symbol of the United States, the five-pointed star.

This ancient symbol is directly connected to astronomy and, more specifically, the planet Venus. When viewed from earth, the shape of Venus's motion in the sky creates a pentagram over a period of eight Earth years. More importantly, within the lines of the pentagram we find the Fibonacci Sequence. When rounded to whole numbers, the sequence proceeds: 1, 2, 3, 5, 8, 13, 21, etc.—each digit being the sum of the previous two. This numerical sequence is most commonly represented by the spiral, and is found in all life, not only on Earth but throughout the Universe. Ancient cultures like the Phoenicians, indigenous people around the world, and the medieval Templars all understood the sacred relationship of Venus and the Golden Ratio as being the key to life and was always associated with the feminine aspect of Creation. Women have always been the life-givers, which is why Venus is considered a feminine Deity in the Heavens. Because of this, it shouldn't be a surprise we see reverence for the sacred feminine throughout the Sinclair/Wemyss Journals, which on its own breathes authenticity into these documents.

The evidence of the Templars revering Venus—both the planet in the heavens and the Goddess herself—is found adorning the magnificent spiritual houses they financed and constructed during their reign of wealth and power in the twelfth and thirteenth centuries. Three such places are found in France and Spain. The first example is in the north transept of the largest Gothic cathedral

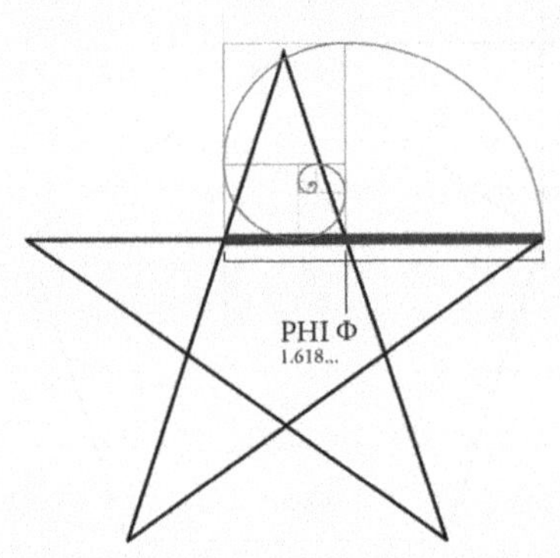

Left: When astronomers track the movement of the planet Venus from earth during its eight-year cycle it creates a pentagram.

Right: The Golden Ratio is imbedded within the five-pointed star symbol as are other mathematical and geometrical aspects which in esoteric circles are called Sacred Geometry. (Internet/Internet)

in France. Amiens has a breathtaking five-pointed star in the rose window of the transept that is pointing down.

This positioning of the symbol certainly flies in the face of the claim by many Christians that it is a symbol of the devil and "black magic." This is hardly the case, and for a time in the past the down-pointed pentagram actually symbolized the "five wounds of Christ." I would also point out the symbol used by the appendant body for women within Freemasonry is called Eastern Star and their symbol is a downward pointing pentagram. This should be the last word on the pentagram being symbolic of anything other than the sacred feminine of Deity, represented by Venus in the heavens and by women here on earth.

Arguably the most beautiful example of the five-pointed star is found in a small Templar church called the Hermitage of St. Bartholomew, which sits in central Spain, nestled in a valley surrounded by towering limestone cliffs that house a stunning cave system. These caves were used for rituals dating back to at least Roman times, when the people practiced a ritual called *Mundus Patet,* which was a festival where the people prayed and worshiped the mother Goddess of the underworld. The underworld aspect of this ritual was connected to the planet Venus when She disappears during the planet's transition from a morning to evening star and vice versa.

At Amiens Cathedral in France the five-pointed star is seen in the north transept window from both the outside and inside. (Wolter, 2024)

Left: One of the appendant bodies of Freemasonry that is primarily for women is called Eastern Star. Their symbol is a downward pointing pentagram that relates back to the planet Venus. (Internet/Wolter, 2024)

Right: On both the north and south transepts of the Church of St. Remy are windows with five hearts interlaced to form a five-pointed star honoring the Goddess in the heavens. (Wolter, 2024)

Another beautiful example is in the rose window of a modest but important church in Troyes, France. The Church of St. Remy in Troyes dates to at least the eleventh century and was where Saint Bernard de Clairvaux reportedly preached to his Cistercian brethren in the early twelfth century. While the five-pointed star was not in the rose window during Bernard's time, it was added during the Renaissance period, most

At the Templar Church at the Hermitage of St. Bartholomew a cave is seen behind it where rituals have taken place going back at least a millennium. (Wolter, 2014)

likely for its connection to Venus and the Goddess. Not far away at Troyes Cathedral is where the charter for the Knights Templar was written by Bernard, and a papal bull was signed by Pope Honorus II on January 13, 1129. These made the Templars an official military monastic order within Christendom and had the Pope's blessing.[64]

The Sinclair/Wemyss Journals begin with a powerful clue to understanding this Goddess ideology of the Scottish clans in the fourteenth century, with the first entry written by the young Henry Sinclair on his eighth birthday, November 5, 1353:

> *My father gave me this journal for the celebration of my 8th birthday. He tells me to write about things I want to remember when I am a man. This year Father Dominic will teach me Latin, French, Gaelic and Norwegian. Father has promised to take me fishing with him in the spring. I can't wait to see the western banks and want to catch lots of fish.*

64. https://templarhistory.com/council-of-troyes/#:~:text=Bernard%20had%20been%20busy%20converting%20the%20rule%20of%20St.%20Benedict,

The five-pointed star is also found in the rose window at the Church of St. Remy in Troyes, France. The pentagram was added to the window during the Renaissance period. (Wolter, 2014)

Later entries continue to display a deep understanding and reverence of these sacred numbers, especially when it came to the crew lists of the ships. There was a total of eight ships on both the 1395 and 1398 voyages that made their way to the western lands. This was no doubt an acknowledgment of the sacred Goddess and a plea for protection from her during their dangerous voyages on the open seas of the North Atlantic to the Western Lands.

In the crew lists for the eight ships on the 1395 Sinclair expedition there were thirteen Templar Knights each aboard the *Accipiter, Itienere, Repostus* and the *Speculator*. There were twenty-one knights aboard the *Perequin* and thc *Ortus*. These numbers are no coincidence and show the level of commitment within the Templar tradition to the Goddess. Any doubt about this fact is removed when considering the number of times Her name is invoked in the journals throughout the 400-plus years of entries.

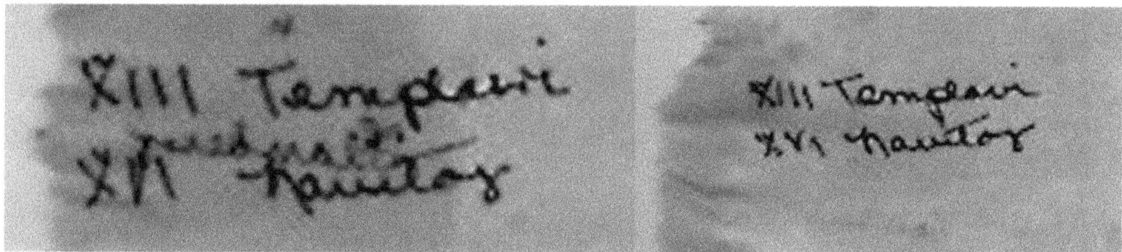

At the end of the crew lists for the *Accipiter* and the *Iternier*, the ships' compliment of Templari and Navitoy. written with the Hooked X symbol in all four examples of the Roman numeral ten (X). Like the sacred numbers, the use of the Hooked X symbol was also an acknowledgment of Deity and a plea of protection for both the men and the mission. (Wolter, 2016)

Here are a couple more examples of thirteen individuals on board a ship written by Earl David Wemyss (1494-1544):

> **October 30, 1518** – *I begin to plan my trip to the Western Lands and have asked 12 of the brethren to travel with me.*
>
> **May 15, 1520** – *We leave in the morrow for the Western Lands. Twelve of the brethren travel with me aboard the Elizabeth.*

I should also point out one more entry with two more sacred numbers found on the Kensington Rune Stone that are part of the Enochian legend of the Secret Vault allegorically embedded within the inscription I named the Cryptic Code. Those numbers are ten and fourteen. This entry was written by John Weems immediately after the treasures left by Earl Henry and his men in Nova Scotia in 1395/1398, were recovered and brought to Mason's Island and placed inside an underground brick vault:

> **July 14, 1770** – *A group of 10 and 14 masons encircled the tomb and we blessed the vault and asked Heavenly Father to bless and protect this place against time and the ravages and greed of war.*

Why this group of Freemasons and Patriots chose to divide themselves into ten and fourteen men, and not simply twenty-four men, must be related to the Enochian legend of the Secret Vault. For a group of men initiated in Masonic traditions they deeply honored who were involved in such a secret and sacred mission, and literally standing above the secret vault they had just filled with treasures that would help bring the Covenant to completion, performing a ritual prayer to protect it would be expected.

Both numbers are vital to the cosmology of Templar ideology and the veneration of the Goddess numerically expressed in the Fibonacci sequence. This numerical expression of the Templars' sacred core beliefs provides a powerful argument for the veracity of both sets of documents.

HOOKED X

What has become the definitive symbol of authenticity in the Sinclair/Wemyss journals, as well as in the Cremona Document, the Kensington, Narragansett and Spirit Pond Rune Stones, and other Templar documents, is the Hooked X. It is the secret and sacred symbol used by the descendants of the suppressed Knights Templar order that represents their true ideological beliefs of Monotheistic Dualism. The symbol was also used by initiated scribes as an acknowledgment of God, and as a plea of protection for the members of the order and their sacred documents and maps.

We've already seen the Hooked X symbol within the Roman numeral ten, and the "x" in the name "Alexander" in the Templar Knights and crew lists for the ships *Accipiter*, *Iternier*, and the *Repostus*. We can only guess how many Hooked X symbols were made within the pages of entries and crew lists we haven't seen that were thrown away by Diana back in 2016. Regardless, we can't fret over what we have no control over and need to appreciate and carefully evaluate the material we do have. At this point we have a total of eight Hooked Xs within the crew lists, which is very telling. All eight are from crew list photos we have from the 1395 trip to the Western Lands. The only crew list photo we have from the 1398 trip is the front side of the *Somnium*. While it does not contain any Hooked X symbols, it does contain three apparent fish symbols which is also an esoteric symbol I'll discuss in more detail in the coming sections.

Here again we see an extremely rare–yet perfectly appropriate–sacred symbol this group of post put-down Templars involved in a sacred mission used. We will see dozens more appropriately used Hooked X symbols within the Cremona Document material yet to be published. They will not only bolster the conclusions I've reached about the meaning for the usage of the symbol, but will also show its evolution over the centuries.

VIRGO

Still another very subtle yet powerful aspect of the journals is found on the lambskin map I photographed back in 2016 during the one and only time I saw the map and book nineteen written by John Weems Jr. On what would have been the right front leg of the animal skin is a Roman numeral

On the lambskin map, purportedly made by the explorer Antonio Zeno, is the Roman numeral date of 1395 and Zeno's sigla. The sigla appears to incorporate two esoteric symbols used by the Knights Templar, the "M" and the "fish" symbol. These two symbols combined also make the astrological symbol for Virgo (Inset), the sixth symbol in the zodiac. (Wolter, 2016/Internet)

date of 1395 (MCCCXCV) and the apparent initials of the famous Italian navigator/cartographer for Earl Henry Sinclair on the 1395 expedition to the Western Lands: Antonio Zeno.

In book two of Earl Henry Sinclair's journals, beginning with an entry on May 31, 1390, he writes about Antonio Zeno with details that parallel specific information in the *Zeno Narrative*, a document published by one of Zeno's direct descendants in 1558 about the explorer's activities in the North Atlantic and rumored landing in North America. Masonic scholar Robert Cooper published a book in 2004 that included both an Italian and English version of the narrative that includes, perhaps not coincidentally, thirteen specific details that directly match information written by Earl Henry Sinclair in the journals. One item is especially worth noting above the rest since it was wrong in the original narrative, but accurate in the

Sinclair journal. The *Zeno Narrative* mentions a letter written by Nicolo Zeno to his *brother* Antonio. However, in the journals it is abundantly clear that Nicolo is not a brother; he is in fact, Antonio's father. On July 3, 1394 Earl Henry wrote:

> *Captain Nicolo has written to his brother Carlos Zeno in Venice about a voyage of discovery he wishes to make. His ship being destroyed he requests that Carlos send Antonio, the son of Nicolo, to Orkney with another ship. He should arrive in the spring. Captain Nicolo has now left for Groenland to explore the western coastline and will return in 2 months.*

Fish Symbol

Another rather obscure but important fact worth mentioning about Antonio Zeno is a Roman numeral date of 1395 on the lambskin map presumed to have been drawn by Antonio Zeno, who was also a cartographer. Below the 1395 date is the curious sigla of the navigator that includes some interesting esoteric symbols. There appears to be a deliberately made "M" within the artistically made "Z" initial, undoubtedly a reference to Mary Magdalene and the Goddess, as well as a "fish" symbol at the base of the far-right leg of the "M." Fish symbols are also seen in the one picture we have of Earl Henry's entries as well as in a picture of the crew list of the *Somnium*. I wrote in detail about these symbols–which were and still are used by initiates in certain Templar traditions–in *Cryptic Code of the Templars in America*.[65]

One notable example of a famous historical figure who was undoubtedly initiated with the same esoteric "fish" knowledge is the first President of the United States, George Washington. When looking at his signature as a young man it is clear he was highly educated with beautiful penmanship.[66] However, there are notable changes to his signature after he was raised as a Freemason in 1752.[67] The most notable change is the addition of a vertically aligned "fish" symbol above the "g" in his last name. Washington also

65. Wolter, Pages 86-88 and Pages 101-110, 2019.

66. http://www.ubooks.pub/Books/ON/B1/E1583R2959/16MB1583.html

67. http://americanbuilt.us/patriots/george-washington.shtml

appears to change the style of the capital "G" in his first name. Here again the letter "g" appears to be connected to the "fish" symbol just like in Ben's Franklin's 1777 letter, and in the Kensington Rune Stone inscription. Prior to my own initiation into Freemasonry, I likely would not have taken any of this very seriously and written it off as speculation. However, after having gained a much deeper understanding of Masonic symbolism and the esoteric aspects of the Craft, I now understand how to pay attention to certain signs and symbols. Keep in mind symbols like these are designed to be subtle and innocuous, always leaving the door open for plausible deniability by the symbol maker. It is very subtle and otherwise obscure esoteric clues within the journals that breathe authenticity into the documents.

Top: An early example of George Washington's signature at the age of twelve in 1744/5 shows a young, educated man with beautiful penmanship.
Bottom: Notable changes in his signature occur after he was raised as a Freemason at the age of 21, most noticeably a vertically aligned "fish" symbol over the "g" in his last name and within the "W." (Internet/Internet)

Dotted M

Another rare and sacred symbol of the Templar order that occurs on Map Eight and the Neck Map of the Cremona Document material is the Dotted M. This subtle symbol speaks loudly in the esoteric world of the Templars as it alludes to the mother Goddess, represented by many names in the ancient world. While the Templar leadership—namely Saint Bernard de Clairvaux, the charismatic leader of the Cistercians—led the Church to believe they venerated the Virgin Mary, the "M" actually represented a different Mary. That Mary was the wife of both John the Baptist and Jesus, the heretical secret hidden

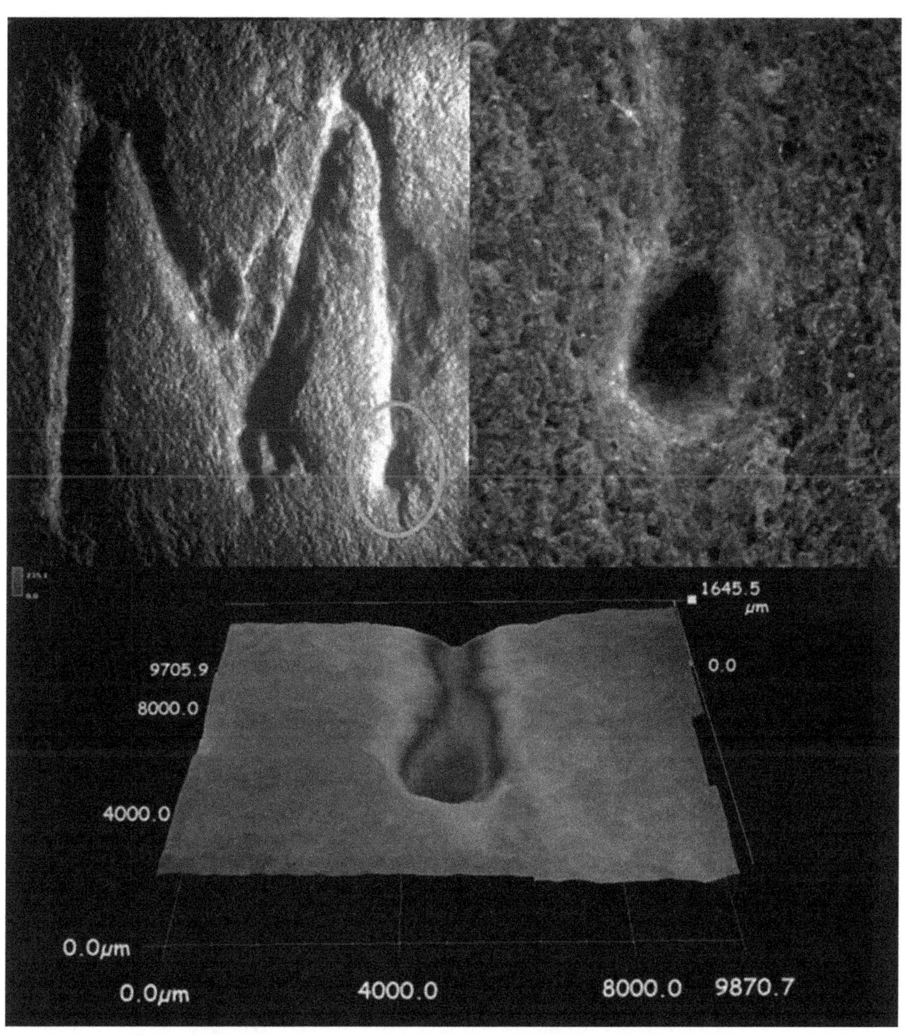

The carver of the Kensington Rune Stone added a deep punch mark on the lower end of the right leg of the "M" in an apparent acknowledgment of the Goddess—in this case, most likely Mary Magdalene—and to protect the Knights Templar land claim. (2002/2011, 2011)

within the first rendition of *Virgin on the Rocks* by Leonard DaVinci in 1483. The woman in the first version of the painting, with auburn hair and wearing orange and green colors watching over her two sons was in fact, Mary Magdalene. She is the one the Templars venerated and secretly memorialized with this symbol. The Dotted M was likely used as an invocation of the Mother Goddess to protect the treasures and the work of the cartographers.

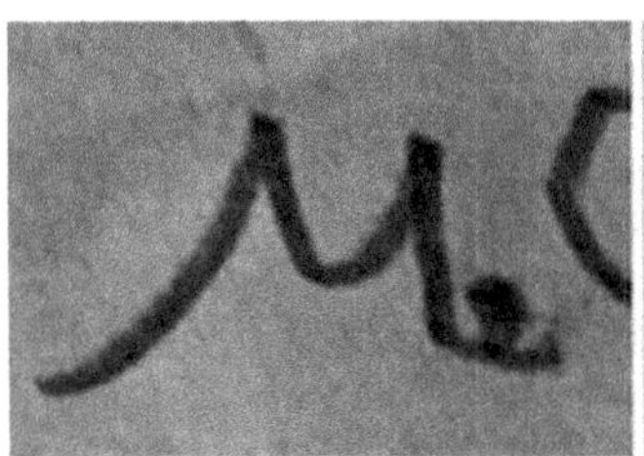
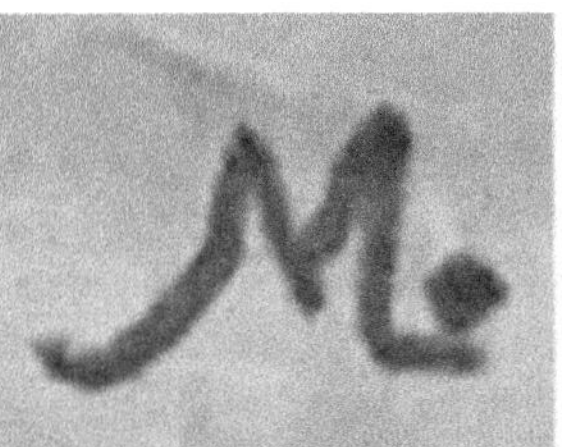
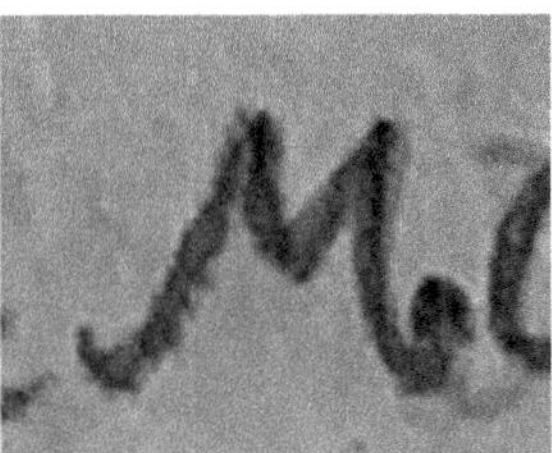

The examples of the Dotted M occur on Map Eight twice (left and middle), and once on the Neck map (right). (Wolter, 2021)

As mentioned previously, the Latin "M" on the Kensington Rune Stone has a punch mark added to the far-right leg. This is a veiled reference to Mary Magdalene and Virgo, the Goddess in the heavens so central to the true Templar teachings and ideology. Therefore, it should come as no surprise find the Dotted M within the Cremona Document material, as it is in Captain Zeno's sigla on the lambskin map.

Father Richards

What might be the most amazing and important entries in the journals was written by a then-twelve-year-old Henry Sinclair. It wasn't until reading the entries a second time that the significance became apparent. He wouldn't learn till later in his life about what we call the Kensington party, which left Norway for the Western Lands in 1358. Armed with this knowledge, reading the entries the second time through led to a starling realization in what Henry wrote on November 22, 1357:

> *I spent the day at the forge with my father learning about the feast of Weyland the Norse God of the Smiths. I am clumsy at the forge but respect those who are very clever. The smiths are creating nails and rivets for a boat to travel to the west banks in the spring. Father Dominic says that Father Richardus will accompany them with the seven new acolytes.*

The only boat mentioned that needed nails and rivets for traveling to the Western Lands in the spring of 1358 was what appears to have been the Kensington party that left from Norway. This discovery is interesting enough, but the real bombshell was in the last sentence. The reader might recall the first line of the Kensington inscription reads, "8 Goths (Gotlanders) and 22

Northmen (Norwegians)..." If the journals are a reliable indicator, the eight Goths might be the "...men of the Craft including monks with herbal knowledge..." mentioned in Henry's July 26, 1368, entry. According to my research into the esoteric and symbolic aspects of the Kensington inscription, it appears the "seven new acolytes" and Father Richardus are being acknowledged and intentionally singled out using what many scholars have called "strange runes."

In *The Cryptic Code of the Templars in America* I discovered what I called the "Confirmation Code" within the Kensington inscription. The code involves the number of strange, never-before-seen runic symbols used throughout the twelve lines of the inscription to confirm the importance of four sacred numbers. These include the eight g/u runes on the face side of the inscription, ten w/v runes, fourteen individual numbers and the twenty-two Hooked X symbols used for the letter "a". If we look carefully at the eight g/u runes we see there are actually seven backwards "g" runes, and one unique "u" rune that resembles the "g" but has a little more going on. There is an extra horizontal bar on the bottom of the vertical stave and two punch marks in the open upper half instead of one. Could these special seven "g" runes be symbolic of the "seven new acolytes" and the even more unique "u" be emblematic of Father Richardus? If so, then it could mean the Master of the eight Goths/monks, Father Richardus, was the carver of the Kensington Rune Stone inscription.

The incredible discovery of Father Richardus was made in July of 2016 when the Sinclair/Wemyss Journals were first brought to my attention. It wasn't until March of 2021, when the Spartan box was opened, that the name Father Richards appeared again. On the back of Map Eight there is a long narrative written by the mysterious "CLY", who reveals himself to be Clyphus Lucinus Yzerbo. He wrote about the map makers and Templar ship captains he and others before him sailed with, beginning in the twelfth century and continuing through his compilation of all the work–now known as Map Eight–in 1908. Roughly a third of way through his narrative he wrote something shocking that could not have been made up or dismissed in any way as a coincidence, "...the acolyte of Father Richards..." Having Father Richards appear in both documents is a powerful, if not conclusive, testament to their authenticity.

The Newport Tower in the spring of 2021. This two-story stone and mortar structure that sits on eight round heavy columns contains numerous solar and lunar astronomical alignments as well as keystone solar illumination events on the winter solstice and on May 1st. The current accepted narrative is that it was built as a colonial windmill. It is, in fact, an observatory and settlement structure built by the Templars circa 1400 CE. (Wolter, 2021)

NEWPORT TOWER

What is arguably the crown jewel of evidence of the ideological descendants of the medieval Templars in North America should not come as a surprise to be mentioned in the journals, but when I first read the following entry, I was still taken aback. As I read the Earl Henry entries about their activities in 1395 and 1398, I kept looking for some kind of allusion to construction or mention of the Newport Tower. He did write about traveling 'far south' to what was likely Narragansett Bay, the largest and best natural harbor on the East Coast of North America, but never anything that could be directly referencing the structure we know was already there or under construction at the time. It is possible Earl Henry did not mention the Tower intentionally to keep it secret. We simply don't know. It wasn't until 371 years later when a then 28-year-old John Weems Jr. wrote the following about the structure on June 25, 1769:

Brother Peleg has shown us what is called the Newport Tower. It has been here longer than the village has been founded. Some say it is a grain mill while others say it was built by the Templars to mark the seasons and to claim the surrounding area for settlement. It is the most unusual place I have ever seen, and I am fascinated by the methods in which it was constructed. As an engineer I can see how it must have been difficult to construct the tower using pressure points. It has 2 stories and has recesses in the stone for a fire and small windows that look out to all the directions of the compass. The sun enters through a different window each season and whomever built the tower had a great knowledge of astronomy. The watcher Baraqijal would have been proud.

The quarry stone used is also unusual and must have taken a great amount of effort to bring to this site. I have sketched a picture of the tower for my wife as I'm certain she would love to see it. After staying the night, we will be returning to Philadelphia. I am anxious to talk to my father about what I have seen. I wonder if his recollections are the same as mine.

It is worth mentioning the Cremona Document has multiple mentions of the "observatory" that can only be the Newport Tower. In March of 2021, when Don Ruh received the box full of artifacts, letters and maps from the estate of Dan Spartan, the most important item in the box what we named Map Eight. Originally on animal skin, Dan and his teenaged son recopied the 3'x2' map onto paper, as the original was rotting away.

The map has thirteen parts, each being separate maps of important locations many where treasures were hidden. Some were familiar as they were different versions of the Nova Scotia, Connecticut, Cape Cod and Narragansett Bay maps Bill Jackson has sold to the Vatican in 1994. This realization was comforting knowing Bill made sure the most important material ended up in safe hands. It was the Narragansett Bay map on Map Eight that provided a shocking piece of information that was not on the Narragansett Bay map the Vatican got. What it showed was a dot at the exact location of the Newport Tower on Aquidneck Island in Rhode Island, and a line leading from the dot

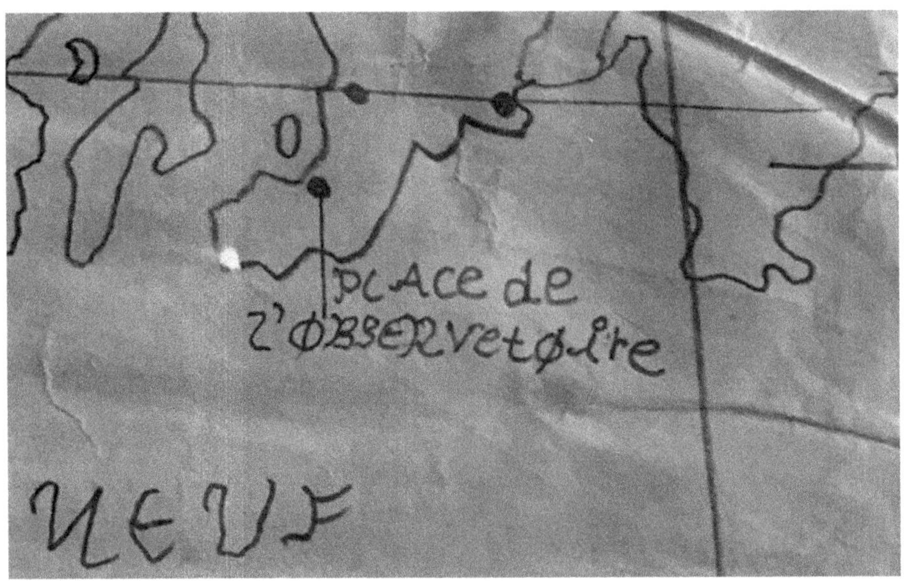

On Map 8, there are thirteen individual maps and on map nine ("Neuf" masculine form) is the same map of Narragansett Bay as seen in the photograph of the Cremona Document Bill Jackson sold to the Vatican in 1994. At the bottom of Aquidneck Island at the exact location of the Newport Tower a dot is present with a line identifying the location in French as "Place de Lobservetoire" (Place of the observatory). (Courtesy of Donald Ruh)

to the words written in French, *"Place de L'observetoire"* (Place of the observatory). This left no doubt that any mention of the "observatory" within the documents is a direct reference to the Newport Tower.

Two of the five encrypted messages Don received in 2023 make important references to the observatory that shed new light on when it was constructed and who was directly involved. The first message shared at the beginning of this chapter (page 319) contains vital information that includes a reference to the observatory:

> *He also carries Ibrahim Muhammad Al-Zacara, maker of structure. Caption Juan de Alvarez from Garda Portugal in Le Vallant with chart maker Sotomon Yzarbo son of Licinius and a crew of LXVIII* [68] *with V chests of gold and silver coin completes the trio. They ar*[r]*ive at the observatory in Juin* [June] *XXI* [21] *and leave Jillet* [July] *XXI* [21] *for the land of the Wasuta and the Mickimacks."*

Could this message be telling us who was brought to North America, presumably from a Muslim country based on his name, to oversee construction of the Newport Tower at some point in the fourteenth century? If there is any doubt about what structure Al-Zacara was the maker of, it is removed in the last sentence as they arrive at the observatory in June of an unknown year. The fifth encrypted message received in 2023 contained two very telling passages. It begins with the following:

> *The Saconnet contract MCDLXXVI* [1476] *years the use of the observatory as gifted from the people to the Poor Knights of Christ. We leave the observatory construction for the northland as Nahookan points south after Tachkanum.*

This indicates construction was on-going close to the time the message was written. We find out the answer to the key question as to when it was written at the end of the 6,600-plus character message: "*It is MCCCXCV* [1395]." This date fits perfectly with the first of two trips to the Western Lands led by Earl Henry Sinclair that same year. It also fits with the vague reference to his visiting the southern-most point on the eastern seaboard of North America which was most likely Narragansett Bay and the colony building the Newport Tower at that time.

We have even more details about construction of the observatory in two pages of notes Don received in 2019 from the estate of his deceased colleague John Drake. On the second of the two pages of notes, written in French, is notation number twenty-two which conveyed some amazing information about construction that is completely consistent with the vast number of astronomical alignments that have been documented in the structure in recent years:

> *The observatory is built here. The hut of the day observers is on the right and the night observers on the left. The field of measurement surrounded by a stone wall separated them from numerous slabs and wooden poles. Henri remains here to oversee the construction.*

This incredible information from the Cremona Document breathes stunning new details about this historically important structure. The

Newport Tower and the Kensington Rune Stone were interconnected via a long-range astronomical alignment that served as land claim devices created by the Templars after their suppression in Europe. The mission of the Covenant was passed onto our founding fathers and modern Freemasonry, who finished the job. I'll have more to say about that shortly.

Here again, mention of the Newport Tower in conjunction with the pre-Columbian activities of the Templars in North America doesn't prove the journals are authentic, but mention of it is consistent with what was already known about the structure prior to the journals coming forward in 2016.

Dog Island

Some of the most compelling entries in the journals were written by Earl Henry Sinclair after his fleet of ships were besieged by storms off the coast of Nova Scotia, costing him men and ships both in 1395 and 1398. One particularly interesting passage made by Earl Henry on August 1, 1398 brings in the name of an island we could find no reference to anywhere on the Internet:

> *We have labored for many weeks to free the Katherine and are unable to do so while her cargo is onboard. We have felled trees to the west and have attempted to dig a ditch filled with water that she might slide into the harbor on the other side of the island which we have named "Dog Island". The island is uninhabited and has no evidence of having been visited by the native people recently. At this time five other ships have been located and lodge in the harbor which we have named for Queen Margaret, Margaret's Bay. In our search for the other ships, we have located the wreck of the Ortus midway across the bay and are still searching for survivors, two of my own kinsmen amongst them.*

We have identified "Dog Island" as McNab Island near Halifax, Nova Scotia, but nowhere can we find it ever being called that in the past. It took six years before we found a reference on Map Eight, which contains a total of thirteen maps. Map twelve (Deuze) is labeled in French as *Le isle de Chien* (The Island of Dog). This discovery was shocking to say the least and provided a huge independent boost of credibility to the Sinclair/Wemyss Journals.

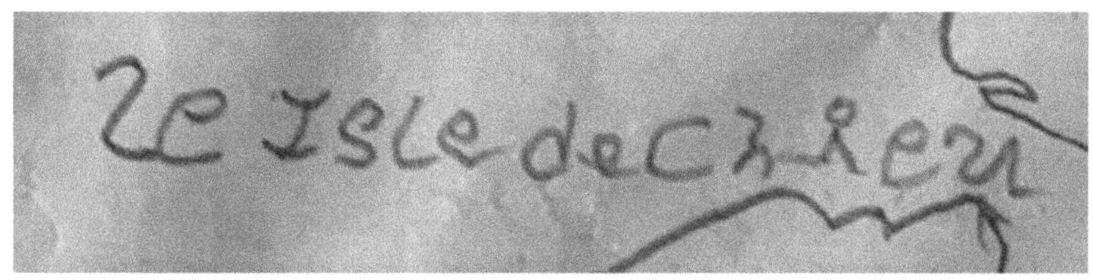

The name given to map #12 (Deuze) of 13 on Map 8 of the Cremona Document material to what is clearly known today as McNab Island, was called "Le Isle de Chein" (The Island of Dog). The only other known reference to McNab Island being called "Dog Island" is found in the Sinclair/Wemyss Journals. (Wolter/2021)

William "The Builder" Sinclair

In the August 16, 1432 entry made by William Sinclair there were subtle translation differences between that of Sister Harkin and Google Translate which Diana used that ended up having profound implications to the message. The important differences between the two translations were outlined on pages 171-172 and it is these facts that are extremely important in providing independent corroboration supporting the veracity of both documents.

Brother Joseph Peters

On August 31, 2017, Janet and I traveled to Nova Scotia to meet with the Grand Archivist of the Masonic Knights Templar courtesy of our friend and then Grand Master of the Knights Templar in Canada, William "Bill" Mann. Our purpose was to try to establish if there was a record of Joseph Peters existing in Halifax in 1766, and if he was involved in

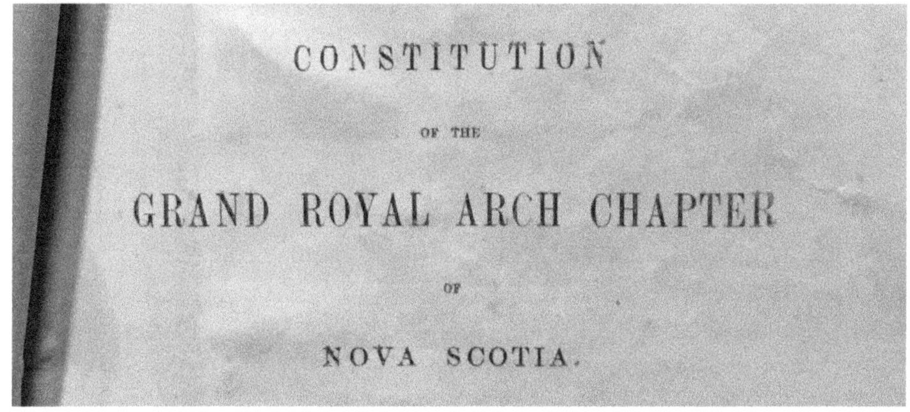
CONSTITUTION

OF THE

GRAND ROYAL ARCH CHAPTER

OF

NOVA SCOTIA.

The title page of the Royal Arch records from 1782. (Wolter, 2017)

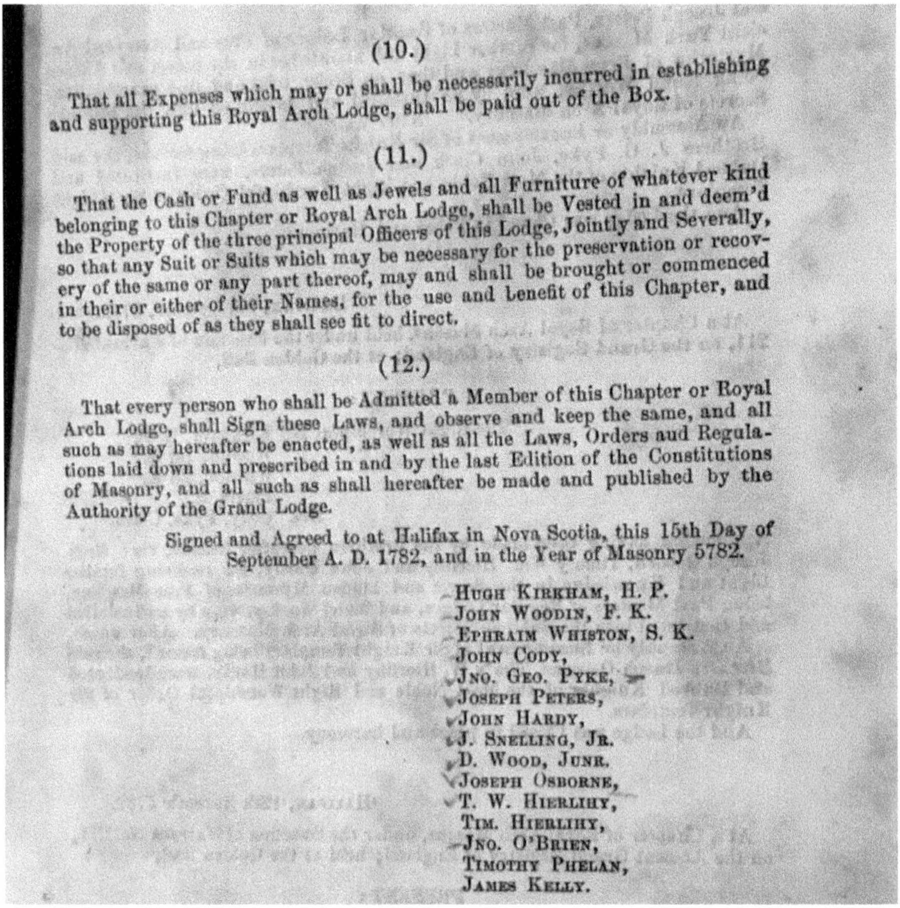

(10.)

That all Expenses which may or shall be necessarily incurred in establishing and supporting this Royal Arch Lodge, shall be paid out of the Box.

(11.)

That the Cash or Fund as well as Jewels and all Furniture of whatever kind belonging to this Chapter or Royal Arch Lodge, shall be Vested in and deem'd the Property of the three principal Officers of this Lodge, Jointly and Severally, so that any Suit or Suits which may be necessary for the preservation or recovery of the same or any part thereof, may and shall be brought or commenced in their or either of their Names, for the use and benefit of this Chapter, and to be disposed of as they shall see fit to direct.

(12.)

That every person who shall be Admitted a Member of this Chapter or Royal Arch Lodge, shall Sign these Laws, and observe and keep the same, and all such as may hereafter be enacted, as well as all the Laws, Orders and Regulations laid down and prescribed in and by the last Edition of the Constitutions of Masonry, and all such as shall hereafter be made and published by the Authority of the Grand Lodge.

Signed and Agreed to at Halifax in Nova Scotia, this 15th Day of September A. D. 1782, and in the Year of Masonry 5782.

HUGH KIRKHAM, H. P.
JOHN WOODIN, F. K.
EPHRAIM WHISTON, S. K.
JOHN CODY,
JNO. GEO. PYKE,
JOSEPH PETERS,
JOHN HARDY,
J. SNELLING, JR.
D. WOOD, JUNR.
JOSEPH OSBORNE,
T. W. HIERLIHY,
TIM. HIERLIHY,
JNO. O'BRIEN,
TIMOTHY PHELAN,
JAMES KELLY.

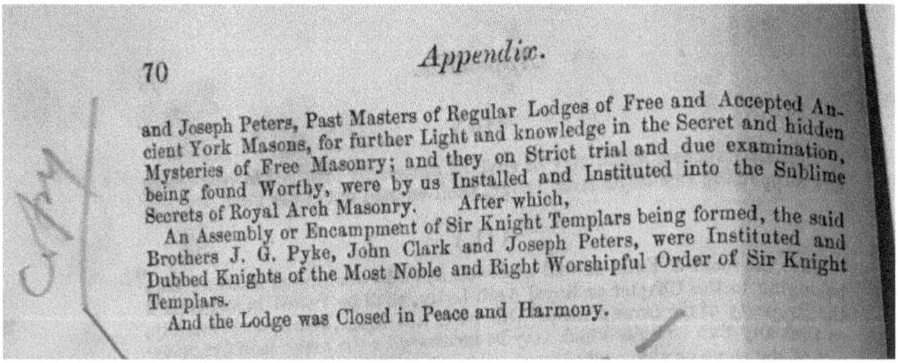

70 *Appendix.*

and Joseph Peters, Past Masters of Regular Lodges of Free and Accepted Ancient York Masons, for further Light and knowledge in the Secret and hidden Mysteries of Free Masonry; and they on Strict trial and due examination, being found Worthy, were by us Installed and Instituted into the Sublime Secrets of Royal Arch Masonry. After which,

An Assembly or Encampment of Sir Knight Templars being formed, the said Brothers J. G. Pyke, John Clark and Joseph Peters, were Instituted and Dubbed Knights of the Most Noble and Right Worshipful Order of Sir Knight Templars.

And the Lodge was Closed in Peace and Harmony.

Pages 69 & 70 of the Masonic Royal Arch Lodge record. Brother Joseph Peters is documented as having been admitted into both the Royal Arch Lodge and Order of Sir Knights Templar in September of 1782. (Wolter, 2017)

Freemasonry as everyone else mentioned in the journals who was involved in any aspect of the secret mission of the Covenant. The Grand Archivist shared records from the Grand Royal Arch Chapter from 1782 that lists among other names, Brother Joseph Peters. We are very confident this is the same Joseph Peters mentioned in the June 28, 1766, entry as he, too, was a strong and forceful man, lived in Nova Scotia at that time, and was both a Freemason and later knighted as a Masonic Knights Templar in 1782.

While visiting with the Grand Archivist, we asked if anyone during his thirty years in the position had inquired about these records or about brother Joseph Peters. The question was prompted by the concern that Diana had possibly found the information and perhaps used it to create or embellish the journals. His reply was that first and foremost, only a brother Freemason would have been allowed access to these records. Second, he said he would have only allowed access to the records if a brother had a legitimate research reason to see them. It became obvious that Diana could never have accessed these records no matter how hard she tried. He also added, "In the past thirty years, no one had ever requested to see these records."

Final Thoughts

As you read these final words after digesting the incredible tale, the words my friend and longtime investigative journalist, Don Shelby, wrote in an email to me after reading the journals sum things up pretty well, "Goddamn! What a great read. If it is true and can be established as true, it is the story of the century, of two and a half centuries, more."

I completely agree with Don and know this is the most important and interesting story I have ever worked on. I remember being gobsmacked after reading them the first time. This amazing story dovetailed perfectly with the Templars in America research I have been immersed in and written five books about since the Kensington Rune Stone came into my lab a quarter of a century ago.

That said, because of the historical implications of the story and what it means to my own research, and that of others I work with, I have had to be extremely careful and thorough as I have vetted the various aspects. That process has gone very well even though it has taken almost a decade. There is still a lot more to do in the form of searching for carvings, rock piles, and evidence of excavations in the past at locations the journals talk about. We also plan to find at least two shipwrecks that would prove the story true beyond any reasonable doubt. You can bet there will be more written about those adventures when we get around to them.

The other factor that has weighed heavily over the journals and my investigation into them goes back to the person who brought them to me in the first place. The need for intensive vetting and researching every historical fact possible is because of the cloud of suspicion that hangs over Diana Muir—and by association, the journals—because of her questionable past. This begs the obvious question, could Diana Muir have created this vast amount of content? I have come to know Diana very well and consider her a close friend. That said, there have been some contentious times. I have never been shy about calling her to the carpet when I felt it appropriate. This has only happened a few times, but each time Diana took responsibility for her actions. She is genuinely a good person who made mistakes in her early life that occasionally come back to bite her.

Other researchers and internet trolls have sometimes aggressively pointed the finger at Diana as the creator of the story, with only her past as evidence to support their claims. Her history is proof of nothing regarding the journals' authenticity. It is simply something that needed to be considered, and I was unable to find anything to support Diana being involved in their creation. There is also no evidence that Don and Diana somehow conspired together. Most notably I was the one who introduced them, years after I first met Diana and had already read the journals multiple times. While hardcore skeptics will be quick to point the finger at Diana, they will be hard-pressed to find any evidence to support their claims. I know this because I have already looked and come up empty.

At this point, I am prepared to say that based on all the research completed to date, it is my opinion the historical information contained in the Sinclair/Wemyss journals is more likely true than not. Obviously, I feel comfortable enough to publish this book to share with the world. That said, I reserve final judgment until we've had a chance to investigate what we believe is still out there to be discovered and confirmed. Stay tuned for more information to come!

References

Alan Butler & Janet Wolter | America: Nation of the Goddess: The Venus Families and the Founding of the United States | Destiny Books | Rochester, Vermont | 2015

Robert Cooper | *The Voyages of the Venetian Brothers Nicolò & Antonio Zeno to the Northern Seas in the XIV Century: The Northmen in America Before Columbus* | Masonic Publishing Company | Glasgow, Scotland | 2004.

Hayley A. Ramsey | *The Bringer of Life: A Cosmic History of the Divine Feminine* | Adventures Unlimited Press | Kempton, Illinois | 2023.

Donald A. Ruh | *The Scrolls of Onteora: The Cremona Document* | Donald Ruh, Dover Plains, New York | 2017.

Gerald Sinclair & Rondo BB Me | *The Enigmatic Sinclair's: A Definitive Guide to the Sinclair's in Scotland* | St. Clair Publications | McMinnville, Tennessee | 2018.

Scott F. Wolter | *Oak Island, Knights Templar, and the Holy Grail: Secrets of the Underground Project Revealed* | North Star Press of St. Cloud | St. Cloud, Minnesota | 2024.

Scott F. Wolter | *Cryptic Code of the Templars in America: Origins of the Hooked X* | North Star Press of St. Cloud | St. Cloud, Minnesota | 2019.

Scott F. Wolter | *Akhenaten to the Founding Fathers: Mysteries of the Hooked X* | North Star Press of St. Cloud | St. Cloud, Minnesota | 2013.

Scott F. Wolter | *The Hooked X: Key to the Secret History of North America,* | North Star Press of St. Cloud | St. Cloud, Minnesota |2009.

Scott F. Wolter | *The Kensington Rune Stone: Compelling New Evidence* | Lake Superior Agate Inc. | Minneapolis, Minnesota | 2005.